Working the Navajo Way

Published in cooperation with the William P. Clements Center
for Southwest Studies, Southern Methodist University

Working the Navajo Way

LABOR AND CULTURE IN THE

TWENTIETH CENTURY

Colleen O'Neill

 University Press of Kansas

An earlier version of Chapter 4 first appeared as "The 'Making' of the Navajo Worker: Navajo Households, the Bureau of Indian Affairs and Off Reservation Wage Work, 1948–1960," *New Mexico Historical Review 74* (October 1999): 375–405. Copyright © University of New Mexico Board of Regents. All rights reserved.

Portions of Chapter 6 first appeared in *Native Pathways: American Indian Culture and Economic Development in the Twentieth Century,* edited by Brian Hosmer and Colleen O'Neill (Boulder: University Press of Colorado, 2004). Copyright © University Press of Colorado. All rights reserved.

Simon Ortiz's poem, "Starting at the Bottom," portions of which appear in chapter 4, was originally published in *Woven Stone* (Tucson: University of Arizona Press, 1992). Copyright © Simon Ortiz. All rights reserved. Used by permission.

Published by the University Press of Kansas (Lawrence, Kansas 66049), which was organized by the Kansas Board of Regents and is operated and funded by Emporia State University, Fort Hays State University, Kansas State University, Pittsburg State University, the University of Kansas, and Wichita State University

Library of Congress Cataloging-in-Publication Data
O'Neill, Colleen M., 1961–
  Working the Navajo way : labor and culture in the twentieth century / Colleen O'Neill.
      p. cm.
  Includes bibliographical references and index.
  ISBN 0-7006-1395-1 (cloth : alk. paper)
  1. Navajo Indians—Employment. 2. Navajo Indians—Social conditions. 3. Navajo Indians—Government relations. I. Title.

  E99.N3064 2005
  979.1004'9726—dc22

2005011125

British Library Cataloguing-in-Publication Data is available.

Printed in the United States of America

10 9 8 7 6 5 4 3 2 1

The paper used in this publication meets the minimum requirements of the American National Standard for Permanence of Paper for Printed Library Materials Z39.48-1984.

For James P. and F. Gay O'Neill

CONTENTS

ILLUSTRATIONS

I would like to acknowledge the many people who significantly guided the direction of this project. First and foremost, I would like to thank the Navajo people who generously trusted me with their stories. I owe a great deal to Clarence and Margaret Kee and their daughters, Juannita Brown and Annita Fonseca, for sharing their memories with me. I would also like to thank Tsosie Blackgoat, Burton Yazzie, and Joe Lee Watson and Rebecca Tazbah Lee Watson and their son, Earl Lee Watson, for their recollections about living and working in and around the Window Rock coal mine. I am deeply grateful to Lawrence Oliver, who introduced me to those families and on occasion served as a translator. His nuanced insight into the labor and political history of the area helped me to better understand the context of their stories. The few accounts I gathered from these conversations recall an important part of a larger history that the Kees, Watsons, Blackgoats, and Yazzies made. I was honored that Kenneth White, a man who profoundly shaped the course of Navajo labor history, agreed to talk with me. I hope this book approaches his exacting standards and honors his unshakable spirit.

I owe a great debt to the Navajo families living in the Hogback community near the northern edge of the reservation. Special thanks to Harris Cambridge, Helen Duncan, Evelyn John, Betty Harvey, Harry John, Julia John, Tom Jones Jr., Alice Jones, Charlie Jones, and Juanita Jones. I deeply appreciate the considerable help I received in locating miners and their families. In particular I am grateful to Charlie Jones Jr., president of the Hogback Chapter of the Navajo Nation, in allowing me to discuss my project at a chapter meeting. None of these interviews would have been possible without Minnie Hamstreet's and Paul George's good humored and patient translation assistance. When I was in Farmington I decided to look up my husband's old air force "buddy," and she turned out to be Ethelinda Corley, a wonderful person whose family had for years offered their insight and translation help to people like me. I truly appreciate Ethelinda's hospitality and her continued friendship. Last but not least, I would like to thank Tom Wheeler, the owner of the Hogback Trading Post, for his help and encouragement.

I am thankful to have had the opportunity to interview the late Charles Mattox, who remained a true revolutionary and innovative artist into his late eighties. His memories supplied some of the harder-to-document facts about the 1933 Gallup strike. I also feel very lucky to have met Lavine Bennally White, a Navajo woman who lived a few blocks from me when I lived in Highland Park, New Jersey. Her engaging spirit and generosity continues to inspire my work.

Archivists supplied me with what seemed like life-saving help locating sources and arranging research trips. I would like to thank Kathlene Ferris and Nancy Brown from the Center for Southwest Research at the University of New Mexico. By suggesting that I take a look at the Albuquerque and Cerrillos Coal Company papers, Kathlene changed the course of my original research plan. Allowing me liberal access to that collection, she made the task of sorting through unprocessed papers a plausible undertaking. Nancy Brown tirelessly worked at locating obscure sources. Her diligence and thorough efforts to find materials made me feel that she was as committed to this project as I was. At the New Mexico State Records Center in Santa Fe, Sandra Jaramillo and Al Regensberg were incredibly generous and helpful. Equally accommodating were the staff at the National Archives: Joan Howard from the Rocky Mountain regional branch, Ann Cummings and James Cassedy at Archives II in College Park, Maryland, and Paul Wormser at the Pacific Coast Branch in Laguna Niguel, California. I also appreciate the help I received from Brad Cole, currently head of Special Collections at Utah State University, who during the course of my research helped me locate sources in special collections at the Cline Library at Northern Arizona University. Thanks to Diane Schenk and Denise Conklin at the Labor History Archive at Pattee Library at Penn State, who steered me toward the relevant materials in the United Mine Workers records and arranged affordable accommodations while I was in University Park conducting my research. Christine Marín, Pat Etter, and Edward Oetting at the Hayden Library at Arizona State University, and the curatorial staff at the Historic Hubbell Trading Post, went beyond the call of duty to help me locate relevant materials. Eunice Kahn from the Navajo Nation Museum graciously helped me locate the Milton Snow photos that appear in the book. Thanks to Terry Reynolds, Curator of Collections and Exhibits at the University Museum, New Mexico State University, for her work on Emma Reh and for guiding me to the Red Lake Trading Post records. Last but not least, I am grateful to Roger Myers of the University of Arizona Special Collections for his prompt response to my research questions over the phone.

The staff at the New Mexico Bureau of Geology and Mineral Resources, Robert Eveleth and David Love, gave me unprecedented access to another unprocessed collection, the Gallup American Coal Company records. I also owe a huge debt to the late Carl Yost of the Bureau of Land Management in Farmington, New Mexico, who—convinced of the historical significance of Navajo coal mining records—made sure that those papers and photos did not end up in the recycling bin.

A number of anthropologists provided me with valuable lessons born from their own research experience and knowledge of Navajo history and culture. I am particularly grateful to Eric Henderson, Lynn Robbins, David Brugge, Louise Lamphere, and Ralph Luebben for sharing their insights with me. I owe the largest debt to Klara Kelley, whose work is a model of historical depth and complexity. Her advice was instrumental in leading me to the important archaeological data on file at the Navajo Nation Historic Preservation Department in Window Rock. I would like to say thanks to the staff at that office for putting up with my presence as I prodded and sorted through the archaeological reports housed in their office. I appreciate the Navajo Nation Historic Preservation Department's granting me ethnographic research permits to conduct interviews on the reservation. In particular I would like to thank Ronald P. Maldonado, the program manager of the Cultural Resource Compliance Section, NNHPD, for his innovative archaeological research and his eleventh-hour assistance in preparing this manuscript for publication.

Many people have read all or parts of the manuscript, including members of my "dissertations anonymous" group at Rutgers University, which included Glen Kuecker, Martin Summers, Ron McGee, Peter Messer, and Michelle Brattain. Thanks to Chris Stacey, Erika Bsumek, and Jan Lambertz, who also read parts of the dissertation. As I moved the manuscript from a dissertation to a book, several colleagues offered me helpful advice, including Peter Iverson, Brian Hosmer, Clyde Ellis, Chris Friday, David Myers, Michael Honey, Richard Boyden, Zaragosa Vargas, Jeff Garcilazo, Marsha Weisiger, Edward Countryman, and David Salmanson. Thanks to Jorge Lizárraga for his map-making expertise and to Phil Roberts for preparing the index. In particular I appreciate Nancy Scott Jackson of the University Press of Kansas for her patience and continued support for this project.

Joan Jensen, who oversaw my M.A. thesis at New Mexico State University and then served on my dissertation committee after I moved on to Rutgers, has been more than a mentor to me. I'm glad she took the initial risk by offering me my first academic resting place in Las Cruces. Alice Kessler-Harris, my doctoral adviser, consistently exceeded my expectations with her perfect balance of nurturing guidance and challenging criticism. I am truly blessed to have had the opportunity to work with both of these distinguished historians. I hope my work in the future merits the confidence they have shown in me.

I am also grateful to Carolyn Brown, Sue Schrepfer, and Dee Garrison for their thoughtful reading of my work. I have also benefited from discussions with Alan Howard, Elizabeth Jameson, Clare Lyons, John Daly, Jennifer Denetdale, Nancy Gabin, Ramón Gutíerrez, Karen Brodkin, Neil Foley, and Kathy M'Closkey. The innovative scholars I met during my brief stint at Temple University, Kathy Le Mons Walker, Thomas C. Patterson, and Peter Gran, have had a profound influence on my thinking. I appreciate their willingness to welcome me into their intellectual community.

David A. Reichard, a close friend and treasured colleague, kept me inspired throughout the entire process. Working laptop to laptop in the archives in New Mexico and in Washington, D.C., sharing the elation of each other's discoveries and the frustrations of the seemingly endless searches, made the work a complete joy. His high standards will always keep me honest and our friendship will always anchor my sanity.

This research would not have been possible without the financial support from the many educational institutions with which I have been affiliated over the years. A fellowship from the Rutgers History Department and smaller supplemental grants enabled me to conduct archival research and my initial oral interviews in New Mexico. I would like to thank Stephen Reinert and the Rutgers History Department office staff, especially Mary DeMeo, Beth Polelle, Karen Bryant, and Dawn Ruskai, for their good-natured encouragement. Helen Putsmueller, who provided me with a home away from home in Denver, significantly diminished my expenses. I'm also grateful to the Western Historical Association for awarding me the Walter Rundell Graduate Student Award. The financial and intellectual support I received from the Center for the Critical Analysis of Contemporary Culture at Rutgers gave me the time and analytical space to make considerable progress on the work. The interdisciplinary atmosphere and the intriguing criticism offered by the members of the weekly seminar, particularly Neil Smith, Paige West, and others, encouraged me to think in provocative new ways about my topic. An NEH Faculty Development Grant from the College of New Rochelle, several state faculty support grants from California Polytechnic State University, release time from teaching in the Ethnic Studies Department at CalPoly, and a John Topham and Susan Redd Butler Faculty Fellowship from the Charles Redd Center for Western Studies at Brigham Young University provided me the essential resources to conduct interviews and additional research. Kathy Teufel and Al Marks supplied essential research assistance. Thanks to Manzar Foroohar, Debra Valencia-Laver, Susan Opava, and Harry Hellenbrand for their unyielding support for my project, even when my requests undermined their own administrative goals.

This project took wings in Dallas, Texas, at the Clements Center for Southwest Studies, where the great gift of time and intellectual companionship helped launch me into the final stages of revising the manuscript. My life and work are enriched by the enduring friendships I made at the Clements Center, including those with Sherry Smith, David Weber, Benjamin Johnson, Michelle Nickerson, Flannery Burke, and Tisa Wenger. I will never forget the overwhelming experience of the manuscript workshop where my "dream team," which included Sara Deutsch, Fred Hoxie, and Maureen Schwarz, along with Dave Edmunds of UT Dallas and Richard V. Francaviglia of UT Arlington and other members of the SMU History Department, helped me see what needed to be done to bring the work to fruition. The people I met in Dallas, including Andrea Boardman, Ruth Ann Elmore, John R. Chávez, James Hopkins, and Alexis McCrossen, made my brief introduction to Texas exceedingly positive.

Thanks to Marguerite MacIntyre, my lifelong friend, whose exacting questions often demanded that I reexamine my polemical impulses. And to Salle Sherrod, who seems to draw from a limitless supply of love and wisdom to offer shelter and guidance to those who are lucky enough to know her. My mind and soul grow richer from their friendship with each passing day.

John Nelson, with all his intellectual rigor and warped sense of humor, has provided me the incalculable strength to see this work through to its completion. He has read every word in this manuscript several times, provided research assistance, offered constructive criticism, and made more pots of coffee than I can count. I continue to marvel at my good luck in meeting him and in the wonderful journeys we have taken together. He and his children, Laura, Stephen, and Angela, have provided my academic gypsy life welcomed moorings. They have helped me recognize "what good looks like."

Finally, thanks to my parents, James P. O'Neill and F. Gay O'Neill. Their continued support allowed me to travel some very unconventional paths. I dedicate this project to them. In their name, I would like to donate royalties from the sale of this book to the Navajo Uranium Miners' project.

AFL-CIO	American Federation of Labor–Congress of Industrial Organizations
BIA	Bureau of Indian Affairs
CCC	Civilian Conservation Corps
DNA	Diné Bee'iiná' Náhiilnah Bee Agha'diit' aahii
FBI	Federal Bureau of Investigation
FERA	Federal Emergency Relief Administration
IRA	Indian Reorganization Act
NCWA	Navajo Construction Workers Association
NLRB	National Labor Relations Board
NMU	National Miners' Union
SCS	Soil Conservation Service
UMWA	United Mine Workers of America

Navajo History and Western Capitalist Development

Some Navajos worked on the railroad in places like Winslow (Béésh Sinil) *and Flagstaff* (KinLání). *They supported themselves very well because they owned livestock and cornfields back home. The womenfolk had wool, sheepskins and rugs which they sold. Everything was used for self-support. At that time the land was rich and grass was plentiful.*

—Tillman Hadley from Blue Canyon, Navajo Nation, Arizona[1]

In June 2001, while I was browsing in a curio shop on Gallup's famous stretch of Route 66, a young Navajo woman who was working there asked me where I was from and what brought me to Gallup. At first I felt a little awkward and embarrassed to reveal my research interests to her, hesitant to leave behind my anonymous tourist identity. But she persisted. I told her that I was writing a book about Navajo workers, how they adjusted their lives to the market economy, and how they shaped that economy in the process. Leaning over a glass case filled with silver, turquoise, and beaded ornaments, she smiled and said, "That's good, that's important history to tell. Most people think we are just silversmiths and drunks."

Her insights reflect, in a nutshell, some of the pivotal issues in American Indian scholarship. For this young Navajo woman, the images reflected back to her from American history portray her people as quaint museum objects or as pathetic social problems. That image has been heavily influenced by the work of anthropologists, who for many years have collected, analyzed, and attempted to "preserve" her culture, often for the consumption of a non-Indian audience.[2] And then there are the sociologists who have been concerned with the problems of assimilation, poverty, and social dysfunction. Of course this simplifies a vast array of scholarship—good and bad—that over many years has provided significant insight into Navajo history and culture. But I do not think she was commenting directly on the state of ethnographical research. Instead, she was reflecting on how that

[1]

research has filtered into the American popular imagination in ways that have reinforced a narrow perception of American Indians, Navajos in particular.

Why then would a history of workers be a welcomed relief for the "most studied people on earth"?[3] For that curio shop worker, such a book would be a positive corrective to the rather limited, stereotyped images of Navajos in the Gallup area. The people I interviewed echoed her feelings. When they signed release forms at the conclusion of the interviews, they often reflected on their role in this project, commenting that the history of Navajo workers was an important story to be told. After our first conversation, Margaret Kee, a master weaver and miner's wife, said—as if to justify her participation in the interview—"I'm doing this for the miners."[4] She and other people I interviewed remembered the work they had done with great pride, whether it was operating a dragline in a massive strip-mining venture, picking potatoes in Idaho, or weaving a rug in exchange for groceries. As workers they were productive members of society, contributing to the welfare of their families and communities. Including that experience in the historical record was a testament to the strength of their culture and communities.

To them, history was a story of their efforts to improve their condition and how well they conducted their lives according to the teachings of their elders. It was a memory of their achievements, something from which they could draw self-esteem and community pride. Some differentiated history from anthropology, where they were often the objects of study rather than the experts sharing their knowledge of the past. This distinction became clear to me when I interviewed Julia John from the Hogback community on the Navajo reservation. She was willing to share her story with me, including the personal details of her life, because as she stated, "This is history." As the wife of a miner, a former weaver, and a wageworker, Julia John tells a story that is intermingled with others in this book, a testimony of heartache, hard work, and perseverance. She told me how she first found solace in the carrot fields near Phoenix, where she worked after fleeing a violent home life. While she was picking and bundling carrots, she met her husband, Harry John, who was loading produce into trucks. Both had experienced a great deal of hardship and had struggled with families torn apart by alcohol and poverty. Together they vowed to live a different life, one devoted to love and mutual care. Their work in the fields initially drew them away from the reservation, but the wages they earned enabled them to come back. As Julia John remembered, "Here we had a family, a home, a farm. We both worked in the fields, and now we benefit from that."[5] John's story, as well as those related to me by other Navajo elders, reveals an understanding of history as a "process of what is constantly in the making."[6] For Julia and Harry John, that process included picking carrots, mining coal, weaving rugs, herding sheep, and operating a backhoe. They were making a living and making history, the Navajo way.[7]

This book examines that history, in particular how Navajo cultural practices and values influenced what it meant to work for wages or to produce commodities for the capitalist marketplace. I focus on the period between the 1930s through the early 1970s, a time when Navajos saw a dramatic transformation of their economy. Navajos worked for wages and produced for the surrounding market before that period, but until the 1930s they were not dependent on a single strategy to make a living. Most pooled their income from a variety of sources, including wages they earned working on the railroad, herding sheep, or selling rugs and other craft items. Beginning in the 1930s, partly as a result of declining wool prices and federally enforced livestock reduction, Navajo households became increasingly dependent on wages to survive. In 1930 wages made up about one-third of the income for Navajo households.[8] By 1960 that share had increased to 60 percent.[9] This book examines how Navajo cultural practices shaped and were shaped by that transition.

This work is part of a new and growing scholarship that features American Indians as significant historical actors in shaping their economic worlds. Since the 1990s, historians and anthropologists have published a variety of studies that examine the innovative ways in which American Indians engaged the capitalist market. Such research reinforces what many American Indians know: American Indian cultural practices played a very important role in shaping the terms of incorporation into the modern capitalist economy. Whether it was through the development of tribal capitalism or a creative redistribution of federal welfare, American Indians crafted resourceful ways to make a living without abandoning their cultural values and traditions. In the early colonial era, they shrewdly negotiated trading agreements and established a "middle ground" where they could balance European demands with their own economic needs and cultural values. In the nineteenth century, Native American lives and lands were turned upside down by the encroaching consumer market and the rush for western gold.[10] In the twentieth century, they worked for wages, migrated to cities, and struggled for economic parity like other workers, yet they did so in ways that made sense within their own cultural frameworks. For example, kinship—a central organizing principle of many American Indian societies—continued to shape the ways they found jobs as well as how they conducted themselves at the workplace. They balanced the demands of the job with their attendance at cultural events such as ceremonial gatherings, sings, and powwows. Gendered obligations shaped how workers incorporated wage work into their survival strategies. Hierarchies of power, born out of specific reservation conditions that included the legacy of Indian Reorganization Act (IRA)–era tribal governments, the ever-present Bureau of Indians Affairs (BIA), and tribal political factions, continued to inform American Indian priorities.[11]

Even though American Indian history is flourishing, it seems that the story of Indian workers still remains marginal to the broader questions of economic development, labor, and working-class history in the U.S. West.[12] Since I began this project in 1994, my work has often evoked quizzical looks from my colleagues. They have often asked me whether I considered myself an American Indian historian or a labor historian. Apparently one could not be both. U.S. labor historians did not write about the experience of "pre-modern" or pre-industrial peoples. And American Indian historians did not seem to be concerned with the working lives of native peoples in the twentieth century. The intellectual paradigms for understanding workers and American Indians seemed to be mutually exclusive.

Yet there have been Native American workers throughout the expanse of American history. They emerge out of the historical documents: cleaning the houses of colonial administrators, laying railroad ties, guiding military expeditions, picking produce, and packing fish in canneries.[13]

In this study I argue that Native Americans are indeed relevant, if not central, to the history of economic development in the United States. But their importance to the history of U.S. economic growth cannot be measured solely in terms of the land they lost to American frontier expansion. As Alice Littlefield and Martha Knack pointed out, "It has become a historical commonplace to decry U.S. wealth as built on the theft of Indian land and the enslavement of African labor." Both tragedies dramatically shaped the development of the U.S. economy. But, as Littlefield and Knack suggest, those "assertions also oversimplify by ignoring the diversity of local circumstances that led employers to seek out a wide array of labor sources and to subject laborers to varying degrees of coercion."[14] This study is an effort to bring Native Americans to the center of that history, not only as one of the groups defeated in an epic drama but as significant actors who shaped the regional dynamics of U.S. economic development. When and how Native Americans participated in the market economy, as producers and as wageworkers, largely defined the terms of local economic conditions.

Colonialism, Class, and Western History

The theoretical paradigms that historians employed to understand the history of economic development in the United States have rendered American Indians marginal to the large questions of capitalist transformation. In western history, the familiar narrative is a story of eastern entrepreneurs dominating the western landscape and bringing with them Euro-American and European immigrants to work for wages in various extractive industries. Class formation, resistance, and power are issues that are teased out in the context of these industrial islands, appropriate categories for studying whoever historians define as workers and/or management. The impetus bringing change arrives from the East, either as investors from New York and Boston or as a workforce that challenges, in sometimes radical ways, the power of those industrialists.[15]

Framing an analysis of the capitalist transformation of the American West within these theoretical perimeters marginalizes Native Americans, clearing the land, so to speak, for the central struggle between eastern capitalists and Euro-American workers to be played out. But, to understand the context of this struggle, it is necessary to address not only what is displaced but also how indigenous alternatives persist and influence the shape of that history. The motor of change may be the encroaching capitalist system, but the road that it travels may indeed be shaped by the cultural, social, and economic systems that lay in its path.

In the 1960s and 1970s, Latino scholars broadened our understanding of capitalist development in the United States when they looked to developing nations for comparison. Inspired by social movements at home, as well as the national liberation movements in the Third World, they found the theoretical models used by Latin American scholars useful for understanding the links between capitalist development and the degraded conditions of Latinos and other people of color in the U.S. West.[16] Influenced by dependency theorists, Rodolfo Acuña, in his first edition of *Occupied America,* argued that Chicanos suffered from the conditions of "internal colonialism."[17] Historians writing within this framework stressed themes of resistance and focused on the displacement of the Mexican population from their land and their decline in status brought about by U.S. occupation.

Rejecting the internal colonial model as a "quintessential victimization framework," a number of historians responded with scholarship that celebrated the survival of indigenous traditions and Mexican-American institutions such as *mutualistas,* Las Gorras Blancas, and border culture.[18] Others continued to wrestle with colonial models by applying Wallerstein's world systems analysis to the U.S. Southwest. Tomás Almaguer found that California's movement into the world system transformed labor from a type of Indian slavery into the ranchero system and finally into a segmented workforce where Mexicanos were relegated to unskilled positions. In his view, California moved from periphery, semiperiphery to core status during the course of the nineteenth century.[19] Although Almaguer's application of Wallersteinian analysis seemed appropriate for California, David Montejano found the world systems approach lacking explanatory power for Texas. Montejano argued that world systems analysis could only at best provide a topographical view of uneven development. A close analysis of the specific historical conditions of developing class and race relations, and not a market-driven approach alone, was needed to understand economic development in the U.S. West.[20] Montejano's argument was consistent with that of other Chicano scholars who have rejected the internal colonial model as too simplistic.[21] By the 1990s, Chicano scholars seemed to abandon the search for totalizing theories; they have focused instead on working out the specifics of colonial power and resistance, including the regional development of race and the role of gender in shaping borderland identities and class-based struggles.[22]

The "new western" historians, including the generation of feminist and Chicano/a scholars writing in the 1970s, 1980s, and 1990s, unearthed the experience of women, workers, and ethnic minorities who had been largely absent from the narrative.[23] In clarifying their agenda, Patricia Limerick wrote that these scholars rejected the concept of the frontier, with its attendant nationalistic and racist connotations. Instead, they viewed the West as a place where "invasion, conquest, colonization, exploitation, development, [and] expansion of the world market" defined its history. She explained further that those events involved "the convergence of diverse people—women as well as men, Indians, Europeans, Latin Americans, Asians, Afro-Americans—in the region, and their encounters with each other and with the natural environment."[24] Others were exploring the connections between class, ethnicity, and gender and thinking about how and why diverse groups of people in the West gained power in relation to each other. For example, in her book *No Separate Refuge,* Sara Deutsch examined how federal policies and the worldwide economic crisis of the 1930s undermined the survival strategies of Hispano villagers in northern New Mexico. As their regional community contracted, Hispano men and women developed alternative ways to arrange and give meaning to their lives. When the village waned in significance, women lost power in relation to men.[25] Peggy Pascoe similarly linked structural questions to gender issues. In *Relations of Rescue,* she showed how specific ideas about gender formed the basis of middle-class identity and provided women missionaries with impetus for their work on the frontier. Thus the power relations between Anglo women and women of color were defined along class and racial categories that were sharply gendered. But these divisions were not necessarily exclusive and impenetrable. In much the same way that Linda Gordon described immigrant women in the early twentieth century utilizing repressive social welfare programs to their own advantage, Pascoe showed how some Indian, Chinese, and working-class Anglo women found relief from the gender oppression they faced in their own communities by participating in rescue efforts sponsored by the missionary societies.[26]

Bringing American Indians out of the margins inspires new questions about the nature of capitalist development and class formation in the United States. Their stories, which often find them in "unexpected places," reveal a much more complicated history where American Indians are agents of change and not simply casualties of some sort of preordained clash between modernity and tradition.[27] That duality itself needs exploration. Is tradition a product of precapitalist culture, automatically sacrificed in the name of modernity? If not, how have traditions survived, changed, or emerged as part of the development of a wage-based economy? If traditions are lost, does that mean that they are replaced by some sort of universal culture of modernity? Or have American Indians crafted ways to live and work within a system that offer alternatives to the individualized and consumerist values of American capitalism? If so, might there be multiple pathways of economic development?

Rethinking "modernity" in this way also means reexamining standard notions of class. For some scholars the historical development of a working class is the foundation on which capitalism rests. It is a historically complex process, and one that labor historians have been debating for decades. On a basic level, a working class develops when economic and political forces transform people into workers, a population that has nothing but its labor to sell in order to make a living. This historical process distinguishes "class" from other forms of coerced labor and capitalism from other types of economic systems. The debate in labor history centers on how and when workers understand their fate and what they do with that knowledge.

Much labor history has focused on the development of "class identity," a collective self-perception that workers derive from their common experiences on the shop floor. This model for understanding "class" is particularly limiting, since it privileges the industrial, wage workplace and imposes a historically specific construct on populations for whom it may not be particularly relevant. And according to this definition, American Indians and other workers who move in and out of the workforce, and who may perform labor that is marginal to the "shop floor," fall outside the definition of "class" and, by extension, exist beyond the realm of modernity.

Other labor historians turn to "culture" to explain the development of class identity. This paradigm assumes a contradiction between "culture," or "old-world ways," and the demands of the "modern" workplace.[28] At first glance, this seems to provide a possible way to bring American Indians into the narrative. But this approach tends to reproduce the modern/traditional dichotomy that freezes American Indian culture in the pre-industrial past. Since cultural practices that contradict a capitalist worldview not only persist but may be created by capitalist development, a paradigm that equates culture with a precapitalist existence cannot accommodate the persistence of American Indian tradition within the framework of an industrialized economy. Furthermore, privileging "culture" tends to neglect the role of trade unions and the shop floor, conflates class with ethnic and racial identity, and thereby obscures class divisions and other hierarchies that may divide ethnic communities.

Households, Class, and Gender

Feminist labor historians offer insights into class that might prove instructive to those exploring the issue of wage work among American Indian communities. Using gender as an analytical category has encouraged historians to think about class in radical, new ways. As Alice Kessler-Harris argued, "we have to lay siege to the central paradigm of labor history. . . . We must challenge the notion that paid work, as a fundamentally male activity, inevitably reproduces itself in a closed system in which men derive their identity from the process of production (and then reproduce themselves by training other men), while women act in the household and in the workplace as the hand-maids of the male reproductive system."[29]

The shop floor paradigm not only excludes women from the defining experience where workers derive their class identities, it marginalizes others who were not permanent wage workers. Since working-class women, white and American Indian, may not fit the "shop floor" criteria, their experience of class remains either—at best—derivative of male industrial workers' history or—at worst—invisible. American Indian men are as marginal to the industrial formula as white women and women of color. And as a result their story remains similarly obscure.

The historical debate over class formation seems to hinge on where people formulate their collective identities and how that experience helps them interpret their place within a broader economic system. For many American Indians, Navajos included, kinship serves that purpose. Clan membership, for example, significantly mapped relationships among Navajos, offering guidelines on hospitality, marriage, and cosmological origins. Fulfilling one's kinship obligation, whether that meant a child respecting a grandmother's wishes, a man taking care of his wife's fields, or an uncle contributing a sheep toward an Enemy Way ceremony, might determine how one might view the wage work force and his or her place within it.

An obvious place to begin looking for kinship is in the household. In the 1930s, Navajo households generally included a woman, her husband, her daughters, sons-in-law, and grandchildren. Many diverged from this matrilocal residential pattern and settled wherever they could, depending on their wealth and personal needs. Although modest urban communities developed in such places as Shiprock, Fort Defiance, and Tuba City in the 1950s and

1960s, most Navajos on the reservation lived in small family clusters, with great distances separating them from their neighbors.

Using the household as an analytical framework provides a method for examining the connections among gender, culture, and class formation on many levels. Defining the parameters of class in household terms is a more comprehensive framework that neither obscures gender conflict nor characterizes culture as existing outside economic relationships. One example of this approach is Earl Lewis's work on African Americans in Norfolk, Virginia. He used a household framework to explain why, up to the 1930s, African Americans united around the priorities of securing political rights and equal access to city services rather than organizing trade unions. Lewis argued that blacks focused on improving the home sphere when discrimination at work seemed insurmountable. For African Americans, the "home sphere" encompassed more than the single family dwelling unit. Far from being a private space where blacks lived a "balkanized existence," it represented a merger between the household and the community, one that spawned collective strategies pursued by the African American population.[30] Lewis's formulation highlighted the need to view workers' identity and actions within the historical context of their communities. He provided further evidence that the creation of separate spheres, the division between home and work, may not have been a universal condition experienced by all members of industrialized society.

Framing an analysis of class in this way is an inclusive approach that considers the variety of resources exploited by the members of the household. Wage labor is not necessarily privileged, and the household members' domestic responsibilities become important variables when considering questions of class identity and collective action. Thinking about class in this way sheds light on why Navajo workers did not see their jobs as permanent, leaving them behind when their household obligations demanded their attention. Also, by focusing on the household, as opposed to the shop floor, we can see how workers and their families, especially in a period of economic transition, navigated through the constraints and contradictions of the expanding labor market.

For Navajos in the mid-twentieth century, the "home sphere" was the reservation household. Infused with gendered expectations and cultural responsibilities, their commitments to that household framed their experience in the market. As Kenneth White, a Navajo labor activist, explained to a congressional committee in 1973, "we have a livelihood that we make our living with[,] also besides working elsewhere."[31] To White, "making a living" meant more than collecting a paycheck or paying one's bills. It was doing what was necessary to maintain the reservation household according to the Navajo way. For a Navajo man like White, that meant leaving jobs working on railroads, picking carrots in Arizona, or mining coal in Colorado to herd his mother's sheep, to help in the shearing, or to make sure she had enough wood to keep her warm in the winter. For his wife, and other Navajo women, "making a living" meant weaving rugs, taking care of their sheep, their gardens, as well as teaching their children and grandchildren how to manage themselves, their kin, and their land in a harmonious manner. White wanted employers to understand that and not to penalize Navajo workers who put their familial and sacred duties first before their obligations to the workplace. "Working elsewhere" meant picking carrots, cleaning railroad tracks, or building a natural gas pipeline. That was labor they did for wages, and although it did not constitute making a living, it contributed to the survival of the reservation household as its economic base was shifting.

Making a Living the Navajo Way

This book examines how Navajos negotiated the sometimes conflicting demands between making a living the Navajo way and "working elsewhere," or engaging the capitalist marketplace. I explore this tension by focusing on three stories I managed to piece together from anthropological and historical sources. Data culled from archaeological surveys, mine inspector reports, and ethnographies, read as contemporary eyewitness accounts, establish the specific cultural context within which Navajo families formulated their household strategies. Archival documents, correspondence, and Bureau of Indian Affairs reports add the federal government to the story, providing insight into the motivations of BIA bureaucrats, who in the 1930s tried to impose market-oriented production methods and an "appropriate" work ethic on the Navajo population. Finally, oral interviews I conducted between 1995 and 2002 add the personal recollections of Navajo workers, weavers, and coal producers. In their retelling of their stories, they offer a complex narrative of cultural re-invention, crucial for understanding the motives and actions of Navajo workers in this period.

The first story is about the development of a small-scale, Navajo-controlled coal mining industry on the reservation. Mining coal like herding sheep, these miners and their families negotiated the terms of the capitalist market on and off the reservation. Mining diversified their pastoral/agricultural ways of making a living in a manner that adapted their notions of land use and household production to the needs of a growing market economy. Although the Navajo coal producers participated in the market, their ideas and production methods remained rooted in a pastoral livelihood.

While Navajo men were mining coal, most of their wives were weaving rugs. The next story looks at the women's side of the household economy. These women experienced the realities of capitalism, not necessarily in the coal mines or through their permanent membership in the wage workforce, but in their homes on the reservation. The trader, with whom they negotiated their prices, was the arbiter of the capitalist market, exchanging consumer goods and the staples of life for what Navajo women produced at home. As a result, Navajo households existed in two types of capitalist economies at once: the trading post system and a broader market that consumed Navajo coal and paid workers wages for their labor. These markets often overlapped. Both men and women worked for wages, and both engaged in trade at the trading posts. But for most Navajo women, into the 1950s, the trading post served as their primary interface to the growing capitalist economy, whereas their husbands, brothers, uncles, and sons largely engaged the market as wage workers. Navajo women's work and the cultural values that shaped it, including Navajo and non-Navajo concepts of gender, delineated the specific landscape of capitalist development on the reservation, one that would involve men and women in different ways.

The next story follows Navajos off the reservation in search of wage work. Unlike the independent miners, Navajos who could not make a living by working their own land negotiated the demands of the labor market by working for wages on a limited basis. To successfully pull them into that market, commercial farmers, mining companies, and other western capitalists had to adjust to Navajos' demands and figure out ways to accommodate their culturally defined work practices. For southwestern industrialists, commercial farmers, and railroad recruiters, the Navajos appeared to offer an attractive labor pool. But poverty and the close proximity of the reservation to commercial farms and mining operations did not necessarily transform Navajos into permanent wage workers. Entering the workforce may have been unavoidable, but wage work did not necessarily bring about an automatic transformation of Navajo society. For the Diné, becoming wageworkers required a negotiation between culturally defined ideas of work, gendered definitions of household responsibilities, and options created by the global market.

A final story looks at the increasing development of a Navajo working class on the reservation after 1950, when the economic landscape began to change. Corporate development of Navajo mineral resources such as oil, coal, and uranium created new sources of wage work, and the reservation household assumed new meaning. Between 1930 and 1950, it had served as a cultural buffer, a place that would draw people back after their brief sojourns into the world of wage labor. Now, instead of migrating to work and returning home to fulfill their household responsibilities, some Navajo workers could remain on reservation land year-round, finding work in nearby strip mines, on construction projects, or in the expanding tribal bureaucracy. Workers who had access to more highly skilled wage jobs, although few in number, constituted a new social class on the reservation, challenging older patterns of livestock and land-based economic stratification.

Changing economic conditions offered Navajo households new ways to make a living and created new sites of cultural contestation. The workplace, the hiring hall, and the picket line became arenas where Navajo workers and Navajo elites constructed competing definitions of "Navajo-ness." Joining a trade union and participating in collective actions organized along class lines were no longer experiences confined to the world beyond reservation boundaries. They were evidence of increasing industrial development and corporate exploitation of Navajo natural resources. Navajo workers, tribal council members, traders, industrialists, and union organizers used racial categories to define the nature of emerging class relationships on the reservation in the mid-twentieth century.

These stories inspire a reframing of the history of Native Americans and economic development in the United States. The Navajo case suggests that economic development in the American Southwest between the 1930s and 1960 was a fluid process, one that shaped and was shaped by local systems of power and culture specific to the region. This story counters the classic modernization tale that assumes that as soon as indigenous peoples encounter the capitalist market, their cultural traditions erode and subsistence economies decay. The Navajos negotiated the encroaching world market selectively, participating in it when it suited their purposes, but refusing to allow capitalist cultural and economic logic to significantly undermine the basic premises upon which they had shaped these new economic strategies.

Certainly American Indians suffered tremendously as they were drawn into the market economy. The Navajos were no exception. The U.S. government attacked Navajo subsistence as a military strategy in 1863. The military destroyed reservation crops and livestock and subsequently attempted to remake Navajos into sedentary farmers while they were being held in captivity at the Bosque Redondo. Seventy years later and well within the living memory of the Long Walk, the BIA enforced draconian measures to reduce the Navajo livestock herds, a policy that helped to undermine their mixed-subsistence household economies. Navajo uranium workers and their families are still suffering from the effects of exposure, poor working conditions, and the toxic contamination of their lands.[32]

Despite—or perhaps because of—these direct assaults on their livelihoods, the Navajos consistently created new ways of making a living within the expanding U.S. economy that were distinctly their own. I hope this book offers a version of Navajo history much broader than what the curio shop worker described. In this book Navajos are union organizers, carrot pickers, coal miners, weavers, and railroad workers. What kinds of work they did, how they did it, and why they made choices they did add up to a story that is more than a sum of its parts. They participated in the "reworking of modernity" in their region, strategically weaving an alternative history of capitalist development that was as culturally specific as the patterns in a Navajo rug.[33]

1

The Diné and the Diné Bikéyah
Navajo History and Navajoland

At the time of stock reduction those who did not have grazing permits and had only a few livestock were promised jobs, and the federal government introduced several work projects on the Reservation. Some Navajos were employed on those projects, but they didn't last long; and many others were recruited as migratory workers and railroad laborers. That was the beginning of wage-earning employment for our people. They had to learn how to earn money and to support their families with it.
  —Thomas Clani, from Teec Nos Pos, Navajo Nation, Arizona[1]

In 1946 Charlie Jones was just sixteen years old when he found a job working as a mucker for the Argentine Mining Company.[2] Traveling more than 100 miles north from his home in Waterflow, New Mexico, he joined his uncles who were working and living in Rico, Colorado, a nonunion mining town that was primarily made up of Navajo labor. Jones quickly learned about the mining process, and his knowledge of drills, jackhammers, and timbering would serve him well for the rest of his work life. After leaving Rico and mining lead, zinc, and coal, he moved on to work in uranium. He and his fellow workers thought the change in metals might be an improvement. He would no longer fear cave-ins and flooding. He did not discover, until much later, the danger involved in uranium mining. After working thirteen more years in Colorado, he returned home to the reservation and settled with his family near Shiprock, New Mexico.

  When I interviewed Mr. Jones in his home in July 2002, I asked him what had brought him back to the reservation. He did not emphasize Utah International, a large coal strip-mining operation near Shiprock, where he worked for more than thirty years. Instead he said, "There is no place else to go, I guess. You gotta go home. You can't leave the places. You can't leave the land. You gotta be there."[3] Jones was like many other Navajos in the mid-twentieth century who ventured off the reservation to find work, only to be drawn back by the land and responsibilities to their kin. To understand their stories, we must first understand the place: the land and culture that brought Jones and his family back home.

The Land

According to the Navajo creation story, First Man and First Woman formed the four sacred mountains out of soil they brought with them when they emerged from the lower worlds.[4] These mountains would signify the boundaries of Diné Bikéyah, the homeland of the Navajo people. Holy people dwelled in these places and endowed them with ceremonial colors and objects that have come to signify the mountains themselves. They first created Sisnaajiní (or Blanca Peak in Colorado) in the east on a bed of white shell and assigned it the color white. In the south they created the blue mountain, *Tsoodził* (or Mount Taylor in New Mexico) and adorned it in turquoise. To the west they formed *Dook'o'oosłííd* (or San Francisco Peaks in Arizona), the sacred yellow mountain, and infused it with abalone shell. The northern boundary is *Dibé Ntsaa* (or Big Sheep Mountain, Hesperus Peak in Colorado), the black mountain, veiled in darkness and decorated with obsidian.[5]

These mountains embody tremendous power for the Diné. They provide the stories, life lessons, and values that are central to their culture. As respected elder and storyteller George Blueeyes described, "This is how they sit for us. / We adorn ourselves just as they do, / With bracelets of turquoise, / And precious jewels about your necks." They mark the places that signify Diné origins and reaffirm their cultural identity. As Mr. Blueeyes continued, "These mountains and the land between them / Are the only things that keep us strong. / From them, and because of them we prosper. / It is because of them that we eat plants and / good meat."[6]

Today, each of the four sacred mountains lies beyond the political boundaries of the Navajo Reservation, which encompasses 25,000 square miles, crossing the borders of Arizona, New Mexico, and Utah and is often compared

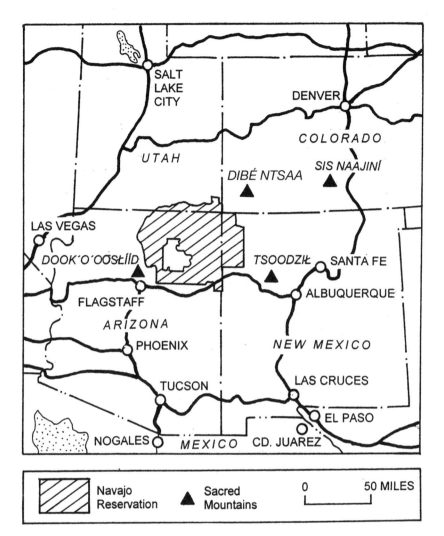

Map 1.1. *Diné Bikéyah map drawn by Jorge Lizárraga.*

in size to the state of West Virginia. In 1930, the Navajo population numbered between 39,000 and 40,000 people. A generation later, by 1960, that number increased to 60,000.[7] By 1972, over 120,000 people lived on the Navajo Reservation. Today, the Navajo nation is one of the largest American Indian communities in the United States, and its reservation is one of only a few that encompass ancestral lands.

Diné Bikéyah, the Navajo homeland, is spectacular and varied terrain. In the mid-1940s, the noted anthropologists Clyde Kluckhohn and Dorothea Leighton attempted to describe its totality, likening it to a massive landscape painting. They encouraged their readers to imagine "the sagebrush interspersed with groves of small evergreens . . . against a background of highly colored mesas, canyons, buttes, volcanic necks and igneous mountain masses clothed in deep pine green, [and] roofed over with a brilliant blue sky."[8] In 1982, N. Scott Momaday remembered the places such as Chinle, Tuba City, and Shiprock, where he had spent a large part of his youth. From the vantage point of a hot air balloon, he described this landscape:

> Directly below was a long sandstone spine, a succession of great red walls like vertebrae curving out toward the sun. In every direction I could see distant mountains, sacred mountains. Here and there were hogans far below, flocks of sheep grazing, dogs barking faintly across the long vertical and diagonal distances. Innumerable facets of rock caught fire in the west. I inhaled the thin, cold air, and I was again glad in my heart.[9]

Three ecological zones contribute the depth, color, and texture to such a beautiful scene. Eight percent is mountainous, carpeted in fir, pine, spruce, and aspen forests and reaching from 7,000 to 10,000 feet in elevation.[10] The temperature in this region averages between 43 and 50 degrees Fahrenheit (commonly falling below zero in the winter) and receives 16 to 35 inches of annual precipitation. Thirty-seven percent of the land is steppe terrain and averages between 12 and 16 inches of moisture, a quarter of which falls as snow. In these "tablelands covered with pinyon and juniper and cut by sage-floored valleys," the temperature falls as low as 10 degrees in the winter and rises as high as 88 degrees in the summer. The remaining 55 percent of the land is desert, a harsh place that only receives between 7 and 11 inches of rain annually but can get as cold as 11 degrees in the winter and as hot as 110 degrees in the summer.[11] This land can be forbidding, accented only by "the bleakness of desert flora except when relieved by lone or clumped cottonwoods along intermittent watercourses." As arid as it is, the desert too contributes its suggestion of color to the Navajo landscape. As Kluckhohn and Leighton remarked, "even the desert is yellow with the bloom of dodgeweed or spotted with stalks of white yucca blossoms and red and yellow cactus blooms."[12]

Over the years Navajos adapted their lives to these environmental conditions, developing a livestock-based economy along a "broad C-shaped belt" of steppe and desert landscape that stretched from the north, west and into the southern areas of the reservation.[13] Since the lack of rain in these regions made farming very difficult, most Navajos depended on their sheep and cattle for their livelihoods. This was also true for some parts of the eastern border, except in the checkerboard area where land tenure problems diminished the accessibility to open range.[14] At higher elevations in most of the eastern and central areas, Navajos developed a household economy centered on dry farming. In the lowlands, where rain was less plentiful, they found ways to take advantage of flood waters. In those areas, where irrigation allowed intensive agricultural development, farming assumed a more central focus of Navajo life.

Many Navajos made use of the diverse landscape by moving between seasonal residences. In the summer, farming households tended their crops, usually located near their primary residential areas. In the winter, they were likely to move to winter camps in higher elevations where firewood was more plentiful. Similarly, families who relied more heavily on herding moved to the high country in the summers to find better pastures for their sheep.[15]

The proximity of border towns, roads, missions, and trading posts could be as important as climate in shaping the ways Navajos made a living.[16] People who lived near the BIA agency headquarters in Window Rock or near Gallup, where government projects were concentrated, might rely more heavily on wages and less on livestock or farming. In contrast, on the Kaibito Plateau, a region largely disconnected from the broader market, wages constituted 15 percent of Navajo household income. Still, access to government jobs did not completely transform Navajo households in the 1930s and 1940s. For the most part, in the 1930s most Navajos lived in semisubsistence-based households. They had adapted to the vagaries of the landscape and made their living with what they could grow, herd, or weave.[17]

Subsistence Culture

By "subsistence," I do not mean to imply that the Navajos lived a noncommercial, precapitalist existence, completely cut off from surrounding wage and commodity markets. Instead, the term refers to a way of life that Thomas Berger described as "an array of activities and deeply embedded values . . . that enables the people to live directly from the land."[18] The line between subsistence and commodity production is highly permeable. What is produced for household and village consumption is often indistinguishable from products sold on the market. The tools and production process as well as the social organization of labor may be the same, incorporating a mixture of methods and resources gained from the larger market as well as those passed down through generations of cultural innovation. For example, the Inupiat Eskimos in Berger's 1985 study developed a system of hunting that incorporated tools, such as snowmobiles, with knowledge "about lore and skills preserved through countless generations."[19] In some cases, the cash they earned from selling commodities and working for wages contributed to the survival of a subsistence lifestyle. That way of life involved continual commitment to making a living from the land, redistribution of resources among village members, and social reciprocity among kin (including sharing labor, hospitality, and wealth). According to Berger, those "activities link the generations and extended family into a complex network of associations, rights and obligations. This network both reflects and recreates the social order and gives meaning and values to each person's contributions and rewards."[20] Subsistence is not simply an economic classification. As Berger continued, "[i]t also involves cultural values and attitudes: mutual respect, sharing, resourcefulness, and an understanding that is both conscious and mystical of the intricate interrelationships that link humans, animals and the environment."[21]

The cultural universe that shaped Navajo households in the 1930s and 1940s resembled what Berger observed about the Inupiat Eskimos in the 1980s. Many Navajos maintained subsistence households even as the material base for that way of life was shrinking. They compensated for the loss of their livestock and increasingly limited access to range and farmland by incorporating resources from the wage and market economy. The cash they earned from those markets helped to bolster the reservation household. At the same time, cultural values about household responsibility informed the behavior of Navajo wageworkers and producers of commercial products such as coal, jewelry, and rugs. Navajo cultural values such as a son's obligation to his mother, or a husband's responsibility to his wife's family, for example, continued to shape wageworkers' migration strategies. Railroad work dispersed Navajos as far as Oregon and Kansas City. But after a few months away from home, many Navajo workers would return to the reservation and tend their wives' fields, help their relatives with sheep shearing, participate in a sing or other ceremony, or make sure their mothers had enough wood to get them through the winter. In the early 1950s, Navajos bought cars and trucks with the wages they earned picking produce on commercial farms and made use of the new roads that were starting to cut across the Navajo landscape with greater frequency. Although those cars took Navajo workers away from the reservation, they also brought them back.

Since the mid-nineteenth century, Navajos have been struggling to retain as much land as possible within the boundaries set out for them by First Man and First Woman. In 1863 the governor and commander of the New Mexico Territory dispatched Kit Carson to force the Navajos to submit to U.S. authority. Carson, a famous trapper, soldier, and former Indian agent, brutally carried out his task; by burning the Navajos' crops and orchards, killing their livestock, and contaminating their water supplies, he made it nearly impossible for them to continue living on their land.[22] The troops destroyed the Navajos' livelihood, then forcibly marched the Navajos more than 300 miles east to Fort Sumner or Hwéeldi in New Mexico. There they spent four miserable years, suffering from hunger, disease, and—as some Navajos remember—broken hearts. Many families recall how their grandparents managed to flee the troops and remain hidden for many years. Others remember the violence and the severe hardships they endured on the journey to Hwéeldi. Such stories of suffering and resistance are a vital part of Navajo oral tradition and remain a significant part of their collective memory to this day.[23]

In 1868, as a condition for their release from captivity at Fort Sumner, Navajo headmen signed a treaty with the United States, setting aside nearly 4 million acres of land in New Mexico and Arizona for the Navajo Reservation.[24] Although many Navajos left Fort Sumner thinking that they were returning to where they had lived prior to the Long Walk, the treaty reserved at most 10 percent of the land they had originally occupied. Many Navajo families simply returned home to where they had lived before, regardless of treaty agreements. Some families occupied the lands within the treaty's boundaries, whereas others sought out relatives and friends who had successfully evaded capture by Kit Carson's forces by hiding out in canyons in the far western region of what is now the Navajo Reservation. To accommodate the Navajo families living outside the boundaries of the original treaty and to settle disputes among Navajo, Anglo, and Hispano ranchers over land rights, between 1878 and 1934 U.S. presidents enacted a series of executive orders that increased the size of the reservation to nearly 7.5 million acres.[25]

Livestock Reduction

In the 1930s Navajos faced yet another assault on their subsistence. But this time the attack did not come at the hands of governors or military officials. Instead, scientists and well-meaning reformers delivered the devastating blows. In 1934, as part of a New Deal program to improve grazing lands and to limit soil erosion on the reservation, agents from the BIA and the Soil Conservation Service (SCS) began enforcing measures to limit the size of Navajo livestock herds.

With the election of President Franklin Delano Roosevelt came a dramatic shift in American Indian policy. He gathered around him reform-minded individuals who set out to tackle monumental issues such as poverty, unemployment, and environmental degradation. With great optimism, they believed that government could solve the major social problems of the day and do so through the use of technology, science, and grand public works projects. Leading the effort in Indian policy was John Collier, a man who was determined to repeal assimilationist policies of the past and preserve American Indian cultural practices and communal land holdings.[26]

John Collier had been a vociferous critic of the BIA, particularly the "autocratic" way it administered its policies without regard to what Indians themselves wanted or needed. Now that he was in the position to make changes, he proposed sweeping legislation that aimed to reverse allotment, increase the amount of communally held tribal lands, and promote the cultural expression of indigenous peoples. Although he did not advocate complete sovereignty for American Indians, he did hope that they would have a larger voice in the administration of their resources and their communities.[27]

Before his tenure as commissioner of the BIA, Collier had had some contact with Navajos while he was in New Mexico working to defeat the Bursum bill.[28] Later, he had publicly condemned what he saw as corruption within the BIA, specifically the rerouting of Navajo oil royalties into pork barrel projects—such as bridges built off the reservation to assist the developing tourist industry—that brought little benefit to the reservation community.[29] Many Navajos found him to be a promising candidate to head the BIA. His cultural pluralist philosophy and his ideas about Indian self-governance initially won a significant amount of their support.[30]

That enthusiasm would wane substantially as Navajos started to feel the personal impact of his policies on their daily lives. Not all of Collier's initiatives were unwelcome, however. Many Navajos appreciated the extension of the Civilian Conservation Corps (CCC) on the reservation and the jobs that accompanied it. They were also grateful for federal initiatives that developed wells, improved roads, and controlled pests, such as prairie dogs, that gnawed away at their crops. Others even found the agricultural extension services helpful and applied what they learned to improve the quality of their livestock and to increase their crop yields. But livestock reduction, Collier's plan to preserve the long-term viability of Navajo grazing lands, created so much resentment that his credibility was severely shattered. Navajos registered their opposition by voting against the implementation of Collier's premier piece of legislation, the Indian Reorganization Act.[31]

BIA officials had been worried about soil erosion for many years before the New Dealers arrived on the Navajo Reservation. Scholars have well documented the laments of Indian agents who worried about the degraded condition of the grasslands and the widening arroyos as far back as the late nineteenth century.[32] But as historian Marsha Weisiger has pointed out, the advent of a new, reformist administration offered a unique opportunity to revisit this dilemma. The soil experts, climatologists, agricultural economists, and sociologists who descended onto the reservation in the 1930s to preserve Navajo rangelands enjoyed unprecedented political support in Washington and unwavering faith that science would offer an acceptable solution.[33]

These scientists examined all aspects of the Navajos' problem. They tested the soils, studied the climate, and inspected the livestock. They assessed the carrying capacity of reservation land and divided it into eighteen land management districts and calculated how many sheep, goats, and horses each could support. They then issued permits to livestock owners that granted permission to graze a specific number of "sheep units."[34] By significantly reducing their herds of sheep, goats, horses, and cattle—by up to 50 percent—SCS officials predicted that the range would be restored and provide Navajos with a viable economic base in the future. In the end, however, stock reduction policies had the opposite effect. The action undermined the Navajos' subsistence economy, a blow that hit the poorest families the hardest.

According to anthropologists Klara Kelley and Peter Whiteley, prior to stock reduction in 1930, Navajos held about 760,000 sheep, 21 per capita, or about 107 per household. After stock reduction, in 1949, that number fell to a total of 414,000, 8 per capita, or 44 per household.[35] For the large stock holders, mandatory livestock reduction actually improved the quality of their herds by forcing them to cull out their weakest animals. Small holders were the hardest hit by these measures. Since an average Navajo household needed at least 100 sheep, goats, or cattle for survival, reducing their stock below that number was devastating. Desperate economic conditions forced many families to consume their livestock, further reducing their herds to below self-sustaining levels. By 1937, large holders had lost 5.4 percent of their stock, whereas those households with 100 animals or less suffered a 23 percent reduction.[36] The result was increased economic stratification throughout the reservation.[37]

It is not clear if, in the long run, the stock reduction program improved range lands. In 1955, the noted anthropologist Gladys Reichard reflected on the poor state of the range. Traveling in the same areas as she had in 1934, she found that "[t]he condition of the land is rapidly worsening despite the deprivation of the People who are far from convinced that the short-lived effort helped them." According to Reichard, Navajos thought stock reduction amounted to "pouring money into the arroyos."[38] We do know that the BIA and SCS efforts did not improve the economy of the reservation as a whole. When federally enforced stock reduction ended in the 1940s, the subsistence base for many Navajo households had been severely undermined.

There is some debate about what caused the soil erosion in the first place. Historian Richard White argued that up to the 1920s, Navajos had avoided a serious ecological crisis by spreading out and grazing their livestock to off reservation lands. But, as the federal government and Anglo cattlemen limited their access to those ranges, Navajos were forced to graze their livestock in a more concentrated manner.[39] This caused what geographer Robert Allan Young termed "hogan grazing" and reflected the pressure on Navajos to curtail their seasonal migrations and settle in one place year-round. He thought the problem was not so much ecological as economic. Young argued that by 1931, the Navajo population had grown at such a rate that it outpaced the value of its livestock.[40]

Many Navajos agreed that their range was suffering from severe erosion. But many did not believe overgrazing was at fault. Instead, they saw it as part of a cycle of drought. They remembered years when the rain fell and those years when it did not. They had faith that erosion was not permanent. In fact, drought served a purpose by making people appreciate the rain.[41] The rain would come back, but only if the people attended to their responsibilities. Reflecting on the horror of stock reduction, Deescheeny Nez Tracy recalled:

All was going well, and people had increased their livestock very rapidly, when along came John Collier and stomped his big foot on our sheep, goats, and horses—and crushed them before our eyes. We believe that is when the rain went with the sheep. Now we have only small units to our permits, and the sandstorms erase a herd's hoof prints in seconds. The people are partly at fault by some of them ceasing to care for the sheep. They have forgotten the songs and prayers which produce more livestock.[42]

A combination of factors, including a growing Navajo population, a long cycle of drought, and the increasing limitations on where Navajos could graze their animals, seemed to have taxed the rangeland beyond its regenerative potential. Both Navajos and BIA officials knew something needed to be done. But BIA officials did not include Navajos in the decision-making process in any meaningful way. As a result, they failed to recognize the broader social and cultural implications of their policy. Therein lies the tragedy of stock reduction.

BIA officials did not fully understand the role of sheep in Navajo culture. To them, as Iverson has noted, "Grass was grass. Sheep was sheep. Soil erosion was soil erosion."[43] Compelling Navajos to give up their sheep was akin to forcing them to abandon their fundamental values about parenting, gender, and notions of security. Livestock meant power and responsibility. For example, Navajos used herding as a way to teach self-reliance to their children. They would learn tremendous life lessons from taking out the sheep in the morning and bringing them home at night. The herds signified a family's social status in the community as well as the power of women overall. They were the material basis of Navajo matrilineal culture. For the most part, sheep belonged to women, and mothers passed down their herds to their daughters, which provided them a source of income independent from their husbands. Finally, to most Navajo livestock owners, sheep and cattle were an investment in their future. Many families taught their children that if they took care of the sheep, the sheep would reciprocate. The wool clip was something they could depend on year after year. It also provided women with the materials they needed for weaving their rugs. Sheep were not just sheep. They were life.

The days that Rose Mitchell, a respected midwife and weaver from Chinle, remembered were over. She recalled how, "In those early times, we moved back and forth with our sheep; it was all open range then and there were no fences anywhere. The land was there for everyone's use and the People moved around, sharing the land. No one was permanently settled and no one thought any family owned any particular place."[44] Now their land was divided into land management districts, and they were prohibited from moving from one to another, according to the season. Such restrictions were a constant source of frustration. Council delegate Manuel Denetso voiced his concerns at a Navajo Tribal Council meeting in 1940. He said, ""What is true with my particular family is true for other families. . . . Heretofore we were allowed to move here and there and always respected the range rights of our fellow man, but now we cannot do that although we have hogans established in other districts than the district to which we are assigned."[45] Restricting their access threatened their basic assumptions about how they used the land and how they interacted with each other. Now they had to respect boundary lines and grazing permits instead of the traditional use rights of their neighbors.

Federally sponsored projects aimed at easing the pain of stock reduction also prepared the way for Navajos to become wage workers. New Deal programs, such as the CCC, were supposed to provide people with jobs to substitute for the income they lost when they gave up their sheep. In reality, CCC jobs were temporary and often did not go to those people who suffered the most from stock reduction policies.[46] Nevertheless, many Navajo workers earned their first wages working on short-term construction projects such as building roads, schools, dams, and serving as interpreters to development "experts." These New Deal programs, however limited, constituted an initial phase of economic development (or underdevelopment, one might argue) that further integrated parts of the reservation into the larger U.S. market. For example, CCC crews built roads that accommodated large trucks hauling coal between the small truck mines to reservation boarding schools and surrounding reservation border communities. The Depression and World War II kept those types of structural improvements rather modest, however, until the 1950s, when the federal government poured millions of dollars into the development of the Navajo Reservation under the auspices of the Navajo-Hopi Rehabilitation Act.[47]

Sacred Landscapes

In late April 1996, Irene Yazzie, a ninety-six-year-old Navajo woman who lived in a hogan on Rocky Ridge, near Big Mountain, Arizona, had a vision.[48] Two Navajo Holy People, one dressed in blue, the other in white, approached her and warned that there would be no relief from a relentless drought that was devastating the land and people in the Southwest. Only if the people returned to the "traditional" ways would rain come. The Holy People disappeared as suddenly as they had come, leaving a circle of corn pollen and their footprints behind.[49] Rain finally did grace the parched land, although not in enough quantities to bring an end to the drought.

Irene Yazzie is one of the Navajos living on the land that had been designated a joint use area by a lawsuit initiated by the Hopi tribe against the Navajo Nation in 1963.[50] But in 1974, an act of Congress changed the boundary lines, granting the Hopis sole rights to parts of the land where many Navajo families had lived for generations.[51] Since then Congress has passed laws requiring Navajos living in the disputed area to relocate. To force the Navajo residents to comply with federal orders, the Navajo Tribal Council has deployed various strategies, from confiscating livestock to enforcing measures preventing families from making improvements on their properties.[52] In 1997, the Navajo Tribal Council attempted to initiate a compromise by negotiating seventy-five-year leases with the Hopis for the resident families.[53] Led by Navajo women elders concerned about preserving their land for future generations, many of the families have refused to sign leases and continue to fiercely resist efforts to move them.

Irene Yazzie's vision and her appeal to the "traditional ways" may be interpreted within this explosive conflict as a challenge to those forces of modernity that have ordered families like hers to relocate. As a messenger for the Holy People, she blames the drought on those Navajos who have abandoned the "Navajo way."[54] In some ways she is drawing her authority from the Holy People, asserting indigenous knowledge over the power of the Navajo Tribal Council and their modern law enforcement procedures, lawyers, and grazing permits. Since she had her vision, her hogan and the place where the Holy People appeared to her have become shrines where hundreds of Navajos have gathered to leave gifts and say prayers. Even Albert Hale, the president of the Navajo Tribal Council, visited Yazzie to pay his respects. He issued a memo encouraging all tribal employees to make the pilgrimage, giving them four hours of paid leave to do so. Hale stated, "We must give thanks for the many blessings that we have and to pray for our land, for abundance of rain, for our future and for our children."[55] Hale issued this memo as the elders at Big Mountain were preparing to hold a Sun Dance, a pan-Indian ceremony that is embraced by some American Indian activists as a way to prepare themselves spiritually for the relentless battle with the federal government over land and civil rights.[56]

Perhaps Yazzie's implied criticism of Navajos who had abandoned their traditional ways was intended for Hale and the tribal council. Navajo Nation and Hopi police had attempted to prohibit the elders from holding their ceremony, arguing that the drought made the land highly vulnerable to fire. Despite efforts to close off the reservation from non-Navajos and to stymie organizers' efforts to prepare for it, the Sun Dance went on as planned.[57]

At the same time the Holy People visited Yazzie, Hale had been riding the range to assess the drought damage. Wearing his black hat and mounted on his sorrel gelding, Hale and his entourage rode 18 miles north from Tó Haach'i' (Tohatchi), 24 miles north of Gallup on Highway 666 to Nahashch'idí (Naschitti). He then ventured east from To Łaní in Canyon de Chelly to Tsét-soh in Chaco Canyon, making surveys of the parched land and suffering livestock. After his repeated trips on horseback, Hale concluded that the land suffered from overgrazing. When asked "How do you tell people that the sheep and cows and goats and horses that define their security, prosperity, and order of their world are destroying the very land they hold sacred?" Hale replied, "It is very difficult. No Tribal leader has wanted to deal with this."[58]

Indeed, Hale was running the risk of political suicide by attempting to enforce grazing restrictions. Memories of federally enforced livestock reduction continue to influence the Navajo political landscape, creating a legacy of distrust and resentment for the Navajo Tribal Council and the BIA. Any resemblance to the range riders who tried to enforce stock reduction in the 1930s would not sit well with his constituency.

Yazzie's story illustrates the way that struggles over land, resources, and political power have been articulated on the reservation, since at least the 1930s.[59] Beginning with New Deal–era soil conservation programs through the large-scale construction projects initiated by the Navajo-Hopi Rehabilitation Act in the 1950s, political and economic conflicts between and among U.S. federal officials, the Navajo Tribal Council, and various Navajo communities have often been framed in cultural terms. Although what is considered "traditional" and "modern" has changed over time, and the amount of tension between the two categories varies historically, Navajos have consistently used those terms to define "Navajoness."

For many Navajos the land could not, and cannot, be measured by the price of the commodities produced on it. The land was and is sacred. But, as Klara Bonsack Kelley and Harris Francis pointed out, the land is not sacred in and of itself. The way people interact with the land infuses it with spiritual significance. Sacred places "concentrate power from the landforms on which they sit, whether those landforms are the powerful religious preserves or the lifegiving areas outside them where people have their homes, farms and grazing lands." [60]

Home, itself, can become sacred as Navajos enact the everyday rituals that give life meaning. For example, where one buried a baby's umbilical cord was tremendously important. According to Rose Mitchell, if the parents wanted the child to be a good weaver, they would bury it in the ground next to the loom. If they hoped for the child to have strong livestock, they placed it in earth next to the sheep corral. That decision was pivotal because, as Mitchell explained, "It ties you to that place, your home, because that's where your cord is buried. We have believed that and gone according to that *for a very long time.*"[61]

After stock reduction, Navajo relationships to the land began to change dramatically. Federal livestock reduction created a crisis for those households that lived close to the edge of survival. Without enough sheep, goats, and horses to make a living, many Navajo household members were forced to venture far from their homes in search of wages. Yet, the reservation household persisted long after the land-based economy declined. Even though it was becoming increasingly difficult to make a living off the land, for its members, the reservation household continued to serve important economic and cultural functions. For those Navajo men and women who worked on the railroads, in the large corporate mining operations, and on commercial farms, the reservation household became a pooling station for the redistribution of resources and income among family members. Far from destroying the reservation connection, off-reservation wage work helped to strengthen it.

The land no longer provided the material base for subsistence. Yet its cultural meaning, derived out of pastoral and agricultural land use, informed the construction of Navajo identities in the world of wage labor. Navajos engaged broader wage and consumer markets in ways that resonated with past practices and in that experience created new expressions of Navajo cultural identity at home.

2

Mining Coal like Herding Sheep
Navajo Coal Operators in the Mid-Twentieth Century

We used to do farming there and at the same time he used to work at the
mine too. When we were old enough to work on our own, we used to go
down to the mine to help him. We did all the farming too so we know how
to take care of ourselves. But we still had to be careful. We used to load
those cars that they pull out. We used to help one another.
>   —Evelyn John from Shiprock, Navajo Nation, New Mexico[1]

Describing the small, underground coal mine developed by his father
and uncles in the 1930s on the Navajo Reservation, Burton Yazzie remembered that his family performed ritual offerings to the earth to
restore the harmony that their mining threatened to upset. Yazzie recalled that there was "[a] lot of living on the mountain. Even insect
got to. So you have to make an offering to her when you disturb her,
[when you] ... disturb mother earth." For Yazzie, performing the necessary prayers restored cosmological balance while reaffirming cultural values of reciprocity among kin. Yazzie's references to the earth
as "mother" throughout his description of the ritual indicated that
his family's prayers and offerings might be understood as symbolic
labor they performed out of obligation to kin, and one's mother in
particular. Mr. Yazzie stressed the importance of such ceremonies,
"[b]ecause this was our livelihood. So we had to ask the great spirit
for protection." These prayers and rituals reinforced the centrality
of the family and the necessity of continuously tending to kinship
obligations. Mr. Yazzie explained that they diligently performed their

prayers and offerings on a consistent basis. "We just don't say a little prayer for this and then forget it for the next 20 years," Mr. Yazzie said. Portraying time in generational terms, Mr. Yazzie continued, "[d]uring them times, during my mother and my father, . . . [t]hey used to have this almost every year. Almost every year." Burton Yazzie thought that his family's observance of "the native ways" ensured safe working conditions. "Maybe that's why we never did have very much accidents," Yazzie concluded.[2]

Yazzie's family was like others living on the Navajo Reservation who, during the era of stock reduction, shifted their primary economic strategies from raising sheep and cultivating the land to working for wages and pooling a variety of other income sources. But, unlike other families that derived most of their livelihood from off-reservation work on the railroads and in Anglo-controlled commercial agriculture, the Yazzie family and other small coal producers continued to make a living working their land. The land they used had rich coal deposits, minable with a minimum of capital investment. They were part of a group of Navajo coal producers who, up until the late 1940s, managed to maintain relative autonomy from the wage market.

This chapter pieces together that part of Navajo history that neither fits the victimization paradigm nor follows a dependency narrative. It examines a strategy used by Navajos that allowed them to engage the capitalist market while maintaining their autonomy from it. What follows is not a story of decay or decline of Navajo cultural traditions. Rather, it is a tale of dynamic cultural innovation where ideas arising from a pastoral, mixed-subsistence lifestyle shaped the development of an industry that was clearly linked to the broader U.S. market economy.

Indigenous Coal Mining Industry

The development of a small-scale, indigenous coal mining industry on the reservation emerged out of the Navajos' participation in the capitalist market. Although there is evidence that a few individual Navajo men operated mines in the 1880s, archaeological studies of abandoned mine lands show Navajos opening coal mines in significant numbers in the 1920s, with development intensifying in the 1930s.[3] When asked by archaeologists to describe when a specific coal mine first opened in an area south of Shiprock, New Mexico, Edmond Henna, a Navajo man who operated the mine between 1932 and

1935, said that coal mining did not become "popular" until the 1920s. Henna attributed this trend to Navajo households acquiring coal-burning stoves. They did not have much need for coal before that time, Henna explained, because most Navajos used juniper and other varieties of fuel in wood-burning hearths.[4] When Navajos began purchasing coal-burning stoves from trading posts and/or retailers in nearby border towns, they created a domestic market on the reservation that a small-scale industry emerged to supply.[5]

Navajos produced coal in ways that resembled a cottage industry, especially when compared with the large commercial coal mines operated by Anglo-controlled corporations such as Gamerco near Gallup and the Albuquerque and Cerrillos Coal Company in Madrid, New Mexico, a small town between Albuquerque and Santa Fe. Those companies employed 200 to 400 men year-round and used the most "modern" equipment the industry had to offer.[6] The Navajos, by contrast, worked their mines in small, family groups on a seasonal basis. Generally, seven to nine Navajo men worked a coal outcropping, each opening mines directly adjacent to the others.[7] In 1936, F. W. Calhoun, a mine inspector from the U.S. Geological Survey, noted that "[t]his class of mines constitute the greatest number of coal mines on the northern Navajo Indian Reservation in New Mexico." In his survey of the area he counted seventy-two Navajos operating thirty-four mines, producing a total of 3,300 tons of coal per year. Although these small mines appeared throughout the reservation, most of the independent operations were concentrated in northern New Mexico, in three clusters of about eight mines each, near Shiprock in the Hogback and Fruitland coal fields. The most extensive workings were along the San Juan River, just south of Fruitland, in a mountainous area called the North Hogback and to the south just outside of Chaco Canyon Wash.[8]

Some mines resembled little more than a surface-level gouging of the coal outcropping, whereas others were more elaborate, complete with 200-foot tunnels reinforced by timber supports.[9] Through the 1930s and into the early 1950s, miners separated lump coal from the slack in the mine, loaded the most marketable sizes into wheelbarrows, then dumped it into a coal car, if they had one. A horse or mule would then pull the coal car up the slope to the surface. By 1943, at least one group of Navajo miners used more sophisticated methods. Fred Begay and three brothers, Gene Funston, Frank Funston, and Tom Pashlakai, hauled the coal out of their mine, designated North Hogback No. 11 by U.S. Geological Survey (USGS) mine inspectors, in one-ton mine cars

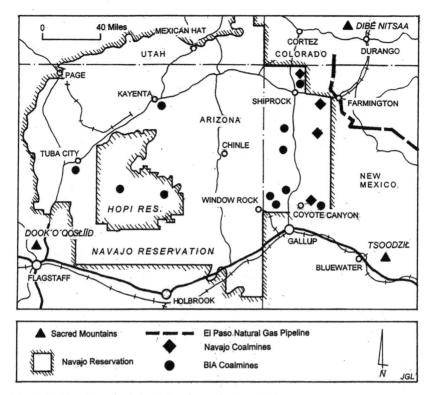

Map 2.1. *Navajo coal mining. Map drawn by Jorge Lizárraga.*

attached by rope to a "single drum hoist constructed from an old truck to which the drum has been installed upon one of the rear axles."[10] But most Navajo miners used more rudimentary methods, loading and hauling their coal by hand and using animals for the heaviest work. Henna told archaeologists that in the 1930s he used picks, axes, and wedges to dig out the coal and then loaded it onto drag sleds that horses pulled to the surface.[11] Miners and their kinsmen would then unload those cars into horse-drawn wagons or later into trucks that would transport the coal to various points on and off the reservation. The miners either sold their surplus at the mine to Anglo truckers, or they loaded the coal into wagons and sold it to their neighbors, BIA agency officials, or residents of the nearby reservation border towns such as Farmington, where, as Henna remembered, he could get six dollars for a wagon or pickup load.[12]

Independent Navajo coal mine. North Hogback. No date, probably 1937. Photo courtesy of the BLM.

Truck mining in this manner was not unusual for the region. Mexican-American and Anglo men operated similar mines throughout northern New Mexico and Colorado in the first half of the twentieth century.[13] They used similar equipment and probably struggled with comparable technical and environmental problems. But the Navajo miners brought something else to their mining processes. They developed their coal mines out of a pastoral tradition, a cultural system that defined land and labor in relational terms. Although coal mining seems at first glance to be an antithesis to the work of herding sheep, the same principles that guided the work on the range shaped the way Navajo men and women viewed themselves in relation to the coal. They were mining coal in the same way they herded sheep.

In their livestock-based economy, a family's relationship to the land was determined by how they used it. Navajo shepherds recognized ownership of personal property, but land was not something that was "owned" in the sense that it was alienable, could be sold, or inherited outright. Everyone recognized a family's claim to use a particular area for a specific purpose, and they could

Hoist constructed from the rear axle of an old truck. Ben Begay and George Funston's mine, North Hogback, 1943. Photo courtesy of the BLM.

pass down that right to the next generation. Survivors could continue using the land, grazing livestock, or growing crops in the same way that their parents, spouses, and grandparents had before them. But, if they did not want to do so, the land would become available to anyone else who wanted to use it.[14] Anthropologist Gladys Reichard noted the fluid nature with which Navajos distinguished the perimeters of land use for individual families and/or households. In 1928 she observed that, "[t]hey set up no boundaries, each goes where he will, each uses all the water he needs. If the supply becomes exhausted he moves to another place where it is better. And all this without dissension or bad feeling."[15]

Mine inspectors' words echo Reichard's observations about Navajos' use of the land for sheepherding. Like Reichard, the inspectors noticed a relative lack of concern among Navajo coal producers about private property lines. B. W. Dyer, J. J. Bourquin, and C. L. Dyer noted that "when ever a mine is opened, the Indians decide among themselves as to the boundaries of the operation." As of 1928, as far as the mine inspectors knew, "no disputes over boundary lines" existed. Their observations also noted Navajo miners' respect for land use rights, a tradition clearly linked to pastoral lifeways. Astonished by the mix of communal decision making and individual initiative, they commented that, "[b]y mutual agreement, the mine is recognized as belonging to the person or persons who developed it as long as they care to operate it."[16] Although they noted that Navajo men worked their mines individually, or with the help of one or two kinsmen, the small mines seemed to them to be "owned by a group of individuals."[17]

Working the mines blended well with the seasonal rhythms of farming and sheepherding.[18] Attempting to describe Navajo work habits to the National Bituminous Coal Commission, E. R. Fryer, superintendent of the Navajo Agency, explained, "[w]hen it's time to plant or tend to other agricultural matters, most coal production would come to a halt."[19] Similarly, R. H. Allport noted that at times the demand for coal could not be supplied "on account of labor conditions . . . [that would] probably continue until such time as the crops are all harvested."[20]

Called "subsistence mines" by one Navajo Agency superintendent, these small operations primarily supplied coal for the miners' own household use. They sold what was left over to their neighbors and/or residents in nearby border towns. During the winter, when coal was in great demand, it served as a kind of seasonal crop that miners could produce in the period between harvests in the fall and planting in the spring when the labor of maintaining their reservation households demanded less of their time.

Winter was also a time when Navajo men who worked on the railroad or in commercial agriculture faced long periods of unemployment. For those Navajo men who stayed on the reservation or returned from working elsewhere, mining coal became a lucrative occupation at times of the year when other opportunities for earning a living were rather limited. Instead of relying on credit advanced by the trader against the next season's harvest or wool clip, selling their coal carried them through the winter and provided them with some autonomy from the cycle of debt that plagued so many Navajo families in that period.

Even though the mine inspectors' reports do not reveal much about the personal relationships of the miners, testimonies gathered from oral interviews and archaeological reports suggest that the men the mine inspectors refer to as "employees" were usually related to the individual operator. Fathers,

Photographed by J. J. Bourquin, unidentified Navajo miners working a "strip pit" near Burnham, New Mexico, 1936. Photo courtesy of the BLM.

sons, brothers, uncles, grandfathers, and in-laws worked alongside each other in the mines. The story told by George Barber, a Navajo man who operated a small mine south of Shiprock in the 1930s and 1940s, serves as an example. Mr. Barber worked with his father to produce coal primarily for his family's use, and for sale locally, in an area that had been home to his maternal and paternal grandparents. Sometime in the mid-1930s, a Navajo man named Joe Dick married one of Barber's sisters. Considering Navajo cultural practices of the 1930s, it is reasonable to assume that Dick went to live with his wife's family, which would, in this case, oblige him to work alongside his wife's male relatives in their mine. George Barber's nephew, James, also remembered Joe Dick mining at another site close by. Judging from the archaeological evidence, it seems that after he had established himself, Joe Dick opened his own mine and constructed a hogan for his new family on land adjacent to the Barbers. When Joe Dick's son died at the age of nine, in 1940, in accordance with Navajo cultural practices, they buried him inside the hogan, then abandoned it. It is unclear what happened to Joe Dick and his family after that date.[21]

According to Navajo cultural values in the 1930s, miners were supposed to use the land in a way that honored reciprocal obligations between kin and fostered harmonious relationships within the community at large.[22] For some that meant employing uncles, cousins, and clan relatives, even when it was financially difficult to do so. Helen Duncan remembered that her husband, Shorty Duncan, routinely hired relatives to work in his mine when they were in need of work. Duncan, a particularly successful miner, sometimes based his staffing decisions on the needs of his kinsmen, not so much on his demand for their labor. But, Helen Duncan painfully recalled, when "there was no coal to sell," some of them went hungry.[23]

Hózhǫ́ and Navajo Patterns of Work

Coal was an important crop, but it did not supplant the cultural significance of sheep to Navajo households. Sheep were (and are) more than a source of income. They embodied a sense of connection with past and future generations. Margaret Kee, the wife of Clarence Kee, a miner who in his younger days worked in small underground coal mining operations, traced her flocks back to their ancestors, the original sheep given to her family by the army when they left Fort Sumner. Margaret Kee remembered that "couples were given one sheep or one goat. So from there, they have babies. Now to this day, one of those sheep is still here."[24] One of the lessons her father taught her in his later years, Mrs. Kee remembered, was the importance of taking good care of the sheep. Translating her mother's story from Navajo to English, Juannita Brown recounted her grandfather's advice to her parents: "He constantly constantly, every day every day, remind[ed] [them] to take care of sheeps and goats. Take good care of them. In the future, . . . when you guys have kids between the two, tell them about the sheeps. Let them go on with the sheep." The sheep gave her mother a connection with the past and hope for the future. Her daughter believed: "[I]f the sheep are not around her, she feels empty, so she has to have some kind of sheep around her . . . they're holding that gift from their dad and their mom to this day."[25]

Burton Yazzie, like Clarence Kee, spent his youth working with relatives in a small underground coal mine and eventually found a job working for the large Pittsburgh and Midway strip-mining operation.[26] He too fondly remembers his mother's careful attention to her sheep. Out of a herd of more than one hundred, "[e]nough to make money on," Yazzie recalled, "[w]hen a goat or sheep crie[d] out, she'[d] know . . . which one [wa]s crying." Like the Kees, Yazzie learned that the sheep represented security for the future. "We had to take care of them, and they would take care of you. Vice versa."[27] Even today, when sheep contribute little in terms of household income, Navajos still invest them with deep emotional and spiritual significance. As one daughter of a miner employed at Peabody Coal Company on Black Mesa explained, "the sheep are our culture."[28]

There seems to be an inherent contradiction in a coal miner's daughter referring to sheep as the embodiment of her culture. Coal and sheep seem innately incompatible. Coal mining was dangerous, unpredictable, and seemingly contradicted the cultural values that guided Navajo ideas about the proper use and care of the land. Prior to stock reduction, long-range herding and seasonal migrations helped to conserve the land and its resources.[29] Yet, coal mining was an intrusive and destructive act and required miners to stay in one place for a large part of the year. In the San Juan Basin, an area where the most intensive coal mining occurred, Navajos who herded their sheep as far as 100 miles from their "permanent camp" were by the 1930s limiting their ranging areas to 2 to 3 miles in radius. As a result, more Navajos were beginning to live at one homesite year-round.[30] It is possible that Navajos turned to coal mining as they found their access to grazing land becoming increasingly limited by livestock reduction regulations. After that, while their children tended the herds nearby, men were free to pursue mining during seasons when their fields and livestock needed less care.[31]

Livestock could devastate a landscape, particularly when they were confined to a relatively small area. But coal mining could be disastrous. Land erosion and the potentially hazardous working conditions worried the miners. Their mines were always in danger of caving, catching fire, or flooding, and most miners could not afford to purchase more sophisticated mining equipment that might have improved safety.[32]

Hózhǫ, a central principle in Navajo culture, might have helped them reconcile such contradictions. Commonly referred to as the "Navajo way," hózhǫ describes, in anthropologist Gary Witherspoon's words, a "universal state that defines the totality of life, of all that is beautiful, harmonious, good, healthy and orderly."[33] It can be something experienced on a personal level as a peaceful feeling derived from a harmonious relationship with both the social and natural worlds. It can also take on a broader collective meaning and connote profound balance between forces of good and evil and order and disorder in the world. Navajos trace the idea back to Changing Woman, a beloved holy person and the mother of the Navajo people. She brings about "dynamic beauty," as Navajo land resources specialist Milford Muskett described, and "through her chaos and order meet to find balance."[34] Following in the tradition of Changing Woman, Navajos' efforts to achieve this balance, as Jennie R. Joe and Dorothy Lonewolf Miller argued, have allowed Navajos to adapt to "all types of differences and diffuse experiences . . . despite their inherent contradictions."[35] Burton Yazzie's description of his family's offering suggests that some miners and their kin may have developed rituals to restore the cosmological balance that they disturbed in the physical world. For Yazzie and his family, making those offerings to "mother earth" provided "her" with "nourishment." Fulfilling their reciprocal obligations with the earth maintained an equilibrium that would ultimately protect the miners' health and safety.[36]

The evidence suggested in the archaeological survey of Barber's homesite and other Navajo coal mining areas, as well as Burton Yazzie's reminiscences of the ritual performed by his family to insure "harmony" in the mining operation, implies an intermingling of ideas and cultural practices between "modern" and "traditional" worlds.[37] Coal, particularly in this region, literally fueled large-scale industrial operations such as railroads and copper mines and supplied the "prerequisite feedstock" that made possible the postwar expansion of such major western cities as Los Angeles and Phoenix.[38] The independent Navajo miners supplied a smaller part of that market by selling coal to consumers in reservation border towns, to their Navajo neighbors, and to the BIA, who used it to heat their schools and offices on the reservation. The Navajos were becoming part of the capitalist market, but doing so in ways that made sense to their own cultural and historical context.

The BIA and the Rationalization of Coal Production

Apparently BIA officials did not share the Navajo workers' faith that such ceremonies would protect the miners' health and welfare. The agency had been purchasing coal from the Navajo producers as well as non-Navajo contractors to heat the BIA administrative offices and schools for many years without paying much attention to how it was produced.[39] After 1928, however, at the be-

Unidentified mine inspector in front of the Burnham School "strip pit," 1937. Photo courtesy of the BLM.

hest of the BIA, the USGS initiated annual inspections of the independent Navajo coal mining operations.[40] Five years earlier, the BIA had created the Navajo Tribal Council in order to approve oil leasing contracts. Perhaps after that experience they perceived themselves as the trustees of all Navajo mineral resources.[41]

Ensuring the long-term viability of the mines weighed heavily on BIA and USGS officials, and the Navajo miners' methods did very little to lessen their fears. Mine inspectors argued that if left unchecked, Navajo miners would deplete the most accessible coal deposits in a relatively short time, and the BIA would lose its convenient energy source. In their first detailed survey of the Navajo mines, inspectors B. W. Dyer, J. J. Bourquin, and C. L. Dyer admitted that the Indian service (as the BIA was sometimes called) obtained coal "very cheaply and with very little trouble." But they worried that such ready access soon would be a thing of the past. By then the "thicker coal along the outcrop will have been mined out, and it will be necessary to drive the workings" beyond the parameters of the current operations in order to supply the BIA with the coal that it needed. And that meant higher mining costs.[42]

The mine inspectors had a lot to worry about. In 1928 the job of mine inspector was a relatively new position. In the early 1890s, under the auspices of the secretary of the interior, Congress sent inspectors to the western territories to enforce mining codes and to make sure that the expanding railroad lines would have an available supply of coal. By the 1930s, the industry itself had undergone tremendous change, as mining had become more mechanized and companies drew new immigrant groups into their labor force. The engineers were a new professional corps of men who arrived in the coal fields armed with mining school expertise, ready to administer new safety laws and regulations. They were like the other New Dealers who were eager to apply their scientific knowledge to the social and environmental problems of the day. But they often faced the problem that many regulatory bodies encountered, promoting an industry that they were hired to police. Advocating profitable mining could at times conflict with the job of protecting workers. Stretched thin, the inspectors were in charge of monitoring large-scale operations as well as the small truck mines operated by workers throughout the Southwest.[43]

The mine inspectors were particularly concerned with the amount of "slack" coal the Navajo miners left in their mines.[44] In 1936, the inspectors estimated that it represented 25 percent of all the coal the Navajos produced and resulted from the miners' practice of "forking" the coal inside the mines.[45] In larger, commercial operations off the reservation, almost all the coal was loaded into mine cars and taken to the surface. Separating the coal by size would then be done by dumping the coal onto a tipple. Gravity would carry the coal down through a series of screens that would sort out the coal by size. Alternatively, a mining company might employ "tipple" or "breaker" boys for that purpose. Slack was particularly explosive, and leaving it inside the mine amounted to a great fire hazard. If the mine caught fire, it could burn indefinitely, leaving the miners with no alternative than to seal up the portal and abandon the site.

The problem that vexed the inspectors the most was what they perceived as the Navajo miners' lack of planning. In report after report they complained that they did not follow any particular system of mining that ensured rational, long-term profitability. As early as 1932, mine inspector J. J. Bourquin wrote

Tom Lee's mine in the North Hogback, near Shiprock, New Mexico, 1937. Photo courtesy of the BLM.

that "few if any Indians [in the Southwest] are qualified to plan and to execute the development of a coal mine." But in a paternalistic tone, Bourquin added, "they perform[ed] their work well when guided by intelligent supervision."[46]

One mine inspector noted that Ben Begay, a Navajo miner from the North Hogback region who supplied coal to many BIA facilities in the northern part of the reservation, would soon run out of minable resources. He complained that Begay's "mine is so badly cut up and hogged out that it may be lost through caving before the period of another year has elapsed."[47] Although the inspectors found in many of the mines the "timbering as a whole ... done well," they did not find that it "afford[ed] proper protection of the workman and to the mines themselves."[48]

What the mine inspectors failed to acknowledge, however, was the role the BIA played in creating conditions that encouraged "inefficient" mining methods. With competition from such large-scale producers as Gamerco and other commercial coal companies within shipping distance from Gallup in the southern region of the reservation, the Albuquerque and Cerrillos Coal Company to the east, and the Colorado coal companies in the north, the small-scale Navajo producers had to keep their production costs at a minimum. Without the capital to develop an "economy of scale," one way the Navajo producers kept their prices low was by mining only the coal that was cheapest to produce. The mine inspectors bemoaned the Navajo miners' management skill, whereas the miners were in fact operating mines with a keen eye to market conditions.

Never satisfied with letting the Navajos pursue their own ways of doing things, the BIA and the USGS set out in an attempt to improve conditions. In 1936, as the BIA was in the midst of trying to "help" the Navajos conserve their range land by eliminating 50 percent of their sheep herds, BIA and USGS officials embarked on a program aimed at preserving coal resources as well. After carefully calculating the market demand for Navajo coal, they concluded that the Navajos had "too many" coal mines.[49]

First on the mining engineers' agenda was to limit the number of mines and to centralize production. F. W. Calhoun, a USGS mining engineer, argued that the number of mines should be reduced to what was "required by convenience or necessity to serve the real needs of the population." Calhoun thought there was "no real need for the operation of more than 12 coal mines by individual Indians on this Reservation." To streamline production, he suggested that Navajos abandon twenty-two of the thirty-four coal mines and the remaining twelve, the "more conveniently located mines," be leased out to "individual Indians." In that way, the BIA could gain control of the Navajo miners' production methods. More important, according to Calhoun, the smaller number of mines would "furnish employment to equal numbers of Indian miners and as equal or greater tonnage [would be] produced."[50]

Apparently Calhoun assumed that wage work was an equivalent substitute for owning and operating one's own mine. It is likely that he did not consider the equity of the arrangement at all. As far as Calhoun was concerned, the Navajos were not qualified to operate their own mines. He wrote,

> They are difficult of supervision, pay no royalty, and accept almost no responsibility for safety or good mining practice. The operation of those mines contributes in a small way to the convenience of a few Indians, but on the whole the mines, as operated, are economically a great disadvantage and hazard to the tribal wealth, and are rapidly rendering the recovery of the coal difficult and expensive. Great waste of the mineral resources of the tribe can readily be noted.[51]

North Hogback agency coal mine, New Mexico, 1936. Photo courtesy of the BLM.

Throughout 1936 and 1937, mine inspectors repeatedly suggested that the BIA come up with a plan to limit the number of mines the Navajos were operating. They now placed less emphasis on the need to preserve the agencies' cheap supply lines and assumed a more paternalistic posture, offering arguments for regulating the independent producers in "[t]he interest of the tribal owners of the land."[52] Soil Conservation Service officials were already carrying out their plans to ensure the long-range market viability of range resources. Mining experts had the same thing in mind for the Navajo coal reserves.

In November 1936, F. W. Calhoun provided a detailed plan for restructuring Navajo coal production. The proposal essentially called for the independent producers to relinquish control over their operations and submit to the authority of the BIA. First the report insisted that "all present mining by individual Indians be stopped as detrimental to tribal interests and as economically unsound." In the name of efficiency, Calhoun suggested that central mines be reopened in place of the groups of mines customarily operated by the Navajos. These new centralized "mines [would] be developed on

Coal mining display at the 4th Annual Navajo Tribal Fair in Window Rock, Arizona, September 1941. Photographed by Milton Snow. Courtesy of the Navajo Nation Museum, Window Rock, Arizona. Catalog # NG6-1.

a standard plan approved by a mining engineer or other coal mining men with long experience in the management of coal mines." New mines would open under a permitting system that would grant mining rights for a five- to ten-year term, requiring operators to pay a royalty of ten cents per ton to the Navajo tribal government. Most important, the new mining system would place regulatory authority and enforcement power in the hands of the BIA.[53] Essentially, Calhoun was suggesting the transformation of Navajo coal producers into wage workers.

From the beginning, mine inspectors complained about their lack of power to institute changes in Navajo mining practices. Now they would have the full force of New Mexico and federal mining regulations to back them up. The Navajo miners' leases would be subject to cancellation at the will of the agency for failure to follow the instructions of the agency mining supervisor. Not only could the BIA revoke their permits, it could punish violators of coal mining laws with fines or imprisonment. Encouraged that his proposal would satisfy all parties involved, Calhoun predicted that "under this plan, all individual Indian mine operators could be employed and conservative mining practices adhere[d] to with consequent improvement in safety, supervision and economy."[54]

Acting on behalf of the BIA, the director of the USGS forwarded a copy of Calhoun's report to Washington, D.C. In his cover letter he suggested that Calhoun's recommendations would work "to the advantage of the Indians engaged in mining the coal."[55] Apparently impressed by the mining experts at the USGS, BIA commissioner John Collier suggested that Superintendent Fryer bring this matter to the attention of the Navajo Tribal Council. Collier was concerned that the Navajos had been mining coal "at will" for many years without supervision and urged Fryer to "impress upon the council the importance of proper mining operations" to protect both the resource and the miners' safety.[56] Collier seemed to be advocating a stronger regulatory role for the Navajo Tribal Council. His suggestion appears to have been a mere cosmetic amendment, however, to Calhoun's plan of vesting the BIA with complete authority over mineral development. At this time, the tribal council was having difficulty establishing its legitimacy among the Navajo population. Many held the councilors responsible for the horrors they faced during stock reduction and had voted to reject the Wheeler-Howard Act (the Indian Reorganization Act) two years before. It would not be until the 1970s that the Navajo Tribal Council would begin to assert greater control over its own coal, oil, and natural gas resources. Even then, it would take a series of lawsuits over the next thirty years to renegotiate the notoriously poor leasing agreements that the BIA had established previously.[57]

On July 22, 1937, three weeks after Collier wrote to Fryer, the Navajo Tribal Council passed a resolution giving the BIA the power to regulate the independent miners. The resolution stated:

> Whereas, valuable resources are being wasted and destroyed by careless mining practices, it is recommended that the Superintendent take appropriate action to close such mines that are not being operated in accordance with regulations. Therefore, be it resolved that all mines on the Reservation shall be closed unless operated in accordance with mining laws and regulations, and all Indians taking coal or other minerals from tribal lands shall pay into tribal funds a royalty to the tribe only when they sell coal, no royalty shall be paid on coal mined for their own use.[58]

Four days after the tribal council passed the resolution, Fryer wrote to Collier to request funds to carry out the program. He claimed that the Navajo agency did not have the resources it would need to oversee the changes recommended in Calhoun's report. Fryer suggested that the Civilian Conservation Corps (CCC) make the coal mines a special project. He also requested that $10,000 be allocated to the program and that the BIA's resident mining expert, Oscar Foy, an Anglo, be employed to oversee the operation.[59] After the Navajo Tribal Council passed the resolution requiring Navajo miners to abide by "mining laws and regulations," local BIA officials began issuing permits.

Enforcement was another matter entirely. The BIA officials admitted that with such a limited staff, it was nearly impossible to supervise all the Navajo mines. How could they regulate a couple of men chipping away at an exposed coal vein with their picks and shovels? Was that the same as monitoring the development of a much more elaborate operation where the Navajos had tunneled back more than 200 feet and reinforced their work with timber supports? The latter category of miners worried the BIA the most since they were subject to more dangerous working conditions and were more commercially successful.[60] Many Navajo miners managed to evade mine inspectors and continued to work their mines without a permit until the early 1950s.

Although BIA officials encouraged the Navajo Tribal Council's oversight of the independent producers, they did not do the same for their own operations. As models of safety and efficiency, those mines were supposed to supply coal to agency facilities and offer Navajo workers the opportunity to learn disciplined mining methods from an experienced Anglo supervisor.[61] BIA officials did not think it was necessary to request a permit from the tribal council or pay royalties on the coal they extracted. According to Fryer, since the coal would be consumed by the agency directly, there was no need to consult the tribal council.[62]

The question of royalties stirred up considerable debate within the BIA in Washington and New Mexico for the next two years. In Washington, officials favored cooperation with the tribal council. Frederick L. Kirgus, the legal counsel for the commissioner of Indian affairs, advised the agency to compensate the tribal council for the coal. An avid reformer, he thought taking the Navajos' minerals without their consent was "the sort of thing [for] which past administrations have been severely, and I think justly, criticized." He wanted the current administration to be more scrupulous, even if they thought the coal was to be used for the Navajos' benefit. After all, he reminded local officials, Navajos would see it differently. They would see the agency employees and the U.S. treasury as the chief beneficiaries, Kirgus predicted.[63]

Local BIA officials were less concerned with what the tribal councilors thought. In 1938 one agency official in New Mexico wrote in an exasperated tone, "[w]e have, of course, been using coal from Indian lands for a long time, and we have not paid the Indian tribes for it. Why should we?" In fact, he thought the Navajos were indebted to the agency for its administration of services on the reservation. "Why not," he continued, "get . . . the approval of the councils for the free use of coal, wood, etc.? In that way the tribe is making a partial contribution toward costs of administration."[64]

Washington BIA officials continued to urge cooperation with the tribal council, including compensating it for coal mined on reservation land.[65] But this issue remained unresolved until after World War II, when the BIA turned the mines over to the Navajo Tribal Council to manage. During the intervening years the BIA never reconciled the contradiction of the leasing issue. At the same time it instituted a leasing and permit system for the Navajos to mine on their own land, it did not formally recognize the need to regulate itself or to compensate the tribe for the coal it consumed. Local practices seemed to win out over Washington's policy directives. Writing in 1949, J. M. Stewart explained that the tribe's "resources should be used as a partial offset against the benefits the Indians are receiving from the Government."[66] From the years 1939 to 1948, the BIA did not compensate the Navajo Tribal Council for the 285,211 tons of coal the BIA mined on reservation land. During that same period, individual Navajo operators paid a total of $9,324.50 in royalties.

Issuing permits did not necessarily bring about the changes expected by the BIA officials and mine inspectors. In 1940, BIA officials decided to use their power as consumers of Navajo coal to force the Navajo miners to comply with procedures established by the Bituminous Coal Commission.[67] When the Shiprock Agency began purchasing coal from the independent producers, they did so under certain restrictions. Mine inspectors reported that coal would be hauled by BIA agency trucks, weighed on scales installed by the agency, and mined under the supervision of a mine foreman supplied by the agency. Coal would not be purchased from those miners who did not conform to the mining procedures approved by the foreman.[68]

The Hogback Coal Miners' Association

With or without permits, some Navajo miners did well enough to attract the ire of corporate coal interests whose operations flanked the Navajo miners to the north and east. Company officials and union leaders worried that Navajo miners were producing coal at a lower price and pressured BIA officials to increase their efforts to control the miners. If the Navajo miners did not abide by the 1937 Bituminous Coal Act, their coal would be subject to a nineteen cents per ton tax.[69] The Bituminous Coal Commission initially reassured BIA officials. Since the Navajos produced primarily for their own household consumption and for BIA agency facilities, they would be exempt from the conditions spelled out in the legislation. When the corporate members of the Bituminous Coal Commission complained about the "unfair" competition from the Navajo operators, the commission reversed its decision. In 1939, Robert W. Knox, general counsel for the commission, wrote to Fryer, noting that "[t]he coal sold by a producer on the Reservation does not differ from coal sold by other producers and so [is] subject to the provisions of the Bituminous Coal Act of 1937."[70] But complying with the Bituminous Coal Act was simply beyond reach for most Navajo coal operators. They could not afford to abide by the production, wage, and price standards outlined in that legislation, and paying the tax penalty would have made Navajo coal less competitive against the coal produced by the corporate operators.

Miners in the Shiprock area were not easily deterred. Together they traveled to Window Rock, approximately 100 miles to the south, to officially request permission to mine the land that many of them had been mining for the previous ten years. Soon the Shiprock miners formed the Hogback Coal Miners' Association, and BIA officials were encouraging the Fruitland group to do the same.[71] According to its 1941 charter, the Hogback Coal Miners' Association set out "to improve and assist in every manner possible, the development of the Hogback Coal resources for the benefit of local Navajo Indians and the Tribe."[72] The responsibilities of the body included policing its members to see that they abided by the terms of their mining permits. They also arbitrated disputes between members, set coal prices and wage rates, and ensured that they followed the suggestions made by mine inspectors regarding safe and efficient mining methods. In addition to regulating its members, the association aimed to work for the mutual benefit of the operators, enti-

Harry John, a retired miner and heavy equipment operator from the Hogback Community. Photo by author. Used with permission.

tling each "an equal share of business providing he has coal available on demand." They also established a centralized facility where the operators could take their coal to be weighed and distributed to truckers. By collecting a ten-cent fee per ton, the operators were able to employ a weigher and raise money for capital improvements.[73] The Hogback Coal Miners' Association also represented the interest of the independent miners in the Shiprock area to the tribal government. In May 1939, the association approached the Navajo Tribal Council for a $1,200 loan to purchase platform scales and for building a coal bin to store coal in the Farmington/Shiprock area.[74]

The Hogback miners tried to beat the corporate coal operators at their own game. The Bituminous Coal Commission was an organization made up of industry representatives who wanted to bring about stability to a market plagued by fierce regional competition. Modeled on World War I cooperation among industry, government, and labor, the commission's goals included setting minimum prices, production goals, and labor costs. And they managed to wield enough power to force small, truck miners to comply with their regulations. The coal companies were defining the rules of engagement, making it almost impossible for the Navajo operators to compete on an individual basis. They simply did not have the capital to develop their mines and install the latest labor-saving equipment. They could not afford to install ventilation fans and electricity, to purchase sophisticated new drills and coal cutting equipment, or even to build a tipple. As E. R. Fryer put it, "[m]ost of them would be unable to furnish bond even in the smallest sum."[75] Since the Hogback miners could not survive independently, they too formed a producers' association and adopted an organizational model that was relatively common in the larger market. The coal companies had the Bituminous Coal Commission; the Navajos had the Hogback Coal Miners' Association. Unfortunately for the miners, that was not enough. Despite its promising beginning, the association did not last long. By the mid-1950s, most of its members had closed their mines and stopped mining for good. Even their collective efforts could not stem the global change in the coal market. Like the owners of larger corporate operations off the reservation, they too suffered as their consumers switched from coal to natural gas and other forms of energy.[76] It is ironic that their success can in some ways be measured by their defeat. They had won a place in that market (however small) and thus were subject to the same market conditions that were beyond the power of many small producers—Anglo or Navajo—to manipulate.

One by one, members of the Hogback Coal Miners' Association had begun to close down their mines in the late 1940s and early 1950s. According to mine inspector reports and interviews conducted by anthropologists, permit violations forced many miners to abandon their mines. The permit plan, in

essence, threatened a system of land use and rights established along customary practices adapted from the Navajos' mixed pastoral/agricultural traditions. One might argue that their semisubsistence lifestyle had provided
them a safety net protecting them from the complete submersion in the wage
labor market.

What began as a way to ensure the agency an adequate supply of inexpensive, high quality coal resulted in the extension of the BIA's paternalistic control over another part of the Navajo household economy. Like its strategies
for improving range conditions of Navajo land, the BIA's approach for over-
seeing the development of Navajo coal resources threatened to eliminate one
of the strategies that had previously provided Navajo producers' households
some autonomy.

This story need not end on such a dismal note. The narrative is not necessarily a story about the disintegration of indigenous traditions brought about
by capitalist development. Rather, it is an example of dynamic, cultural innovation where ideas arising from a pastoral, mixed-subsistence lifestyle
shaped early forms of industrial production on the reservation. The emergence of a Navajo-controlled coal industry during the era of stock reduction
offers an alternative narrative for economic transformation on the reservation. By developing the mines, the independent Navajo miner was, in effect,
transforming the land that had been part of his customary use area for several generations. Mining diversified the Navajos' pastoral/agricultural ways of
making a living in a manner that adapted their notions of land use and household production to the increasing needs of a growing market economy.

That experience would surely guide others who faced similar choices over
relocation and working for wages off the reservation. The struggle with the
BIA over control of coal production, like those bitter memories of stock reduction, would become part of the cultural conversation that would shape the
kinds of demands that Navajo workers and political leaders would make in
the 1950s and 1960s. Seen from that standpoint, Navajo coal miners participated in the making of their history.

Conclusion

Anthropologists have shown that prior to the era of federally enforced stock
reduction, Navajos had fashioned an extremely flexible system of social

relations that allowed them to utilize a variety of economic strategies.[77] Although herding sheep remained a central source of subsistence and cultural identity for many Navajos into the 1930s, survival of the household largely depended on the ability of its members to draw from a variety of sources of income, including wage work, silversmithing, and weaving. Ideally, combining multiple sources of income allowed Navajos the freedom and flexibility to adjust to the vagaries of the market, the climate, and other factors, such as the intervention of federal policies, that made their lives and livelihoods unpredictable.

As an indigenous mining industry developed on the Navajo Reservation, it emerged as part of a mixed economy that integrated subsistence strategies with a selective participation in wage and market economies. Even though the Navajo coal producers participated in the market, the ideas and methods remained grounded in a pastoral livelihood. What they received from their coal sales enabled them to maintain their connection to the land and their kinship obligations and potentially to resist the draw of the off-reservation labor market. But, as the federal government chipped away at the source of that subsistence, removing sheep and regulating production methods, that "harmony" was threatened.

The Navajo case illustrates what other American Indian scholars have revealed, that until the relationships of production are transformed, the mere "contact" with the capitalist market does not initiate, necessarily, a complete transformation of a society's culture.[78] The Navajos are significant for how they negotiated the struggle with the encroaching world market, participating in it when it suited their purposes, but refusing to allow capitalist cultural and economic logic to significantly undermine the cultural premises from which they shaped new economic strategies. As long as they could maintain control over their sheep, their land, and their coal, they could participate in the market on their own terms. The encroachment of the BIA on the independent miners' autonomy undermined the viability of the small producer and may not only have hastened the pace of transition of Navajos into wage workers but also have impeded the early development of a Navajo-controlled industrial base. BIA efforts to regulate Diné livestock may have undermined their traditional ways of making a living. Attempting to rationalize coal production threatened to undermine Navajo innovation as well.

3

Weaving a Living

Navajo Weavers and the Trading Post Economy

*It was the women who were the "bread winners." The whole family de-
pended on the women.*

        —John Dick, from Rough Rock, Navajo Nation, Arizona[1]

When Betty Harvey needed school clothes for her children or groceries for her family, she would sit down at her loom and weave. She
rarely received cash for her rugs. Instead, she traded them for groceries and other goods at the Fruitland or Hogback trading posts. The
wool came from her own small flock of sheep, and she did the carding, spinning, and dyeing herself. For Betty Harvey, as for many other
Navajo women of her generation, weaving provided a financial safety
net. Although she could not earn enough from her weaving to support her family year-round, the income she generated often bridged
the gap between starvation and survival.

    Betty Harvey was the wife of a Hogback coal miner and had grown
up in a miner's family. Born in 1926, near Sweetwater, Arizona, as a
young child she and her family moved 65 miles southeast to the Hogback region on the Navajo Reservation, where her family routinely
mined coal to use in either potbelly stoves they acquired from the
traders or in "sheepherder" stoves that they fashioned out of sheet
metal or an old steel oil drum.[2] They filled those stoves with the coal
she and her neighbors mined themselves. According to Harvey, "[w]e
found that coal ourselves. . . . The mine was open to everybody. Whoever wanted coal, they just used to go and get it."[3] She eventually

married John Harvey, who worked with her brother, Harry John, in a variety of mines in the Hogback region.[4] There she raised seven children and while her husband was working in the mines, she would take care of her family's farm 10 miles east of their home in the Hogback.

A complex history of conquest and colonization, the development of labor markets targeting Navajo workers, and paternalistic federal control over Navajo land and resources framed the choices Betty Harvey and her family would make in the postwar era. As a young girl, she witnessed federal livestock reduction. She came of age during World War II, when many of her relatives left the reservation to join the military or to work in defense-related jobs. As western agriculture expanded to feed the postwar population boom in the Sun Belt, she accompanied her family to work in the carrot fields around Phoenix, Arizona, and Bluewater, New Mexico. The traveling stopped when her children were old enough to attend school. After that, she stayed in the Hogback for good, tending her sheep and weaving rugs to make ends meet.

These events brought dramatic changes in the way Betty Harvey's generation made a living on the reservation. In the years leading up to stock reduction, Navajo men and women engaged the capitalist marketplace as producers and consumers, trading wool, livestock, handcrafted items, and sundry agricultural products with traders who operated businesses on the reservation or in nearby border towns. The Navajos were also drawn into the market as workers, repairing and cleaning railroad tracks and picking crops on a seasonal basis. After stock reduction, those jobs became even more important to Navajo men, drawing them away from their reservation households for up to four months at a time. Women occasionally accompanied their husbands, brothers, or uncles off the reservation to work on commercial farms throughout the West. Or, they might work as domestics in border towns or in middle-class households in various western metropolitan areas, where they were recruited directly from Indian boarding schools as part of their vocational curriculum.[5] But for many Navajo women, the capitalist market remained something they engaged closer to home, where they wove the rugs that became pivotal to the trading post economy.

Chapter 2 focused on men's contribution to the Navajo household economy in their role as miners who, like Betty Harvey's husband, developed a small but significant coal mining industry on the reservation. Navajo cultural practices, ethics, and values shaped that effort, even if coal mining was not

Betty Harvey, at her loom in her house in the Hogback Community. Photo by author. Used with permission.

particularly "Navajo" in its origin. This chapter turns toward the women, many of whom were the wives, daughters, sisters, and mothers of the miners. They engaged the market as well, producing commodities that included wool, rugs, blankets, and other handcrafted textiles. But their experience was different from that of their male counterparts. From the 1930s through the 1950s, while Navajo miners were distancing themselves from the trader's paternalistic grasp and earning cash from selling coal, weavers remained entrenched in the trading post economy, a capitalist marketplace that kept them mired in a cycle of debt. Their work was pivotal to their families' survival, a resource that kept starvation at bay. Yet, to Navajo women in the mid-twentieth century, weaving meant much more. By weaving rugs, women found a way to maintain their powerful economic and cultural roles in their households, even as the expanding capitalist market was transforming the land and resources that had shaped their gendered experience in the years leading up to stock reduction. The result was a system of overlapping markets within the same household that reflected the gendered values and expectations of its members.

The Trading Post Economy

Woven textiles had long been an important part of the Navajo economy. Navajos had traded blankets and other handcrafted items with neighboring Ute and Pueblo communities since at least the early eighteenth century. At times, their reach extended into broader markets, including the Great Plains, where Navajo weavings commanded impressive prices, and Chihuahua, where Spanish traders exchanged the weavings for other goods with established merchants. By the early nineteenth century, Navajos were well ensconced in a trade network that linked a variety of American Indian communities with Hispano and Anglo settlers as well as Mexican merchants.[6]

In the mid-nineteenth century, Navajo weavers adapted to harsh conditions and changing market demands by incorporating innovative materials into their work and developing new designs. Incarceration at Bosque Redondo, or Hwéeldi, from 1864 to 1868 severely disrupted the blanket trade. Kit Carson and his men had largely destroyed Navajo herds in his campaign to bring Diné into submission, and the bleak conditions at Fort Sumner made weaving exceedingly difficult to manage. Nevertheless, Navajo women found ways to experiment with what they had on hand, including army-issued textiles imported from Mexico. After the Navajos returned home, weaving became even more important to their economy than it had been prior to the Long Walk. As the market grew, they started to weave rugs that would appeal to Anglo consumers instead of the blankets they had traded in southwestern markets earlier in the century. This does not mean that Navajo women produced for non-Navajo markets exclusively. They might exchange rugs for credit toward the purchase of a Pendleton blanket, but their weavings continued to be important items of exchange within Navajo communities. They might be too valuable to put on one's own bed or floor, but they would be cherished as gifts to relatives or to singers in exchange for performing important ceremonies.[7]

The earliest traders to establish permanent posts on or near the reservation were those who made their money supplying the military posts. Initially, they found the Navajos reluctant consumers, since much of what the trader had to offer, the military supplied in annuities.[8] The first trading post appeared in 1868, but the Navajos remained a secondary market until 1885, when the government stopped supplying them with flour, sugar, tobacco, and other

Painted mural from the original Hogback Trading Post. Photo by author.

staple products. By that time the Navajo economy was recovering from the devastation wrought by Kit Carson's raids and the incarceration at Bosque Redondo, twenty-two years earlier. Traders would try to tap into their new prosperity, and the extension of the railroad into the region provided them with the means to do just that.[9]

By 1881, the railroad's reach extended to the border towns surrounding Diné Bikéyah. The Atlantic and Pacific Railroad connected the reservation to points beyond through Gallup, New Mexico, a dusty crossroads with billboards that now, more than a century later, proclaim it "The Indian Capital of the World."[10] Such it is for the tourists drawn to the region who frequent the curio shops that line Gallup's streets. But for Navajos and other American Indians, such as poet Simon Ortiz, it is where "the heat is impossible, the cops wear riot helmets, 357 magnums and smirks, you better not get into trouble, [and] you better not be Indian."[11] Aptly named after the railroad paymaster, David Gallup, in the 1880s it was a place where railroad workers would go and get their pay. Today the town maintains its notorious reputation among

American Indians as the place to which their pay returns, to either the merchants' hands or to the saloons along Highway 66. By 1889 there were nine trading posts in operation on the reservation and thirty trading posts in border town communities. By 1937 there were eighty licensed trading posts on the reservation and far more operating off the reservation beyond the regulatory authority of Indian service officials.[12]

In 1905, twenty-four years after the Atlantic and Pacific Railroad rolled into the southeastern environs of the reservation, the Denver and Rio Grande Railroad Company built a branch line to Farmington, 120 miles northeast of Gallup, to tap into the rich coal resources of the San Juan Basin. This did not mean that Betty Harvey's family and others like them were going to get rich filling railroad coal contracts. The Hogback miners' markets were much more modest: neighbors, kin, BIA schools, and Anglos in nearby towns who bought their coal from the back of the Navajos' wagons and pickup trucks. Supplying the more lucrative railroad market was left for the larger commercial operations such as the Gallup American Coal company or the coal companies in southern Colorado.

Even though the railroads did not open new markets for Navajo coal producers, they did bring goods to Navajo consumers, such as the coal-burning stoves Betty Harvey described earlier. Navajos mostly purchased food and clothing and other staples at the trading post, however, rather than larger manufactured items.[13] Traders hoped to exploit the promise of an untapped Navajo consumer market, but they soon found out that the real money lay in exporting Navajo wool, textiles, and other products off the reservation.

Since traders were primarily interested in Navajo wool, initially they merely dabbled in the blanket trade, leaving that market for Navajos to negotiate with other American Indians in the region as well as interested non-Indian settlers.[14] But the wool market was volatile, subject to dramatic fluctuations in the global economy. Navajo textiles were a good substitute. They were a reliable commodity that provided attractive long-term profits. In fact, the blanket trade served as a buffer, protecting traders from the fluctuations in the global wool market, an "alternate way to market wool."[15] For example, according to Kathy M'Closkey, Lorenzo Hubbell made far more money on trading Navajos' rugs than he did on marketing their wool. Even though the textiles provided the trader with some financial security, he rarely, however, passed on those profits to the women who produced them.[16]

The most successful traders were those who operated with a respectful nod to Navajo sensibilities.[17] The trader needed to treat his customers like kin, offering hospitality to those who walked through the door to trade or to gossip. Stories about Lorenzo Hubbell, one of the most famous traders on the reservation, abound with tales of his generosity and somewhat larger-than-life role in Navajo history. Some Navajos remember him as fair and benevolent, often recounting how he would treat his customers to a can of peaches or some other treat and offer children candy or a bottle of sweet soda.[18] The letters Navajos wrote to Hubbell, now preserved in the trading post records, testify to the affection many felt for him. They often addressed him as uncle or friend and usually requested some sort of favor: either advancing them a small loan, extending their pawn agreement, or relating some sort of news to their relatives.[19] Other Navajos remember him in a less than positive light; resentful of their indebted relationship to him and frustrated with the small sums and "tin money" he would give them for their weaving.[20]

Hubbell's hospitality, however memorable, does not negate the broader exploitive nature of the trading post system. It is beyond the scope of this chapter to recount the vast scholarship on traders and weaving. Much of that work either vilifies the traders as cutthroat merchant capitalists or romanticizes them as "wooly individualists."[21] Newer research highlights Navajo agency in trading and treats the trading post as "hybrid places reflecting both Euro-American and Navajo value systems."[22] The bottom line, at least for the purposes of this chapter, is that traders and Navajo households were bound together through a system of debt. That Navajo women were able to negotiate amiably or whether the trader was kind and helpful does not negate the overall exploitive nature of the system nor the relative powerlessness of Navajos engaged in it. Until they could get in their pickup trucks and drive to Gallup, Flagstaff, or Window Rock and pay for goods with cash, Navajos were subject to the whims of the trader. The trader could extend or deny credit, and he could deduct the balance of Navajo workers' accounts from their paychecks, leaving them with little left over except for an expectation of credit against their future earnings. The traders even issued a kind of "scrip," similar to the currency that deeply irritated non-Indian miners who lived in company towns across the West at the turn of the century. Navajos received that "tin money" in exchange for rugs and other tradable goods, and it was only redeemable at a specific trading post.[23] Even the miners, whose families earned cash from their coal sales, relied on the traders to purchase their blasting caps and other mining equipment.[24] Although the traders did not mortgage the miners' coal, they did issue Navajos credit against future wool clips or harvests.

Navajos had very little consumer power to force down the prices on goods that were notoriously high. Not until the 1950s and 1960s, when roads improved and Navajos gained ready access to cars and trucks, did their buying power improve. Navajos were now likely to frequent the large supermarkets such as Fedmart or Bashas' that were opening up in the border towns or in developing urban areas on the reservation, such as Window Rock, Shiprock, and Chinle. Although they did not have the same relationship with the owners of those establishments, they were able to buy merchandise at much more reasonable prices than they could at the trading post.[25]

From the late nineteenth century to the 1930s, the trading post dominated the Navajo economy. Navajos began to experience the transformation of their economic worlds when the federal government initiated a reduction in their livestock holdings. By the 1950s, Betty Harvey's household, like the other Navajo mining families on the reservation, straddled two markets: the trading post system, defined by barter and debt, and the industrial economy where Navajos earned cash from either selling their coal or their labor. These two systems coexisted even as making a living from the land had become increasingly difficult. Both men and women conducted business with the traders, negotiating over lamb and wool prices, trading agricultural products and handcrafted silverwork and rugs. They both pawned personal items for groceries and cash and relied on the trader for mail and other services. But as many Navajo men set out to search for wage work off the reservation, the gendered nature of these transactions changed significantly.

The ethnographic evidence suggests that during the transformative years between the 1930s and the 1960s, the two economies overlapped in time and place and engaged men and women in different ways. Navajo men, who left the reservation to work on the railroads or in commercial agriculture, met their household obligations by returning home when they were needed, either to participate in sings and ceremonials or to attend to their womenfolk's needs. Some Navajo women traveled off the reservation, too, accompanying relatives to the agricultural fields, mining camps, or western urban areas to work in defense-related jobs. But, like Harvey, many more women of this generation stayed or came back home to Diné Bikéyah to raise their children.

From there they carved out a place in the trading post economy, one that did not necessarily afford them power in the world beyond the reservation, but could nonetheless help them sustain their high status and authority within the cultural and economic landscape at home.

This does not mean that the trading post and wage economies were mutually exclusive. Nor does it mean that men and women were sole arbiters of their respective domains. The two worlds often collided in the person of the trader himself, who in addition to advancing credit for wool or accepting a rug to pay off a Navajo woman's account might also serve as a labor contractor to commercial farmers and other western employers. But the market experience was generally different for men and women until the 1950s. Men were traveling great distances to work on the railroad, in large mining operations, or in commercial agriculture. Although some men used their wages to redeem their pawned possessions or settle their accounts with the trader when they returned home, their connection to the wage economy was weakening the bonds of dependency and affording them more autonomy from the trading post economy. For the most part, women's experience in the marketplace was limited to negotiating with the trader over goods she and her family produced, including sheep, rugs, and other items.

Women were central to Navajo culture and their household economies. As early as 1915, weavers constituted 55 percent of those Navajos "engaged in gainful occupations," according to a survey conducted by Peter Paquette, the superintendent of the Navajo Agency.[26] As the trading post system developed on the reservation, Navajo women soon found a central place for themselves within it. Unlike other indigenous women who found their productive labor devalued as their communities were drawn into the capitalist economy, Navajo women's roles became even more important, particularly since much of their work involved producing commodities the traders desired.

How did the changing economic climate impact Navajo women? Did Betty Harvey and her husband have a lot in common with men and women in other developing regions who found themselves drawn into the global economy, whether they liked it or not? In many cases, the introduction of capitalist market relations brought about significant changes in indigenous societies by either exploiting existing patriarchal structures or undermining gendered systems that were complementary rather than hierarchical.[27] But the development of capitalism does not necessarily bring about a "predictable and automatic" transformation of indigenous gender systems into patriarchal structures. As historian Florencia Mallon has argued, although patriarchal and class relations may be somewhat autonomous, the intermeshing of the two systems produces a historically specific configuration.[28]

For Navajos, that "configuration" meant the development of new types of gendered marketplaces on and off the reservation. Of course, Navajos did not need new markets to introduce them to the concept of "gender." Prior to their incorporation into the capitalist economy, Navajos generally understood the world in gendered terms, categorizing nature, thoughts, and actions as either male or female. Unlike Western notions of gender where the categories "male" and "female" exist in ranked opposition, Navajos did not establish a hierarchical relationship between them. Navajo cultural categories defined male and female as complementary parts of a whole, each necessary to ensure a harmony and balance in the universe.[29]

Feminist scholars have been examining the link between the history of capitalism, colonialism, and the development of gender hierarchies for many years. They created analytical models that seemed to offer universalizing theories about women's lives, only to find that such a project was, at best, only partially achievable. Mostly, the debates revealed that class dynamics, racism, and colonialism were powerful social hierarchies that undermined any significant shared experience among women. The development of "separate spheres," of private and public spaces, did not impact all women in the same way. Working-class households in general did not become refuges from work to which men would retreat from the evils of industrial society to be nurtured by attendant wives. This feature of industrialization may have defined the worlds of white middle-class women in Western communities and created complicated racial and class boundaries for elites in colonial settler societies, but it has little explanatory value for women whose histories did not follow that particular path. The sexual division of labor in one society or culture meant something very different in another.[30]

With capitalist transformation, many working-class homes stayed firmly in the public, subject to the scrutiny of governmental officials, be it social reformers attempting to clean up the tenements of New York or missionaries setting out to civilize the Indians. For workers, the line between productive and reproductive labor remained ill-defined with the onslaught of industrialization. Labor that a working-class woman might perform for her own household, such as sewing, washing clothes, cleaning, or minding the children, became a commodity, something to be bought and sold in the marketplace. Their households continued to be places of work whether they lived in New York City or Boston, hemming garments and making matchsticks, or in the Hogback, weaving rugs.[31]

Consequently, many indigenous women, the Navajos in particular, did not experience the division of their lives into polarized spheres.[32] Although Navajos did organize their household labor along gender lines, those roles were somewhat flexible and defined in complementary rather than hierarchical terms. According to historian Marsha Weisiger, a balance between men and women was supposed to exist to ensure "the holistic harmony embodied in the concept of *hózho*." Weisiger continued, "[m]ale and female were like two banks on either side of the same stream, and this concept coursed through everyday life, shaping understandings of the actual relationships between women and men."[33]

Rose Mitchell, a highly respected midwife and weaver from the Chinle Valley, described such a scenario in her own household. Reflecting on her life to anthropologist Charlotte Frisbie, Mitchell voiced her frustration with the younger generation's struggle over power in their households. She acknowledged that sometimes women assumed all the responsibilities, particularly if their husbands left them with children to support. But, she said, "if you're making a living with someone, you should share in that, too. Both the man and the woman have jobs to do about all of that; both of them are necessary to make things complete and to raise a family in the right way. That's how things were established by the Holy people at the beginning, and that's how we should be going along, even now."[34] Mitchell described how she and her husband accomplished this. She was in charge of the hogan and all that was associated with it, including directing the labor of her children. Her husband, Frank Mitchell, a very well respected political leader and Blessingway singer, was in charge of their schooling. He was also the one who made the decisions about which singer to consult in the event someone in the household fell ill. They made big decisions together, especially those that affected the future well-being of the family. Day-to-day economic choices were up to the individual to make. Her husband would decide whether he wanted to make additional money hauling wood, presiding over a ceremony, or serving on the tribal council. Mitchell made other types of economic decisions. She recalls,

"I decided how many rugs to weave for the traders, how to spend whatever little money he gave me to use for our children, and even when to stop help- ing women who were facing childbirth. In all those things, we supported and encouraged each other, but we didn't decide them for the other one."[35]

Generations of anthropologists studying the Navajos often lamented the in- evitable passing of such an arrangement. But, as historian Jennifer Nez Denet- dale has pointed out, Navajo women often contradicted anthropologists' pre- dictions and maintained a great deal of cultural and economic power in their households and communities, despite the overwhelming pressures to assimi- late.[36] For the most part, Navajos continued to define themselves according to their mother's ancestral line, passing down land use rights accordingly. And when a couple married, they tended to live with the woman's family if finances and personalities allowed for it. Of course, matrilineal and matrilocal social or- ganization does not always garner women great respect or authority. But such practices reflected the significant power women wielded within Navajo so- ciety even as they adapted to the demands of a new economic universe. When the pastoral economy began to decline, thus limiting the practical importance of matrilineal land use practices, "matricentric" cultural values remained.[37]

Marsha Weisiger's term, *matricentric,* is useful for describing the signifi- cance of women in Navajo households, and in Navajo culture generally. It de- scribes a fundamental value that shaped the ways Navajos organized and un- derstood their lives. Anthropologists have debated the significance of Navajo residential and inheritance patterns for many years. Women were at the cen- ter of Navajo culture, whether they chose to live with or near their mothers or moved in with their in-laws. As Weisiger explained, "[w]omen framed the tap- estry of Diné family and community life. Closely-knit networks of mothers, daughters, and sisters structured Navajo families and gave them cohesion."[38]

Women's Labor in the Trading Post Economy

Navajo women's productive and reproductive labor was pivotal to the trading post economy.[39] As producers, they created objects of trade, most notably the rugs, saddle blankets, and other textiles that have become emblematic of Navajo culture. As mothers, they did what they could to mold their children into people who would provide well for their families and honor their kinship obligations. That daunting task involved teaching children how to take care of the endless work involved in herding sheep and farming. As daughters, they learned to weave, tend their sheep, perform a variety of household tasks important to the survival of their families, and identify useful plants that would be helpful to them as they matured. As grandmothers, they often managed the labor of their households and offered cultural knowledge as well as wisdom born of considerable personal experience to the younger generations. They were responsible for teaching their grandchildren about "'good thinking' (*yá'át'ééh ntsáakéés*) and 'forward thinking' (*naas ntsáakéés*)." According to Karen Ritts Benally, "[t]heir teachings focused on establishing a good life, one in which you have everything you need—no more, no less—and one in which family, relatives, and neighbors live and work together in harmony." To achieve this balance, it was imperative to live a good Navajo life, fulfilling one's responsibilities to kin, clan, and the land.[40] Julia John, a miner's wife from the Hogback region, explained how she would organize weaving around her other obligations,

> There's no time set aside to weave. But, you find times when you know you can weave. One is early; I get up early in the morning, round about 4:00 am when the other family members are asleep. During that quiet time I could either finish a rug or just weave until it was time to prepare breakfast for the family. Then when everybody went off to school or off to work, I would go out to the sheep corral and let the sheep go on their own for awhile and I would weave a little bit more. And then when it was time to follow the sheep, I would put the rug aside. When I came back in the afternoon I'd do the same thing.[41]

Julia John was doing what was necessary to maintain her household on the reservation. Reflecting on how she overcame hardship, she likened her weaving to the work of building her family. "So, you know, I guess weaving's like that. You just find time and you just work at it and you have a finished product. The family, you know, is like weaving. You go through a lot, go to school, and your family becomes a finished product."[42]

Although some scholars might not see this as "economic" behavior, performing this "work" produced commodities for trade and created a strong link between Navajo households and the trading post economy.[43] Navajo cultural practices framed and shaped that work, much of which the women did to produce what their families would consume. Weaving helped them weather the economic and cultural storm brewing around them.

Julia John, at her home in the Hogback Community on the Navajo Reservation.
Photo by author. Used with permission.

It was a hostile climate in many ways. Between the 1930s and the 1960s, Navajos saw their economic and physical worlds turned upside down. Navajo weavers witnessed their herds depleted by federal agents who promised to conserve the land for future generations. They bid goodbye to their uncles, husbands, brothers, and children who left home to serve in the military and to find jobs, work that would draw them far from home for long periods of time. The weavers themselves often left home in search of work. They traveled to Phoenix to pick carrots, followed the potato harvest in Idaho, and packed tomatoes in Oakland. Some women found jobs closer to home. For example, Helen Duncan and Julia John worked in the Fairchild semiconductor plant from 1969 until it shut down operations in 1975.[44] After stints working in Oakland and Idaho, Margaret Kee eventually landed a janitorial position at the Navajo Nation.[45] For Rebecca Watson, the wife of Joe Lee Watson, a coal miner from Black Hat near Window Rock, the transformation of the Navajo economy meant the destruction of her family's traditional use area. The land where her mother herded sheep is now part of the Pittsburgh and Midway strip-mining operation. When I asked her if she had managed to keep her sheep, she sighed and motioned for me to look outside. "Where would they go?" she asked mournfully.[46]

The changing Navajo economy was making it increasingly difficult for women to weave. Livestock reduction depleted their sheep herds dramatically, thus limiting the amount of wool they could weave into rugs. Even as their access to wool was shrinking, their need for weaving income was not. Navajo households were becoming more dependent on the trader for food. Rugs had always provided them with the means to acquire groceries, but now their weaving bought a lot less. During the Depression, weavers received 48 percent less for their rugs than they had in 1928. Women, alternatively, had to weave more rugs to trade with fewer resources at their disposal. As Kathy M'Closkey stated, "It seemed as if the more the Navajos wove, the poorer they became."[47] But even with all these constraints, they kept on weaving, contributing 20 percent or more to their household incomes.[48] Soil Conservation Service workers found this to be true in the Gallup area in 1939. In the 175 households they surveyed, they found 230 weavers who produced 1,551 rugs, for which they received $6,535 in trade from local traders. Navajo women contributed 19 percent of the household income by weaving, whereas wages only supplied 12 percent (see Figure 3.1).[49] Livestock, wool, and agricultural products combined constituted the largest source of income. Of course, those percentages might be different in other parts of the reservation, since these figures reflect the unique concentration of the jewelry market near Gallup.[50]

As the country started to mobilize for war, Navajo women were weaving less. Anthropologists estimate that the rug trade was declining in importance,

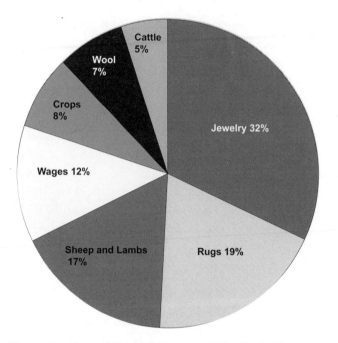

Figure 3.1. *Types of Household Income: Gallup/Two Wells Region, 1939–1940. Source: U.S. Soil Conservation Service Schedule, Areas 16–18 Combined, 1940.*

constituting from 9 percent to 11 percent of Navajo household income in 1940, depending on the region of the reservation. During World War II, Navajo households experienced a brief reprieve as those who served in the military or worked in various defense-related jobs off the reservation sent their wages home. Those resources, along with temporary employment, provided weavers with alternative sources of income and less economic incentive to weave.

The significance of weaving to the household economy continued to decline in the postwar era. According to anthropologists Garrick and Roberta Bailey, women coming of age in the 1950s found that they could make more money working on and off the reservation. For example, in 1954, Navajo women could earn seventy-five cents an hour doing domestic work in Farmington, New Mexico.[51] For these women, weaving rugs did not make much economic sense. "As late as 1959," Bailey and Bailey estimated, "a weaver earned only 6¢ per hour for her labor."[52] A destitute woman might pursue other available options first, including applying for welfare—something that was not available to Navajos before 1950. By the 1950s, Navajos finally gained access to federal welfare programs. As part of the 1950 Navajo-Hopi Rehabilitation Act, the federal government supplied subsidies to the states in exchange for including Navajos in their programs.[53]

Why Weave?

So, why did Navajo women continue to weave when the economic benefits of doing so seemed rather marginal, at best? Indeed, Helen Duncan, a Navajo weaver from the Hogback community, posed this question herself when I interviewed her in the summer of 2002. When I asked her to describe her weaving, she responded in an exasperated sigh, "sometimes I wonder why do I even weave? Sometimes you don't get that much out of it." Helen Duncan was married to Shorty Duncan, a successful miner who worked his mine in the Hogback region from the 1930s to the mid-1960s. She remembered that in those days she received very little for her rugs. Mrs. Duncan could expect the trader to pay between four and eight dollars for a 3-foot rug or up to twenty dollars for a 5-foot rug. But the traders did not pay her in cash. They paid her in groceries or other items they had in stock at the trading post. The rugs made a big difference to her family, since as she recalled, "the coal didn't pay all that much."[54]

Coal, like sheep, agricultural products, and wages, was a seasonal source of income. Weaving was not.[55] Navajo women could weave at any time of the year, depending on their familial circumstances. If they had children to tend the sheep or sisters to share the day-to-day household labor, they could focus much of their energy on weaving.[56] But traveling with their families to work in commercial agriculture off the reservation or finding a job closer to home might force them to put away their looms, at least until they had the time to focus on their weaving once more. Margaret Kee, a successful weaver from St. Michael's, started to weave as a child and continued to weave throughout her adult years. But it was not until her husband started working at the Pittsburgh and Midway coal mine that she could devote all her time to her work. Even then she occasionally stepped away from her loom to travel to Idaho to pick potatoes or to work as a janitor for the Navajo Nation. The top prices her rugs now command at upscale galleries in Durango, Colorado, have replaced the

wages she used to earn cleaning offices or picking potatoes in the Idaho potato fields. Wages bought her first truck; weaving paid for her brand-new
Chevrolet Suburban.[57]

For Helen Duncan and the other wives of the Hogback coal miners, weaving helped to make ends meet between seasons. The groceries from trading
one rug would last until she could finish weaving another. That could take two
months, because as she described, "you had to card the wool . . . wash it and
dye it."[58] Coal generated cash during the winter, but weaving could feed one's
family any time of the year. Economists echoed the weavers' observations. In
1937, B. Youngblood, an agricultural economist with the U.S. Department of
Agriculture, concluded in a report he issued jointly with the BIA that weaving was more important to families than the aggregate numbers suggested. He
said, "It is practically the only income they can normally depend upon between wool and lamb marketing seasons."[59]

By the 1950s, wages replaced livestock and wool as the major source of income for Navajo households. Although the source of income had changed,
the seasonal nature of it did not. For the most part, Navajo men and women
who worked for wages found jobs working on the railroad or in commercial
agriculture, work that was highly seasonal. Women continued to weave, their
income providing a buffer that enabled them to survive when wages dried up.
D. Y. Begay, a master weaver and scholar, remembers that her mother's weaving helped to provide for the family while her father was away working on the
railroad. Not only did weaving provide a buffer for seasonal work, it helped
to make ends meet when men were laid off from their jobs.[60]

Weavers like Margaret Kee, who was eventually able to devote full time to
her craft, or those who balanced their weaving with other household obligations remember their work as pivotal to the economic well-being of their
families. Weaving gave them confidence and comfort, knowing that if all else
failed, they would be able to feed and clothe their children. Weaving was a
safety net. Indeed, for Wesley Thomas's grandmother, the batten, comb, and
loom—her tools—were her "defenders." They were "weapons against hunger
or any form of hard times."[61] Rose Mitchell, a well-respected midwife from
Chinle, remembered how important weaving was to her family. As she related
to Charlotte Frisbee, "My mother taught us that if we kept weaving, if we were
good weavers, we could manage to live by that."[62] By weaving rugs, a woman
would always have something to exchange for food. She remembered, "[o]nce

in a while, after other stores were established, one of us would make one or two small rugs and go to one of the stores around here to trade for food when we barely had enough to eat again."[63]

Navajo women were busily working to meet their largest household expense. Stock reduction had been devastating, depleting much of the food they had originally produced for their families to consume directly. By 1940 they were now dependent on the trading posts to feed their families. Yet the smaller herds meant less wool to weave into rugs, and that limited their income options even further.[64] That forced many Navajo men to leave the reservation, at least temporarily, to search for wage work. In oral histories, in memoirs, and in the interviews I conducted, nearly all the weavers explain that their weaving made the difference. This was particularly important, since, according to Emma Reh, an anthropologist who studied Navajo consumption practices in 1939, Navajos spent two-thirds of their income on food.[65] The Navajos whom David Brugge interviewed in the early 1970s at the Hubbell trading post stressed the specific role weaving played in alleviating hunger. One man remembered that his mother wove all the time: "[T]hat's all she did. She . . . made rugs just to get groceries, you know. Groceries was all she wove for, just to live on, grocery was all, and then she would get a pair of shoes, [and]some cloth to make a blouse." It seems that the groceries would last just about as long as it would take to weave another rug. "We had to struggle for quite a while until my mother starts weaving again and just by the time when she finishes, our groceries would be down and they'd come again," he continued. When "food would be scarce, we'd run out of flour, we'd run out of coffee . . . and she had to weave . . . almost all night sometimes."[66] Others recalled great suffering and described how they used to weave small rugs to take to Hubbell in exchange for food. These women, who lived in desperate poverty, did not have sheep of their own and would get their wool from Hubbell to make their rugs.[67]

Weaving provided Navajo women a sense of security for themselves and their children. Partly answering her own question, Helen Duncan explained, "my dad told me, when I was younger you know, learn how to work with the wool. Learn everything you can about weaving because as you get older, it will make you money and you will be eating from whatever you produce from the wool. It'll feed you. It'll carry you on. That's why, to this day, I still weave."[68] Margaret Kee learned a similar lesson growing up. Her grandparents taught her to take good care of the sheep, because "you could use the wool for rugs . . . and make a living." Her mother and father reinforced her grandparents' teachings and urged her to rely on herself, not necessarily her husband, to provide for her family. Mrs. Kee recalls her father's advice, "don't just look at your husband. Your husband might have a job but don't look up to him because jobs can end and this weaving [is always here]. Stick to your weaving. You can raise your kids on your weaving and you can make money along side your husband."[69] Like Margaret Kee and Helen Duncan, Nancy Woodman gained a great deal of satisfaction from her weaving. In 1954 she reflected on the horrific conditions she endured as a child in an article she wrote for *Adahooníłígíí*, a monthly Navajo language newspaper. She recalled: "When I was out herding, my tattered clothing, made haphazardly out of old flour sacks, would flutter about me. I even went about with my hair filthy and matted with burrs, and I was covered with lice. This is how I suffered day by day. But even so, I had some goats." Herding her mother's goats comforted her, but learning to weave instilled in her a great deal of self-respect. Woodman remembered, "When I learned it I gained my independence. I got so I could support myself by my work, and I kept it up. I made fairly good rugs, and still do. That is how I got along."[70] Her goat herd increased until they fell victim to stock reduction in the 1930s. But it was weaving that gave Woodman her independence.

To be sure, weaving provided Navajo women significant income, and many women like Helen Duncan remember it was key to their families' survival. But answering Duncan's question, "why do I even weave?" requires more than a simple economic explanation. Weaving improved the quality of that survival, providing women a vehicle for creative expression that celebrated their central role in Navajo culture. It informed how Navajo families understood the world around them and how they expressed themselves within it, enabling them to fulfill their gendered obligations to their kin and participate in ongoing cultural invention.[71] For some weavers, a rug was an extension of the self that linked the weaver to the consumer; it was, as anthropologist Maureen Schwarz learned from her interviews of Navajo weavers, "a physical embodiment of the maker's thoughts."[72]

Reproductive and productive labor were not distinctly separate endeavors. Navajo women living on the reservation in the mid-twentieth century did not necessarily make those distinctions in their own lives. Producing for the market did not undermine the cultural significance of rug making. There is a growing consensus in American Indian scholarship that urges scholars to rethink the somewhat arbitrary division between the secular and the sacred. Doing so reveals a great deal about women's household work.[73] The mundane world of household labor was imbued with cultural significance, particularly in maintaining kinship responsibilities and providing the community with the objects, food, and other necessities for sings and other ceremonies. Either for trade or for personal use, weaving a rug involved an interconnected network of kin.[74] To devalue weaving as simply a "commodity," and therefore not sacred, misrepresents the full cultural meaning of Navajo women's work. Weaving was a creative expression that carried with it tremendous aesthetic value. Weaving was a vehicle for passing down cultural knowledge and for reinforcing kinship responsibilities. And finally, weaving produced a product that a Navajo woman could trade for food. The two processes of weaving for trade and weaving for household use were interdependent and heavily imbued with cultural significance.[75]

Examining the relationship between the sacred and the secular, or as anthropologist Tressa Berman termed it, the "ceremonial relations of production," might yield further insights on the gendered work experience of American Indians.[76] As the Navajo weavers' example suggests, much of that is women's work. Everything that went into making a rug, from raising sheep for the wool, developing designs, and teaching children to weave and behave responsibly, was informed by a Navajo worldview—a perspective that was constantly adapting to the demands of the changing economy. Navajo women in the mid-twentieth century were weaving a living. Although that meant trading rugs for groceries, it also meant maintaining the cultural cohesion of the household and women's power within it.

Kay Bennett painted a vivid picture of her mother directing ceremonial household labor in Bennett's memoir, *Kaibah: Recollections of a Navajo Girlhood*. In one example, she remembered how her mother prepared for a Ndáá, or the social dance of an Enemy Way ceremony at Oak Springs. Her son, Keedah, had been suffering from persistent headaches, which according to a medicine man, he had incurred by sleeping on a bed at school where a white soldier had died. Mother Chischillie soon began her preparations and busily finished weaving a rug while Kaibah's older sister, Tesbah, sewed new blouses and skirts for her and her sister-in-law. Mother Chischillie then made the long journey to the trading post, where she exchanged her rug for "more supplies, candy, crackerjack, fruit and materials to give away to her guests."[77] Like Betty

Harvey, Margaret Kee, and Helen Duncan, Bennett's womenfolk always turned to weaving to fulfill ceremonial, kin, and other economic obligations.

The collective labor of the household made weaving possible. Wesley Thomas, a weaver and teacher, remembers it as a "family affair." Family members maintained the herds of sheep and goats that supplied the raw materials for weaving. Children and other members of the household gathered the needed plants for dyes and helped in washing the wool, carding, and spinning it. The weaver's husband, brother, or uncle would help assemble the loom itself. Such cooperation among household members reinforced those relationships and embedded them with cultural meaning. As Thomas reflected, "It is not possible for a weaver alone to produce a *dah'iistł'ó*. Weaving teaches me that these elements are incorporated into the continuum of Navajo life."[78]

Within the social world of weaving, Navajo women and their kin enacted the values and spiritual narratives central to what it meant to be Navajo. They were living out their lives as Spiderwoman, a pivotal figure in the Navajo creation story, had instructed. They would always have clothes if they taught their children to weave.[79] Consequently, the well-being of a Navajo woman's family was deeply connected to how hard she worked at her loom and how well she attended to her kinship obligations, which included retelling the stories that made sense out of their universe. Thus, as historian Jennifer Nez Denetdale explained, "[w]eaving remains a significant activity because it defines meaningful social relationships among members of the community and between the community and the cosmos and because it has roots in traditional narratives." Telling these stories and imparting their knowledge of weaving, Navajo grandmothers socialize younger generations and "remain productive members of the households."[80]

Playing such a pivotal role in the cultural and economic life of Navajo households, weavers in the mid-twentieth century exercised considerable power over their resources. In many ways they were similar to Euro-American women living in eighteenth-century Maine or nineteenth-century Pennsylvania, who managed their own households on the periphery of an expanding capitalist economy. Like Martha Ballard, an accomplished midwife who accounted for her earnings and expenditures separate from those of her husband, or the mid-Atlantic farm women who made ends meet by selling or bartering butter and eggs, Navajo weavers controlled the economic resources earned from their own labor.[81]

Traders' records, ethnographies, and oral histories provide clues on how Navajo women's work translated into household power. For example, one of the best-known traders on the reservation, Lorenzo Hubbell, consistently listed women who conducted business on their own and kept their credit accounts separate from their husbands'. Daughters could also keep their own accounts and trade for merchandise available at the trading post.[82] For example, Hubbell credited Tahchine Yazza's Daughter #1, $18.75 for six lambs, and Tahchine Yazza's wife $35.00 for four rugs she brought in for trade. The contradiction in this ledger entry is interesting. Hubbell simply referred to these women in terms of their relationship to a Navajo man, Tahchine. Hubbell's own gender assumptions, those that defined the oldest male as the head of the household, framed his perceptions of Navajo relationships. Yet, Hubbell was first and foremost a shrewd businessman and understood that Tahchine's wife and daughter made decisions about prices and purchases and assumed debt independently of their father or husband.

What was true for Ganado was also true for more remote areas of the reservation. In 1939 Emma Reh documented this practice for Navajo Mountain, one of the areas of the reservation least accessible to outside markets. She noted that out of the forty-nine accounts listed, 25 percent were women. In nearly every case, the woman's husband maintained a separate account in his own name. When Reh asked about this practice, a Navajo man explained to her that this was normal and that it corresponded to Navajo concepts of personal property. Describing the gendered notions that generally guided livestock ownership, he described why husbands and wives kept separate credit accounts at the trading post: "because the woman owns her sheep and the man his cattle." This did not necessarily imply animosity or a power struggle between men and women, because he added, "the man and woman help each other out."[83] The extent to which men and women did help "each other out" is difficult to conclude from ledger books. Reh's examination of the items purchased noted that they both obtained food for their families, but that each bought his or her own clothing. In some cases a woman might maintain a separate account, as a way to protect herself and her children from a husband whom she thought was not as careful with his money as she was.

Another researcher working for the Soil Conservation Service in 1935 found a similar practice at the Red Lake Trading post, 148 miles northwest of Ganado. Those records list joint accounts for six households, twenty-six accounts for individual women (married as well as daughters and sisters of male household members), and individual accounts for fifty men. Women received an average of eight dollars in trade for each rug and paid off their accounts with those resources and any extra cash or wool they might have at their disposal. In addition to those resources, men used cattle and wages to settle their accounts with the trader.[84]

Women continued to maintain separate trading post accounts into the 1950s. Many who moved into reservation border towns, such as Farmington, New Mexico, sustained this practice, even as their access to the reservation resources that enabled them to weave, such as sheep and kinship networks, declined and their participation in the wage work force increased. In 1954, Seymour Parker, a sociologist studying how Navajos were adjusting to living in Farmington, explained how "even among some of the more educated Navahos," husband and wives kept separate accounts. Some of these women kept sheep on the reservation and would continue to weave, even though they were somewhat removed from their network of relatives. Parker's note of surprise, that "even educated Navajos" did this, reveals his underlying assumptions that Navajo women's independence was a somewhat anachronistic, cultural phenomenon, one that infringed upon the development of a "modern" nuclear family. Navajo women not only maintained separate accounts, but they would occasionally call up the traders and ask them to cut off their husband's access to credit. According to Parker, they worried that their husbands were not spending their money on their families and, in some cases, were using their income to purchase liquor.[85]

Unfortunately these women found they had less authority over their husbands' accounts in Farmington than they did on the reservation. Parker reported that back on the reservation, traders were very likely "to listen to such requests because they know that the woman often owns the hides, the wool and the rugs." Parker continued, "It is well known that back on the reservation the woman often has great power in the family and usually has a financial income of her own." In the urban areas, "the situation is usually reversed." In the border towns such as Farmington, as men generated more of the household income, their power in family decision making increased. He reported that such a role reversal was upsetting to the women in his study, because "they just don't like to have to ask their husbands for money when they want to buy things for themselves or for their children." In Farmington, some traders refused to honor the women's requests. As traders explained to Parker, since "their husbands earn money . . . [we] cannot curtail their credit as long as they are not delinquent in paying their bills."[86]

Navajo women living in Fruitland, New Mexico, 12 miles west, were just as frustrated as their counterparts in Farmington. The BIA established Fruitland in 1933 as a soil conservation experiment. BIA officials, assisted by a committee made up of three Navajo men, assigned 20-acre plots of newly irrigated land to the "male heads" of 191 Navajo families. Many of those families had migrated from other areas of the reservation and felt like outsiders in the larger community, disconnected from their matrilineal networks. Not long after the project began, Fruitland Navajos were disappointed to find that the BIA had decreased the size of their land to 10 acres, hardly large enough to support families by either farming the land to feed themselves or to sell produce in the marketplace. Worse yet, Fruitland Navajos were obliged to give up their sheep, cattle, and goats in exchange for their 10-acre parcels.[87] Now they had to find other ways to make a living. Most found jobs working for non-Navajo ranchers and farmers off the reservation, and others worked for the railroad. By the mid-1950s, many of the men eventually found jobs closer to home, doing construction work on the El Paso Natural Gas pipeline, working for the Four Corners power plant, or at the Kerr McGee uranium processing mill near Shiprock.[88]

According to anthropologist Louise Lamphere, the BIA's experiment involved more than irrigation. It constituted an effort to reconstruct Navajo households into patriarchal nuclear families. Drawing from anthropologist Leila Shurkey's 1951 field notes, Lamphere explained how allotting parcels to male heads of households undermined Navajo notions of land use, practices that previously reserved control of the land to women. Without the resources they had previously, women found themselves dependent on the men for their income, which did not suit them a bit. One woman explained, "You know when we had lots of sheep, we don't care when the husband go away and don't send no money. We butcher the sheep and sell lamb. We make rugs and have money that way. We don't have no sheeps now."[89] The stock reduction program itself did considerable damage to those systems, as many Navajos and others have pointed out.[90]

The weavers' story offers another side to the complicated history of capitalist development on the Navajo Reservation. Weaving may not have provided women with enough income to sustain their reservation households, but it did reinforce their powerful position within Navajo culture regardless of the increasing lure of the wage economy. Within the confines of the trading post economy, women asserted the little autonomy they had at their disposal by controlling their own income and directing much of the household labor. Although a system of dependency resulted, the way it unfolded reflected the persistence of Diné ideas about gender. The women's story shows the uneven nature of capitalist development, a process that reflected the cultural values, economic needs, and gendered ideas of those people who were at the mercy of the market forces but who participated in ways that made sense to them.

4

Working for Wages the Navajo Way
Navajo Households and Off-Reservation Wage Work

*Arizona employers each year spend many thousands of dollars importing
foreign and domestic workers, when in fact, we have within our backyard
a very substantial number of resident Indian workers who should be used.
The problem of getting the Indian to accept the White Man's way of living
will be most difficult, but in several instances, it has been proven in agriculture, mining and lumbering, that over a period of a few years' time a
transformation can be effected which is beneficial to both employer and
the Indian.*

—Arizona State Employment Service, 1948[1]

In 1939, thirteen-year-old Clarence Kee boarded a truck bound for
the carrot fields near Phoenix, Arizona, nearly 350 miles southwest of
his home on the Navajo Reservation. Young as he was, the Navajo
teenager sensed that hardships lay before him. After his father's death,
his mother and seven siblings had supported the family by raising
sheep, selling wool at the trading post, weaving what was left into
rugs, and working at any odd jobs they could find. Even attendance
at a school near Fort Defiance fell by the wayside. With his father
gone, Kee's mother needed her seven-year-old son at home. As Kee
recalled, "she wanted me to take care of the sheep, all my life."[2]

As history would have it, Kee's mother got her wish, but not in the
way that she might have imagined. When Kee climbed into the back
of that pickup truck six years later, the full-time task of herding sheep
would be over. After those carrot fields, Kee worked on a railroad
section gang, a job that took him far from his mother's flocks to

California, Oregon, and Nebraska for six weeks at a time. Yet the familial responsibilities of caring for his mother's sheep and tending to her other needs always pulled him back to the reservation. Employed by the railroad until 1948, Kee returned to work in a coal mine near his family's home, ending his days as a migrant worker. Other family members, however, including his wife and children, would continue to work at seasonal jobs into the 1960s. As Kee's mother had wished, they continued to raise sheep. But it was wage work that provided the family with the resources they needed to maintain their small flock and remain on the reservation.

Historians and anthropologists have argued that federal stock reduction policies and World War II transformed Navajos into wageworkers.[3] Indeed, the federal government played an important role in ushering in this transition. Those who lost the most as a result of stock reduction, the families with smaller herds, now relied on wage work for a larger percentage of their income. They were part of a new Navajo working class who, like the Kees, survived by selectively engaging in the capitalist market as wage earners, producers, and consumers. Most pooled their income from a variety of sources; including the wages they earned working on the railroad, herding others' sheep, or selling rugs and other craft items. Stock reduction and the lure of defense jobs pushed and pulled Navajos away from the reservation, at least temporarily. But how and why people stayed and managed to resist federal initiatives reveals an even more complicated story.

Becoming a Wageworker

Before stock reduction, a minority of Navajo youth probably received their initiation into the world of wage labor at BIA-run boarding schools on and off the reservation. In the late nineteenth century, following the model of the Carlisle Indian School in Pennsylvania, reformers founded several industrial training schools for Indians, including the Phoenix Indian School in Arizona; the Haskell Institute in Lawrence, Kansas; and the Sherman Institute in Riverside, California.[4]

Originally conceived as an answer to the "Indian problem" by promoting assimilation, these schools privileged "industrial" over academic training. School curriculum in the years leading up to the New Deal attempted a cultural makeover of the Indian students, forbidding them to speak their native languages and forcing them to learn Anglo customs and lifeways. School officials enforced these lessons with rigid military-style discipline, an approach criticized by Lewis Meriam as "restrictive rather than developmental."[5] Reform-minded government officials criticized these institutions as overcrowded, unsanitary, and utterly exploitative. Schools saved operating costs by requiring students to perform much of the labor needed to keep the institutions running. Indian students cleaned the dormitories, worked in the kitchens, and tended the school gardens, all under the rubric of vocational education. Such policies drew harsh criticism from Meriam in a 1928 report that served as an exposé of Indian service operations. He argued that such vocational education was, in fact, for "production work for the maintenance of the school." Conditions were so bad, he mused, that such work would be "prohibited in many states by the child labor laws."[6]

Although administrators boasted about their up-to-date equipment and superior training facilities, their schools did not offer Indian students the kind of education that would allow them to find skilled work. In fact, the curriculum was specifically aimed at creating a subproletarian class of workers, grooming them to pick crops and clean railroad tracks and not to compete with white workers.[7] According to Meriam, the schools were providing western employers with cheap, unskilled labor. Those jobs were "mass work, not individualized," and they did not offer potential for advancement or appeal to a worker's creativity.[8] Instead, the most important task at hand was to teach the Indian students the "dignity of work" and that "the government owed them nothing."[9] Alice Littlefield argued that such values encouraged "the formation of subjectivities and dispositions appropriate to workers in the surrounding capitalist economy." The result, according to Littlefield, "was not so much assimilation as proletarianization."[10]

Many Navajos managed to avoid the dehumanizing boarding school experience. They strongly resisted sending their young children off the reservation, preferring instead to enroll them in day and mission schools that were located closer to home.[11] Although that increased school attendance in the 1920s, few Navajo children attended long enough to master rudimentary English language skills. In his analysis of 1943–1946 draft registration records, George I. Sanchez, a noted Mexican-American sociologist, concluded that 12 percent of Navajo men between the ages of eighteen and thirty-eight were literate in English.[12] If they went to the BIA schools at all, they did not attend

Jim Bowman, Navajo gang boss with the Navajo Ordnance Depot,
August 1946. Photograph by Milton Snow, courtesy of the Navajo
Nation Museum, Window Rock, Arizona. Catalog # NO 16-332.

them for very long. That trend threatened to be repeated in the postwar era.
The study Sanchez conducted for the BIA showed that of the 21,000 Navajo
children who were between the ages of six and eighteen, fewer than 6,000 were
enrolled in school for the 1945–1946 school year.[13]

The Reservation Labor System

Navajos did not need to attend boarding schools to get low-paying jobs. They
had been working for wages long before they were learning how to march in

formation at the Carlisle or Phoenix Indian Schools. Some served as scouts for the U.S. Army in the campaign against the Apaches in the 1870s. Many Navajos worked as common laborers on Soil Conservation Service projects, as miners in agency-operated coal mines, and as interpreters at other BIA administrative facilities. From the turn of the century onward, those Navajos with few sheep to tend became extra-gang track laborers for the Santa Fe Railroad or traveled to Colorado to find employment in the sugar beet fields.[14]

Before 1948, Navajos found jobs through a variety of networks. Culturally defined internal hierarchies on the reservation had emerged in response to the encroaching U.S. economy. Traders played a central role in this unfolding process. Since the turn of the century, they had acted as the front-line arbitrators of the capitalist market for the Navajos, buying wool, advancing credit, and supplying them with consumer goods. As it became more difficult for Navajos to produce for the market, the traders assumed the role of quasi-labor contractors for the railroads and other off-reservation employers who were recruiting Navajo laborers.

The trading post offered railroad officials a central place to distribute information about job openings. Recruiters valued the traders' knowledge of Navajo culture and relied on their recommendations to fill their job orders. Traders eagerly promoted railroad work because it was seasonal and Navajos would usually bring their wages back to the reservation to spend on goods at the trading posts. The railroads also offered unemployment benefits to Navajo workers in the winter, assuring them a continued cash income during the months when they had previously depended on credit from the trader.[15]

Other industries sought out Navajo elites to act as go-betweens. In fact, leading Navajos began to challenge the prominence of the trader in negotiating their kinsmen's experience in the wage labor market. Employers might contact a headman from a particular part of the reservation and encourage him to recruit a specific number of workers. For example, during World War II, the Phelps Dodge Corporation approached Howard Gorman, a prominent Navajo leader from Ganado, to bring 200 men to work in the copper mines in Morenci, Arizona.[16] Another tribal council member from Crownpoint recruited workers from his area to work in the notoriously unhealthy farm labor camps in Bluewater, New Mexico.[17]

After World War II, returning veterans and defense workers became an additional layer of cultural brokers. According to one observer, they were "up

Trader at Mexican Water Trading Post taking Navajos to Farmington to work on the
railroad. Elijah Blair Collection. Courtesy of Cline Library, Special Collections.
Northern Arizona University.

to date men who knew their way around the white world."[18] They were part
of a new generation of Navajo men and women who, in the 1950s, would challenge the "old guard" of Navajo politics by questioning the authority of an
elite who derived power from large livestock holdings, relationships with the
traders, and an ability to exploit the labor of their extended families.[19]

World War II brought relief from the suffering associated with stock reduction, drawing thousands of Navajo men and women off the reservation to
serve in the armed forces and to work in defense-related industries. Like other
minority groups, they took advantage of the wartime labor shortage and migrated to reservation border towns and cities such as Los Angeles, Phoenix,
Albuquerque, and Denver, where they found jobs that would have been closed
to them before the war.[20] Navajos were not the only Native Americans to take
advantage of the weakening color line in the industrial labor market. American Indians throughout the United States wanted good jobs and livable wages
and traveled great distances to get them. As a result, the war inspired the first
massive migration of American Indians off the reservations in the twentieth
century.[21] According to historian Alison Bernstein, in 1944 alone, more than
44,000 Native Americans left home in search of off-reservation employment.

Ethel Nofschissy and children at her home near the Morenci Copper mine. Morenci, Arizona. Circa 1950. Photographed by Milton Snow. Courtesy of the Navajo Nation Museum, Window Rock, Arizona. Catalog #NO 16-1026.

Out of that number, 24,000 found work in nonagricultural jobs. Approximately 25 percent of that total were Navajos.[22]

Some Navajos found new opportunities serving in the armed forces.[23] The military provided a kind of occupational training ground where Navajo soldiers gained skills they found useful in the postwar labor market. For example, in 1942 Myrtle Waybenais left her position as an instructional aid at a BIA day school in Shiprock to join the Women's Army Corps. In a medical course, she learned "about food and diets" and at a hospital technical school she studied "the fields of being a nurse."[24]

After the war, federal policy began to shift from Collier's cultural pluralist model to a harshly assimilationist plan that favored the termination of Indian reservations. Part of that legislation included an extensive program to relocate American Indians to urban areas such as Los Angeles, San Francisco, Chicago, and Denver. The Navajos did not have to face the specter of termination and did not suffer the fate of other tribes, such as the Menominee, but they did endure a variety of voluntary BIA programs designed to relocate them off the reservation for good. BIA representatives were particularly interested in stopping the return migration of many Navajos who had left the reservation to find wage work. Officials attempted to create off-reservation settlements that would function as labor colonies, providing commercial growers with a permanent, year-round workforce. The BIA hoped Navajos would be drawn to these communities, leaving behind, once and for all, the homes and responsibilities that had once brought them back to the reservation.

Stabilizing the Navajo Workforce

After 1948, the BIA set out to stabilize the Navajo workforce. The existing reservation labor system brokered by traders, railroad companies, and a few Navajo elites had allowed Navajo workers to dip into the wage market for a limited time and then return to maintain their reservation households. Much as BIA officials had attempted to rationalize sheep and coal production, they now were hoping to gain control of Navajo wage-labor practices as well. They were still concerned about the carrying capacity of the reservation, but rather than further limit the number of sheep, the agency instead decided to reduce the numbers of people living on the land.

BIA officials worried that veterans and war workers would place an unbearable strain on already limited reservation resources when they returned home after the war. In an alarmist tone, they concluded that the land simply could not support them. The officials predicted that "30,000 Navajos need to find a way to live outside the reservation or by some other means than sheep raising and the meager farming available."[25] Congress commissioned a study, later known as the Krug Report, in an effort to find solutions to these problems and assess the reservation's potential for economic development.

The 1950 Navajo-Hopi Rehabilitation Act, the bill designed to implement the study's findings, offered one solution. Sponsors of that legislation allocated $88,570,000 toward implementing the act and hoped federally financed improvements would boost the reservation economy. Indeed, that investment laid the groundwork for a developing infrastructure. Paved roads, electricity, and telephone lines were essential to attract large-scale industry. This type of development, however, would not necessarily create a dynamic internal economy on the reservation. It connected the Navajo reservation to external markets, but it did not provide Navajos with the capital they needed to create their own local enterprises.

Table 4.1 Available Off-Reservation Employment, 1948

Employer	Number of Jobs
Railroads	7,500
Agriculture	3,500
Military depots	625
Mining	350
Logging and sawmills	175
Construction	250
Miscellaneous: Border Towns	850
Total	13,250

Source: Employment Security Commission, Arizona State Employment Service, State Information Bulletin no. 090, Supplement no. 6, March 28, 1949, National Archives I, Record Group 75, Bureau of Indian Affairs, Classified Files, Navajo, Washington, D.C., Box 498 (916–922), File 5764-46-920.

The program embodied contradictory goals. It was supposed to improve the reservation economy and provide relief to the Navajo people who lived in terrible poverty. But, instead of helping to create a vital working class to participate in the development of an internal economy, the program encouraged workers who were at the height of their productive years to leave the reservation for good.[26] BIA officials set out to transform reservation labor practices because they were convinced that Navajo migratory behavior reinforced the Indians' connection to the reservation, a problem that undermined their eventual assimilation into the white world. Encouraging permanent off-reservation relocation would ease the demand on reservation resources and facilitate Navajo incorporation into the mainstream American economy.[27]

According to BIA estimates, demand for Navajo labor exceeded supply. In 1948, Indian service officials reported that approximately 10,000 Navajos were available for off-reservation wage work, a number that barely met the demand for their labor the year before (see Table 4.1). Their relatively large numbers, access to regional commercial agriculture, and availability suggested an alternative source of cheap labor to replace Mexican nationals and other migrant laborers. The BIA, members of the Navajo Tribal Council, and representatives of western industries now had to figure out how to bring Navajo workers to that market and, most important, how to make them stay.

Part of that plan meant imposing gender roles that were the norm in the surrounding U.S. economy. An in-depth analysis of the gendered implications of the BIA's relocation plan is beyond the scope of this chapter. The criteria they used to define potential workers, however, offer a revealing glimpse of the significant role gender played in the BIA's attempts to shape the Navajo working class. The BIA estimated that there was a total of 16,000 men between the ages of fifteen and sixty-five living on the reservation, 6,350 of whom were not available for work because they were either attending school, physically incapacitated, employed, or self-supporting. Fewer women could be considered potential workers because of their "family ties." BIA officials did not list "family ties" to explain why men might not be prepared to join the wage labor market. In addition, "self-supporting" was a category they only applied to men, although we know that women significantly contributed to the household economy by weaving rugs and selling sheep and wool as well as working for wages on and off the reservation. Since most Navajos at this time pooled their resources and valued women's work as crucial for household survival, it appears that the BIA's criteria were less an actual assessment of the Navajo labor market than a prescription for what they hoped it would become.[28]

In January 1948, James M. Stewart, the general superintendent of the Navajo Reservation, outlined a philosophy consistent with federal assimilationist goals, offering a proposal that would guide the BIA's efforts to shape the Navajo labor market. He modeled his plan on how he imagined immigrant communities coped with an unfamiliar and often hostile American cultural environment. In Stewart's eyes, European and Asian immigrants had established neighborhoods that cushioned their arrival with familiar cultural surroundings and simultaneously offered them an avenue for assimilation into the American mainstream. Chinatowns and little Italys "offered points of departure from which the individual and his children could learn the language and customs of America and ultimately assume his place in our national life." Ethnic neighborhoods drew immigrants to them and provided "training grounds for the new arrivals from the old country."[29] He hoped that the new Navajo "colonies" would serve the same purpose. They would supply employers with labor and, in Stewart's words, "rehabilitate" the Navajo people.

Unlike the Navajos, the Chinese and the Europeans lived "too far away to permit them to return as an escape from nostalgia or frustration." As a result, "they were faced with [the] necessity of creating a familiar environment in the midst of the unfamiliar." Because Navajos could return home at any time, the challenge, according to BIA officials, was to make these off-reservation communities an attractive alternative to life on the reservation.[30] Thus, coloniza-

An unidentified Navajo woman working at a WPA-sponsored mattress factory program in Shiprock, New Mexico, 1940. Photograph by Milton Snow. Courtesy of the Navajo Nation Museum, Window Rock, Arizona. Catalog #NO 16-378.

tion would break the connection that pulled so many back to the reservation and create a reliable workforce for western employers. Such a plan resonated well with the federal termination agenda.[31]

For BIA officials and some western employers, Navajo culture was a *problem* that needed to be solved. Stewart noted that the Navajos "subscribe to a way of life, a pattern of thinking, and a system of values which are highly divergent from our own." He knew that transforming those cultural ideas would not be an easy task. He noted that the "customs, institutions, and other characteristics which serve to distinguish one way of life from another are not things which can be shed and replaced at will." Thus, Stewart concluded, any program that the BIA implemented had to address Navajo cultural practices that tended to draw them back to the reservation. He assumed that a continued connection to the reservation household interfered with Navajos' eventual assimilation into the white world of permanent wage labor. Severing those connections was the only answer for ensuring the success of the colonization project.[32] Hence, BIA officials launched an all-out battle to transform Navajo ideas and expectations about work and household responsibilities. With stock reduction, the BIA had intruded into Navajo households and undermined their subsistence base. Now, BIA officials were attempting to control how the Navajos engaged the wage labor market.

The BIA did not wait long to implement Stewart's plan. On January 30, 1948, two days after Stewart released his report, William H. Zeh, director of the BIA's District IV, convened a meeting to discuss off-reservation employment for the Navajo and Hopi people. Attending the meeting were representatives from railroad and lumber companies, commercial agriculture, and traders with operations on the Navajo and Hopi reservations. Placement officials from the Arizona and New Mexico employment services represented the state governments. Also in attendance were various federal bureaucrats from the Department of the Interior, the Navajo and Hopi agencies, and the Veterans Administration. Thirteen Navajo leaders attended to comment on working conditions in industries that employed Indian labor.[33]

Six days later, at a meeting of the Farm Labor Advisory Committee in Arizona, Zeh explained to commercial growers what had transpired at the Phoenix conference. He summarized the conclusions, reporting that the participants confirmed the need for a stabilized Navajo labor force. The challenge they faced was how to "keep them on the job longer." He invited employers and BIA officials to "encourage [the Navajo worker] to become an established workman, established in the community and available to work in whatever type of work his capacities, his limitations, or his strength qualifies him for." He laid out the problems that he thought would face all parties involved in off-reservation colonization. Stressing that Navajos were willing to seek off-reservation employment, he acknowledged to his audience that it would be a challenge for the employers and the Indian service to encourage permanent migration. The problem, according to Zeh, was that for Navajos, "[t]here is a very strong tie to the reservation. The Navajo is in general a primitive sort of individual, the wide world is a foreign world to him, he doesn't feel any happier than we would feel in the Navajo world." In rather paternalistic terms, Zeh encouraged the growers to empathize with the Navajo workers' situation, reassuring them that, in time, the Indians would adjust.

You can see what a difficult situation the Indian has to meet off-hand to adjust to white man's civilization. It will take a period of time under certain conditions, and the primary condition will be right treatment, and then he will respond quite well. . . . In general, the Navajo has been found to be a desirable employee. The comments made which were adverse to the Navajo were primarily directed to his habit of leaving the job and going back to the reservation. That is something that education will take care of. 60 to 80 years ago, the Navajo was a primitive savage. He has come a very long way in a short time. According to our standards, he will have to learn about work habits before he becomes a first class employee of any kind.[34]

According to Zeh, Navajos had to adapt to "modern" workplace practices. Employers, too, had some lessons to learn. They could improve their success with Navajo workers if they made an effort to understand their culture. He noted that "problems created by language and tribal customs . . . [would] be solvable through sympathetic understanding and education of the Indian and the white employer. It is not only necessary for the Navajo to learn, but the white employer must learn about the Navajo."[35]

After holding a series of meetings with interested employers and consulting officials from state employment agencies, the bureau enacted a pilot project to facilitate the creation of off-reservation communities. The BIA established the Navajo Placement Service in the spring of 1948 to secure off-reservation employment, primarily in agricultural and extra-gang railroad work.[36] The employers or state employment officers would file job orders with the Navajo Placement Service, and it would send them suitable employees. The success of the program, according to BIA representatives, required both educating the employers about Navajo cultural values and teaching Navajos how to behave on the job. The BIA, in conjunction with state employment services in Arizona, Colorado, Utah, and California, would coordinate this exchange, protecting the Navajos from exploitation and at the same time offering to industry workers who were reliable and suited to the task.

Agency officials circulated a calendar that outlined what they understood as the important events that marked the Navajo year in an effort to educate potential employers about the types of cultural and familial commitments that might lure Navajo workers back to the reservation. They explained that from June through September, Navajos would be preoccupied with cultivating their fields and from mid-September through mid-October, they would be leaving work periodically to harvest them. March, April, and May would find many Navajos working on spring planting, tending to new lambs, and shearing mature sheep. Herding, of course, was a responsibility that would draw Navajos home year-round when they were needed. The brochure warned employers that the demands of the reservation household would draw employees back home, particularly in the fall, when the piñon crop was ready for harvesting.[37]

Additionally, the Colorado Department of Economic Security informed employers of spiritual and other cultural events in the Navajo calendar. The Shiprock fair, held at the end of September, the powwow in Flagstaff on July 4th, and the Gallup Ceremonial in late summer were specific events that encouraged Navajos to gravitate away from their jobs. The Yeibichai was held in October, November, and December, and other Navajo ceremonies, such as "squaw" dances, took place in August and September.[38] In the winter, other household demands limited the availability of Navajos to take jobs off the reservation. Those who had children in school on the reservation were reluctant to leave. Men returned home in the fall to make sure their families had enough firewood to get them through the coldest months. According to the employment service, understanding these rituals and responsibilities would improve the employers' relationship with their Navajo employees.

Representatives of the BIA's Navajo Service suggested that employers designate English-speaking Navajo men as work group leaders. They could interpret the terms of employment and explain the requirements of the job to their fellow Navajo workers.[39] At the Phoenix conference, employers offered their experience of how successful such a setup could be. John C. Church, a vegetable grower near Phoenix, testified that he always hired Navajos who were bilingual in English and Navajo. As a result, he did not "find the language problem too serious." He explained that he would "pick out leaders from different districts and make them road bosses. All these road bosses speak very good English and they convey our messages."[40]

Some farmers were not as lucky as Church and found out that an interpreter's loyalty did not always favor management. In November 1948, on the Harmon Crismon Farms in Queen Creek, Arizona, a Navajo man named Earl Johnson used his leverage as a go-between to bargain for higher wages and better living conditions for the other seventy Navajos employed to tie carrots. He demanded mattresses for all workers to sleep on, a wage increase from twenty-two to twenty-four cents per crate, and a paid police officer to patrol the camp to "insure that if any of them got drunk they would not wander into town and be arrested." Finally, he insisted on nine dollars a day as compensation for his role as foreman.[41] When his employer initially refused to grant the pay increase, Johnson and the rest of the Navajo workers ceased work. Disturbed, the farmer called the Navajo Service placement officer to intervene. But Johnson stood his ground. He insisted that the increase "was necessary in order for them to make a living wage." The placement officer reported that, despite his attempt to intervene, "Mr. Johnson was very adamant in his demands that the employer would have to pay the higher rate or he would take all of the workers back to the reservation." Much to the chagrin of other growers in the area, the farmer gave in to Johnson's demands after less than a twenty-four-hour standoff.[42]

That same month, another group of Navajo agricultural workers in Cucamonga, California, staged a similar collective protest. On November 20 Navajos who had been employed to pick lemons walked off the job because the farmers refused to employ one member of their group, a man the farmers characterized as "hard of hearing and absentminded." Once again, the farmer called in the Navajo Service representative to "reason" with the workers. Unlike the Queen Creek incident, however, the Navajos carried out their threat and returned to the reservation. Either the farmers hired everyone in the group, or nobody would work.[43]

Conditions in these types of agricultural camps were particularly difficult. In 1950, Navajo families who worked in the cotton fields near Safford, Arizona, were living in an abandoned one-room schoolhouse without even the most rudimentary sanitation facilities. In another camp, social workers found the filth "indescribable." Tents that served as temporary housing were old and dirty, and "flies swarmed everywhere—on the garbage, the excreta, the soiled mattresses . . . and on the children's dirt-encrusted faces."[44] The fields in Bluewater, New Mexico, also caught the attention of social workers. Two thousand Navajos, mainly from the Crownpoint area, worked in Bluewater during the harvest season. Lucy Adams, a BIA official at the Navajo Agency responsible for administering the placement service, noted that the housing and sanitary conditions were bad enough to warrant intervention from the county health service. But despite her protests, New Mexico's Governor Thomas J. Mabry discouraged an investigation.[45]

Navajo agricultural labor camp in Tolleson, Arizona, December 1950. Photograph by
Milton Snow. Courtesy of the Navajo Nation Museum, Window Rock, Arizona.
Catalog #16-949.

Many of the farmers who employed Navajos were Mormon. They lived in
small, rural settlements throughout the West, including southern Utah, Colorado, Idaho, and Arizona. Some owned large commercial facilities, like that
of John Jacobs from the Phoenix area, but most farmers had more modest operations. According to William Adams, an anthropologist who grew up on the
reservation and conducted a detailed survey of Navajo agricultural workers,
the Mormon/Navajo relationship was "no coincidence." He states that employing Navajo workers was part of a larger plan by the church to reach out
to American Indians.[46] Conditions in those camps varied greatly. For Julia
John, a Navajo woman who worked in Jacobs's fields, this provided an instant
network of seasonal jobs. During the winter she found work in Jacobs's carrot fields in Phoenix. When the weather grew too hot, she would move to the
Bluewater Valley, 11 miles northwest of Grants, New Mexico, where she found
work with other Mormon families.[47] Mormons settled in the Bluewater Valley after the railroad arrived in Grants, New Mexico, and employed Navajo,
Acoma, Laguna, and Mexican American workers to pick carrots on a seasonal
basis.[48] But as soon as other job opportunities developed on the reservation,

many American Indian workers abandoned such back-breaking jobs. Simon Ortiz, the noted Acoma poet, remembers the relief he and his fellow American Indian workers felt when they found jobs working in the large uranium and coal mines:

> When the mines came
> to the Laguna and Acoma land,
> the men and their families were glad
> in a way because
> the men wouldn't have to go
> so far away to work
> for the railroad in Barstow,
> Richmond, Flagstaff, Needles.
> Or to pick beets and onions
> in Idaho, Utah, and Colorado.
> Or to work for the Mormons
> in Bluewater Valley
> who paid you in carrots and potatoes.[49]

Those Navajos who could not find work in the mines continued to work in commercial agriculture until the early 1970s.

As these anecdotes about the agricultural fields demonstrate, Navajo workers consistently endured difficult living conditions, and sometimes undermined the BIA's best-laid plans. The growers might have taken the agency's advice and employed bilingual Navajos to communicate their instructions. But that did not necessarily mean that those spokesmen did the grower's bidding. Those work leaders could serve as a mouthpiece for worker's demands, directing the flow of information in the opposite direction.

The BIA As Labor Contractor

Although some employers applauded the BIA's efforts to control and stabilize the Navajo labor supply and attempted to comply with its suggestions, others were less than enthusiastic. Employers' support for the BIA's policies depended largely on whether they benefited from Navajo migratory strategies. Some commercial growers balked at the BIA's suggestion that they build permanent communities near their farms. Unwilling to assume the expense or responsibility, these farmers objected to establishing communities where Navajo workers would live year-round. One Phoenix grower complained: "Our particular business is seasonal and we have not been able to figure out a uniform job for this group over the entire year. We bring them in November and the season runs until June, but fluctuates during that period. . . . We don't know how we can cushion over an entire year, because these people, when the time comes, always want to go back to the reservation."[50]

John M. Jacobs, representing general farming and vegetable growers in Phoenix, raised the problem of establishing schools for Navajo children if permanent communities were developed. He argued that the local schools were resisting enrolling Navajo students. He pointed out that "[o]ne of the greatest problems of our camp is trying to work with the schools in order to get the children into school. Facilities simply are not set up to take care of these children in school. That is a problem that will be basic in your over-all plan of trying to locate these people."[51]

The growers did support a system that would establish off-reservation communities (at government expense) from which they could draw their labor supply. They urged the BIA to create a centralized "pooling" station where they could hire employees according to their labor needs. This, they argued, would solve the problems they had in recruiting enough laborers.

BIA officials may have had the *bracero* program in mind when developing their scheme to relocate Navajos to agricultural labor camps. The Navajo proposal followed the development of the bracero system by six years, and in some ways the two programs were similar. Both programs involved U.S. federal agencies as labor contractors, supplying agricultural workers to the commercial growers in the West. But the aim of the BIA's program differed considerably from the bracero system. BIA officials hoped to encourage Navajos to leave their homes for good. The bracero program, at least officially, expected workers to return to Mexico after staying in the United States for a limited time. It sought to benefit western agricultural interests, whereas the BIA's program aimed, at least in theory, to relieve poverty by easing the stress on reservation resources and to encourage Navajo assimilation into mainstream U.S. society.[52]

It is unclear whether the BIA was working in tandem with the Immigration and Naturalization Service and the Labor Department, the two agencies responsible for administering the bracero program. Whether or not these two programs were officially connected, there is evidence that farmers entertained the idea of replacing Mexican contract workers with Navajos. Yet Navajos'

Navajo agricultural workers at a John Jacobs carrot-packing shed in Glendale,
Arizona, December 1956. Photograph by Milton Snow. Courtesy of the Navajo Nation
Museum, Window Rock, Arizona. Catalog #NO 16-949.

numbers could not possibly have met the demand for labor supplied by Mexican workers.[53] The BIA may have modeled the labor camp plan on the types
of colonies farmers built for sugar beet workers in Colorado in the early twentieth century. In that case, growers tried to cut their recruiting costs by creating permanent communities for their workers near their fields, but separate
from Anglo communities. Each plan had the same goal: to create a permanent
labor supply. But neither scheme would eventually proceed as planned. The
Hispano beet workers would use those communities to launch labor struggles, and the Navajos would return to their homes on the reservation.[54] And
employers would devise other ways to find workers.

Faced with opposition from the farmers, Zeh offered a compromise proposal that abandoned the BIA's ideal of stable, off-reservation colonies for centralized and less-than-permanent labor camps. He argued that it was inefficient for individual growers to venture out onto the reservation to do their
own recruiting. Instead, the BIA would hire five Navajo recruiters to canvas

Arizona State Employment Service mobile unit in Polacca, Arizona. Photograph by Milton Snow. Courtesy of the Navajo Nation Museum, Window Rock, Arizona. Catalog #NO 16-828.

the reservation for available workers. When they found enough candidates to fill the growers' labor orders, the Navajo recruiters would bring them to a central place to be picked up. One of the merits of this plan, Zeh asserted, was that, for farmers, it would "eliminate the necessity of going out and beating the bush for labor."[55] The BIA would not change the labor system that had been in place since the beginning of the century. Its officials would simply attempt to take control of it.

The BIA's relationship with railroad recruiters was not as amiable. Given the choice between placing Navajo workers in commercial agriculture or in jobs working for the railroad, the BIA clearly advocated the former. The agency favored agriculture because railroad employment usually only took men on a seasonal basis, encouraging them to leave their wives and children at home on the reservation. Agricultural work was seasonal as well, but since commercial growers hired whole families, the BIA saw the potential for encouraging entire households to leave the reservation for good. The railroad recruiters were also closely affiliated with the reservation trading posts, an institution that some BIA officials saw as corrupt and exploitative.[56]

Railroad employers were quite satisfied with the system they had in place. Like some of the growers, they opposed creating permanent off-reservation settlements. They preferred recruiting their workers when they needed them, primarily in the spring, summer, and fall, and laying them off in the winter when bad weather slowed track maintenance. Working through the trader allowed them an insider's access to the available workforce and a way to identify and keep track of the most reliable workers. Railroad representatives resented the BIA's bias toward agriculture and argued that their system offered the Navajos more economic benefits, including unemployment insurance, sick pay, and retirement.[57]

Railroad employers presented one of the largest stumbling blocks for the BIA. After discussing the Navajo labor situation with Atchison, Topeka, and Santa Fe officials in Winslow, Arizona, Lucy Adams, director of welfare and placement for the Navajo Service, reported:

> It is very difficult to make this individual or any other official of the Santa Fe realize that they should not have a monopoly on Navajo labor. They are firmly convinced that since they pioneered in using Navajo labor that henceforth all Navajos should be directed to their uses. They also believe that the Indians should be kept as a pool on the reservation during the winter months so that they will be available for their uses commencing in the Spring.[58]

It is not surprising that western mining companies expressed the most interest in what the BIA was proposing. Unlike the agricultural industry and the railroads, mining depended on a stable, permanent labor force. Some mining companies even offered a number of incentives to married Navajo men and their families to encourage them to settle down. For example, the superintendent of the Bingham Canyon mine planned to remodel two old apartment buildings "which, when completed, will provide modern living quarters to between six and eight families." As long as the BIA provided the Navajos with trailers, he was even willing "to provide a camp area, level it off with bull-dozers, and provide water, sewage disposal and electricity."[59] In another example, Phelps Dodge offered to bring a medicine man to Morenci as a way to stem the tide of workers returning to the reservation. That effort failed, however, since the medicine men they approached refused to perform Navajo rituals on land that lay outside the four sacred mountains.

In some cases, Navajos responded to the incentives provided by the mining companies to settle down. In fact, the majority of Navajos who were leaving the reservation to establish permanent communities were in locations that employed them in semiskilled, industrial work. In 1951, compilers of the progress report on the 1950 Navajo-Hopi Relocation Act noted that permanent communities had been established in the Colorado mining towns of Rico, Telluride, and Ophir and in Bingham Canyon, Utah. Other sites of permanent settlement were around defense industries in Barstow, California; Belmont, Arizona; and Wingate Village, New Mexico.[60]

Despite the efforts of BIA officials, tribal leaders, and western industrialists, Navajo workers continued to view wages as a resource to be pooled for the maintenance of the reservation household. In his 1948 investigation of off-reservation wage work, Robert Young reported that Navajos working and living in Bingham Canyon were not committed to settling there on a permanent basis. Even men who had their wives and families with them set their sights on returning to the reservation. For example, Young reported that Ab Harris, a Navajo man from Marble Canyon, was saving fifty dollars from every paycheck, which would soon amount to $2,000. Despite the good wages, he, his wife, and three children were living in part of a small, dilapidated house in the ruins of an abandoned underground copper mine near the Bingham Canyon operation. Instead of using his savings to move into more comfortable quarters, Harris planned to use the money to build his family a stone house on the reservation, a project that he estimated would require twenty days in the upcoming year to complete. When the house was finished, he expected to continue working at Bingham Canyon to raise more money so that he could build a filling station on the highway nearby.[61] By 1955, Young reported Navajos devising similar strategies to keep their reservation households afloat. Husbands or other family members would normally divide their time between their jobs working in the mines, railroads, or agricultural fields and their homes on the reservation, and others would stay behind and tend to their farms and livestock.[62]

For BIA officials, the small mining community in Rico, Colorado, seemed to provide an ideal model for off-reservation Navajo colonies. Rico was a typical company town that experienced cycles of boom and bust from the 1920s through the 1950s. At its height in 1954 the community reached a population of 700 people, 35 percent of whom were Navajos. Located 93 miles north of Shiprock and connected to the reservation by U.S. Highway 666 and Colorado State Highway 145, Rico was within easy reach of Navajo workers. Unlike railroad work and commercial agriculture, mining offered year-round work for wages that would support a standard of living above the poverty line for families residing off the reservation. Ralph Luebben, an anthropologist who conducted a participant-observer study of the Rico Navajos, noted that the mining company paid relatively high wages. He reported that between July 1953 and June 1954, seventy-five Navajo miners employed by the Argentine Mining Company in Rico earned $116,209.08, or an average of $1,549.46 per man, just above the minimum government officials had determined would allow a Navajo man to support himself and his immediate family.[63]

In addition to offering relatively high wages and employment year-round, the mining company offered better housing than other southwestern industries that employed Navajos. Company housing was by no means luxurious, but in comparison to the migrant agricultural camps where workers would be lucky if the growers provided them with tents and cooking stoves, the Rico facilities were an improvement.[64]

Housing was better than what Navajos would find on commercial farms, but it was worse than what the mining company provided Anglo miners and their families. The Navajo homes were clustered around a common sanitary facility that included central washing places, toilets, and showers. Families living in houses without inside cold water taps had to rely on wells, a fire hydrant, and the water overflow of the nearby Atlantic Cable mine. In contrast, Anglos living in company housing enjoyed hot water and indoor, private toilets and bathing facilities.[65] To make matters worse, the mining company paid Navajo workers less than Anglo miners performing the same work. Such racial discrimination was an all too familiar pattern. Rico was just like any other reservation border town.

Despite these difficulties, the high wages Navajos could earn in Rico made it one of the best options available to them off the reservation. Jobs at Rico paid better than what a man could earn working in the reservation mines, on the railroad, or in commercial agriculture. It was also one of the few places where workers could bring their wives and children.[66]

The Draw of the Reservation Household

To the dismay of BIA officials, Navajo workers treated working in the mines like any other off-reservation job. Navajo miners did not view their jobs as permanent. On the average, they worked about four months at a time and returned to the reservation to check on their families, tend to household responsibilities, or participate in Navajo ceremonials or curing sings. Despite the possibility of earning as much as $5,000 a year, most Navajos refused to work for more than a few months at a time. Family and ritual obligations consistently drew them back home.[67]

Despite frequent warnings from mining company officials, Navajo mine workers would leave work when pressing matters on the reservation needed their attention. Luebben calculated that Navajos missed twice as many shifts as Anglo workers, the highest rate of absenteeism occurring in the month of the Shiprock fair and during the Gallup Ceremonial. They also missed a high percentage of shifts in April to return to the reservation to prepare their farm plots for spring planting.[68] One Navajo miner explained to Luebben in a matter-of-fact way, "I'll go down on weekends and farm. Once a month I'll have to take off on Friday evening to get two days of farming."[69]

Navajo absenteeism was so bad that mining company officials complained that it undermined their operation. But despite efforts to carry out disciplinary actions, Navajo workers refused to change their priorities. The company geologist explained to Luebben: "I fired a few [for failing to make the shift]. I did it before, but it didn't do any good. They're not on the job as much as I'd like to have them. . . . What I need is a crew of about 55, with half off and half on. I don't know what would happen if they all showed up."[70]

Luebben argued that this behavior indicated "that Navahos [were] interested primarily in short terms of employment and a subsequent temporary monetary income." Interpreting high absenteeism and turnover as their reluctance to identify as permanent wage workers, he concluded that "[t]o most Navahos mining is just another job and their occupational position does not mean economic security nor does it define their status."[71] With the type of discrimination they faced in Rico, it is no surprise that Navajos did not want to make it their permanent home.

The wages they brought home from their off-reservation jobs allowed Navajo workers to maintain their household-centered survival strategies and to navigate the changing political and economic climate on the reservation with increasing flexibility. With the money they earned working on the railroads, in commercial agriculture, or in mining operations, many Navajos achieved relative autonomy from the traders and developed the means to maintain migratory strategies on their own terms. By the early 1950s, with the federal government building roads with money allocated from the Navajo-Hopi Rehabilitation Act, consumer and wage markets were becoming more accessible to reservation households. With the new roads, wages, and an increased demand for goods that could be acquired off the reservation, trucks and cars quickly replaced the horse and wagon as the main means of transportation. Owning a truck allowed Navajos to bypass the trader and purchase food and consumer goods in grocery and department stores located in places such as Gallup and Flagstaff.

By purchasing trucks with the very wages they were earning from working in the fields, agricultural workers established a stronger bargaining position for themselves with farm labor recruiters. Driving to the fields in their own vehicles allowed them more freedom to come and go as they pleased and easier access to return to the reservation at a moment's notice. Although growers were relieved to some extent by the reduced cost of transporting Navajo workers back and forth to the reservation, they lamented the problem that increased mobility caused for maintaining a stable workforce and for controlling the Navajos' behavior in the labor camps. A Navajo Service representative complained: "To the grower, this increase of cars is a mixed blessing. Though he is not responsible for transportation, the worker is more likely to leave without notice or go into town and get drunk. It has also meant this summer that workers are arriving a week or more before the jobs start, and have to apply to local merchants for credit which they are reluctant to extend."[72]

Clarence and Margaret Kee might have been among those Navajo workers who worried western employers. They traced the lineage of their cars and trucks, like that of their sheep, back to the first two vehicles they purchased with the wages they earned working on the railroad and in the fields.[73] The wages that Clarence Kee sent home from his job on the railroad bought his mother her first truck. A few years later, Margaret Kee and her adolescent son went to work picking potatoes and sugar beets in Idaho. When they had enough money, they purchased a small car and returned to their reservation home near Window Rock, Arizona. Wage work provided the resources that brought them back to the reservation; it did not encourage them to move away for good.

Laborers leaving for the Idaho potato fields, Navajo Fairgrounds, October 1950.
Photograph by Milton Snow. Courtesy of the Navajo Nation Museum, Window Rock,
Arizona. Catalog #NO 16-519.

As much as the Navajo Service hated to admit it, it had not been successful in stemming the tide of return migration. Some Navajos did permanently
leave the reservation, but many came back. In 1953, approximately 375 people
left the reservation for long-term employment and relocation purposes. In
1955, 415 people moved to Chicago, Denver, Los Angeles, and San Francisco,
where the BIA had field offices to assist those relocating. In January 1956, 500
more applications were on file.[74] Approximately 30 percent of those who left
with the aim of relocating on a permanent basis returned to the reservation,
however. Compilers of the report detailing the progress of the 1950 Navajo-
Hopi Rehabilitation Act noted that the Indians returned because they were
"unable to adjust to changing living conditions" and because of "family ties
on the Reservation."[75]

In contrast, by 1953 the Railroad Retirement Board, the BIA's Branch of
Placement and Relocation in Window Rock, and state employment services
in Arizona and New Mexico reported 23,500 seasonal, off-reservation placements. The difference between the number of placements and the number

of people relocating in 1953 suggests that Navajo seasonal migratory strategies persisted. In 1962, responding to a congressional inquiry on Indian unemployment, Glen R. Landbloom, general superintendent of the Navajo Service, admitted that "in spite of the interest of the Navajo people toward economic life, the effects of Indian culture still exist." Landbloom confirmed what commercial growers and railroad employers already knew, that Navajos "still prefer to work at employment which enables them to take part in the numerous tribal ceremonies."[76]

The struggle over relocation amounted to a battle over what would constitute the Navajo household in the postwar era. BIA officials wanted to transform extended, kin-based residential groups into nuclear households off the reservation. They hoped Navajos would leave their hogans and become village dwellers and limit their kin obligations to what was customary for an Anglo-style nuclear family. Navajo men and women participated in those BIA programs but did not accept the ultimate goals of colonization. Instead, in an effort to keep their reservation households intact, they treated those "opportunities"—even jobs that offered them more money and permanent year-round employment—as one more source of income that would allow them to maintain a broader, kinship-centered lifestyle on the reservation. The reservation household provided Navajos with a cultural buffer, offering them relief from the hostile racial environment that many Navajos experienced in reservation border towns such as Rico, Colorado. When Navajos refused to relinquish that space, the BIA's plan failed. What had begun as a grand plan to reconstitute the Navajo household off the reservation, provided, in the end, a way for the BIA to assume the role of glorified labor contractor for southwestern agricultural interests.

Conclusion

Wage work did not remake Navajo culture in the way that the BIA and southwestern employers imagined. Many Navajos withstood BIA efforts to relocate them permanently in off-reservation labor colonies. They insisted on keeping their homes on the reservation and adjusting their wage-work practices so they could continue to meet their household obligations. For southwestern employers, the Navajos appeared to offer an attractive labor pool. To pull them successfully into the labor market, commercial farmers, mining companies, and other western industrialists had to adjust to Navajos' demands and figure out ways to accommodate their culturally defined work practices. BIA officials, reduced to little more than labor contractors, failed to reshape Navajo migratory behavior in the ways they had intended. As the Navajos navigated the pull of the market and the push of the state, they located new ways to make a living; they found work that allowed them to hold fast to their communal and kinship-based values and enabled them to contribute to the survival of the reservation household in whatever form it might take in the post-stock-reduction era.

Resisting permanent relocation and refusing to conform to the BIA's expectations, Navajos made a place for themselves in the southwestern labor market. They participated in that market but did not embrace the assimilationist goals that BIA officials and some employers promoted. Navajos did leave the reservation to find jobs. But for many—like the Kees—that work provided them with the resources they needed to preserve, rather than replace, their reservation households. Margaret Kee now lives in a comfortable house in St. Michael's, Arizona, equipped with all the modern conveniences. She spends most of her time weaving rugs and tending her sheep while her husband, Clarence, is at work at the Pittsburgh and Midway strip mine a few miles east, near Window Rock. Her daughters' mobile homes stand near her house like hogans clustered around family settlement in the days of her youth.

Navajo Workers and White Man's Ways
Race, Sovereignty, and Organized Labor
on the Navajo Reservation

*I guess they called it prejudice, and at the same time it was an unfair
labor practice.*

—Kenneth White, Navajo labor activist[1]

In the late summer of 1958, three white members of the Farmington
Fire Department lured two Navajo men, Harry Pinto and Amos John,
into a car and took them back to the fire station. Why Pinto and John
went with the firemen is unclear, but the events of that night suggest
that they did not know what was in store for them. At the fire station a group of Anglos overpowered the Navajo men, poured paint
over their bodies, and dumped them out onto the streets of Farmington. Harry Pinto and Amos John became the victims of what
Charles E. Minton, executive director of the New Mexico Commission on Indian Affairs, characterized as a "sport" that was "beginning
to flourish in Farmington."[2] As Minton's description suggests, Pinto
and John's experience that summer night was part of a larger pattern
of escalating racial violence in Farmington in the late 1950s. Even
though conditions warranted an investigation by the Federal Bureau
of Investigation (FBI), federal agencies offered little relief to the
Navajos living and working in the Four Corners region. Even Charles
Minton admitted that the "kind of white trash" who were responsible for such crimes were "execution proof."[3]

Navajo Tribal Council members grew increasingly frustrated as
their appeals to federal officials failed to bring about a meaningful

response. Appearing helpless and unable to protect the Navajo workers did little to improve the Navajo Tribal Council's reputation with the reservation population. The council's legacy of cooperation with the BIA and its role in the enforcement of the federal livestock reduction program in the 1930s and 1940s still haunted the minds of many Navajo people, who, as a result, were reluctant to view the council as a legitimate governing body. As Congress poured millions of dollars of federal money (allocated by the Navajo-Hopi Rehabilitation Act) into projects aimed at developing the economic infrastructure of the reservation, the Navajo Tribal Council needed to find ways to create an identity that would be independent of the BIA and have the power to control what economic development would mean for its constituency.

Recent literature that explores race as historically constructed, as a fluid category that acquires meaning in relational terms, is helpful for understanding the racial hierarchy that characterized the Farmington working class in the 1950s. In this vein, using David Roediger's paradigm of race reveals a great deal about the nature of white working-class racism at that time and place. The brief vignette with which I opened this chapter illustrates how race was defined in relational terms and how those racial categories shaped the meaning of class in Farmington, at least from the perspective of a person from the white, bureaucratic elite, such as Minton. For instance, the "white trash" that Minton referred to consisted "mostly of Texans, who received low salaries and are of the type which regards an Indian as lower than a Negro, and a Negro as lower than a Mexican."[4] According to Minton, the white workers conceived of race in relational terms. "Negroes" served as the racial yardstick against whom the Texans assessed the status of the rest. White workers, or the Texans, were at the top. They derived their status because they were not Mexican, black, or Indian. Mexicans came next because they were neither white nor black. Since African Americans represented the lowest level on the racial hierarchy, Indians occupied a place in the racial order that was lower than the lowest category. Such a racial hierarchy produced an extremely hostile climate for Navajo workers and was indicative of the conditions they faced in the 1950s and 1960s when they visited, worked, and/or lived in towns, such as Farmington, that bordered the reservation.

It is difficult to assess how the white workers viewed their own class and racial standing in this hierarchy. Minton's description helps us understand the complicated racial landscape Navajo workers faced in border town communities. But that is only part of the story. If whiteness is purely a construction of white middle- and working-class anxiety, then the historical significance of what workers of color do or think becomes at best referential, or at worst, irrelevant. Although central to understanding the "'Texans'" identity, Navajo workers and tribal leaders remain faceless, nonactors in the historical process of class formation. Thinking through how people of color confronted "whiteness" and how their ethnic and/or racial identities informed how they engaged the world of wage labor, however, complicates the picture in a way that brings them to the center of the story, not just as reference points but as participants in the making of the historical narrative.[5] Exploring how Navajos perceived whiteness as the "white world" tightly incorporated them into its orbit raises larger questions about how subaltern peoples engaged dominant cultures in ways that gave them room to negotiate alternative strategies of resistance and survival.

This chapter examines a critical moment in the history of economic development on the reservation as trade unions emerged as part of the newly industrial Navajo landscape. It was a pivotal time when the class experience of Navajo workers was changing dramatically. Before the 1950s, working for wages was usually a temporary pursuit, largely confined to the world outside reservation boundaries. But, with development brought about by uranium mining and processing and the corporate extraction of other energy resources, permanent access to wage work at home was starting to become within reach of the reservation household. A relatively stable working class was in the making.

Racial Segmentation and the Gallup Strike of 1933

Like Farmington, Gallup was a reservation border town that offered possible sources of wage work for Navajo workers. And Gallup employers, like their counterparts to the north, relegated Indians to the bottom of a multitiered racial hierarchy. In the 1930s, Gallup was the most highly industrialized region in New Mexico, supplying the state and the surrounding Southwest with coal. It was second only to Colorado, which fed the copper industries, railroads, and growing communities such as Los Angeles, Phoenix, and Albuquerque. But, prior to the Depression, which forced a drop in coal production in the 1930s, Navajos remained on the fringes of that extractive economy. The coal-mining region attracted migrants from Mexico, Europe, and other places throughout the United States who were looking for work. The Navajos, with perhaps the least distance to travel, did not make up a significant part of that labor force. On the reservation, only a few miles to the northwest and to the northeast of Gallup, those who mined coal either worked in their own small diggings or worked in mines operated by the BIA. On their own land on the reservation they could be miners. When they crossed that boundary line into a racially segmented setting, their status changed. In Gallup they were no longer coal miners, they were Navajos hired to do "Indian work." That status would become a point of contention in one of the most explosive labor struggles in New Mexico's history.

In the early 1930s, the labor movement in Gallup and Madrid, a mining area south of Santa Fe, was growing in strength. Radical miners who were critical of the highly centralized United Mine Workers of America (UMWA), and those who were dissatisfied with its role in a strike in 1922, were gaining influence. Many of those who joined the National Miners' Union (NMU) were Mexican immigrants with ties to radical politics in Mexico.[6] Charles Mattox, an accomplished Albuquerque artist who moved to New Mexico in 1934, remembered the Mexican labor activists as "true revolutionaries."[7]

Throughout the region, workers voiced their dissatisfaction with a variety of coal company practices. Miners complained about wage cuts, discrimination, payment in company scrip, and the lack of compensation for "dead work." Those who were paid by the ton thought company officials routinely cheated them at the scales and unfairly penalized them for loading coal mixed with rock. The miners and their families felt that company housing was expensive and substandard.[8]

This discontent provided fertile ground for NMU organizers, and by late summer in 1933 they had enlisted the support of a large majority of the miners working in the Gallup district. On August 29 the union set up picket lines and successfully shut down the major coal mining operations. In the three months that followed they endured opposition from the United Mine Workers of America (their rival union) and other obstacles, the most damaging of which included Governor Arthur Seligman's use of the National Guard to maintain order. The guardsmen did so by prohibiting workers from assembling in groups of larger than five.[9]

Despite the intimidation tactics, on November 22 the union claimed victory when company officials finally agreed to some of its demands. Coal companies offered to increase wages, eliminate scrip, and rehire workers who had been fired during the strike. But the NMU failed to gain their most important demand: official recognition. Not long after the strike ended, workers grew increasingly impatient when the mining companies failed to deliver what they had promised. The union won the first battle, but the war was far from over.[10]

One year later, when the mining companies failed to make good on their agreement, the NMU widened the scope of the struggle to include the unemployed. Many of the miners who had been out of work since the strike were receiving aid from the Federal Emergency Relief Administration (FERA). So, the NMU mobilized those workers, too, and staged a strike when federal officials cut wages on a public works project.

This move sparked a conservative backlash. As historian Harry Rubenstein argued, FERA jobs were important sources of political patronage, and politicians were not willing to cede influence to a left-wing union. After the FERA strike, conservative groups in Gallup, such as the Elks Club, the American Legion, and the Veterans of Foreign Wars, responded by protesting against extending FERA benefits to aliens. As Rubenstein stated, this was "a move directed primarily against Gallup's Mexican community."[11] On April 6, 1935, three people, including the sheriff, were killed outside the county courthouse as observers assembled for the arraignment of an NMU organizer who had been arrested for leading an anti-eviction campaign.[12] Local and state authorities responded with mass arrests, deportations, and house-to-house searches. Vigilantes used "extralegal" tactics to intimidate defense witnesses and to undercut support for the union.

Despite winning initial wage concessions, the NMU's organizing efforts ended in eventual defeat. One hundred miners were deported to Mexico, the NMU local was in shambles, and the union failed to achieve collective bargaining rights.[13] With the NMU gone, the UMWA continued with its efforts to organize the miners in the Gallup area. But they would not achieve victory until 1943, when the Bituminous Coal Commission and wartime politics would finally force the major coal producers in Gallup to negotiate a collective bargaining agreement with the UMWA.[14]

Throughout the 1933 strike, relations between union members and Navajo workers were tense, at best. Leaders of the National Miners' Union were particularly angry when Navajo workers crossed their picket lines. In a letter to Arthur Seligman, governor of New Mexico, NMU leaders stressed that the

Navajos were "inexperienced" and "improperly equipped according to state mining laws" and demanded that the state mining inspector come to investigate.[15]

That investigation did not yield what the union members had hoped. The mine inspector "found the inexperienced indians [sic] to be working under the supervision of six experienced men, one of whom was the mine foreman" and that "every precaution possible is being taken to prevent an accident and there are no violations of the law."[16] When Seligman confirmed that the Navajos were not working in hazardous conditions, he sent in the National Guard to protect the strikebreakers.[17] Stuart Hines, an employee at the Mentmore Mine, complained:

> Since the strike the management has employed Indians until now about one-third of the crew are Indians. I am told that the number of Indians now in that mine is twenty eight. These Indians have never worked in a mine before. . . . These Indians live in hogans and of course pay no rent and receive all the benefits which the Government extends to all other members of the tribe. This is most unfair competition to white miners who have spent their lives in the coal mines.[18]

On May 17, 1934, a mine operator named George Kaseman anxiously wrote to Oscar Huber, the superintendent of Kaseman's coal mine in Madrid, New Mexico, to warn Huber about the tactics union organizers were using at his mine in Gallup. Kaseman suspected that union activists were surreptitiously posting wage rates that were below what the company usually paid its miners and surface laborers. If those flyers were to make their way back to Madrid, Kaseman worried, they would fuel the smoldering labor situation there. "Of course, these rates are awfully bad," he admitted, "because we pay much lower wages than this to our outside men who are practically all Indians."[19] At his Madrid operation, Kaseman employed primarily Mexican immigrants and native-born Hispanos. He did not want those workers to think their wages were going to be reduced to what he paid for "Indian work" in Gallup. Kaseman's operation in Gallup participated in a regional dual wage structure that defined categories of work along racial lines. In Gallup, those lines were rather fluid, changing over time to distinguish "Old-Mexicans" from "New Mexicans" and those groups from European immigrants and native-born Euro-Americans.[20] But the category of "Indian work" would persist at least through World War II, despite gains made by unions in the district and wage mandates imposed by the Bituminous Coal Commission.[21]

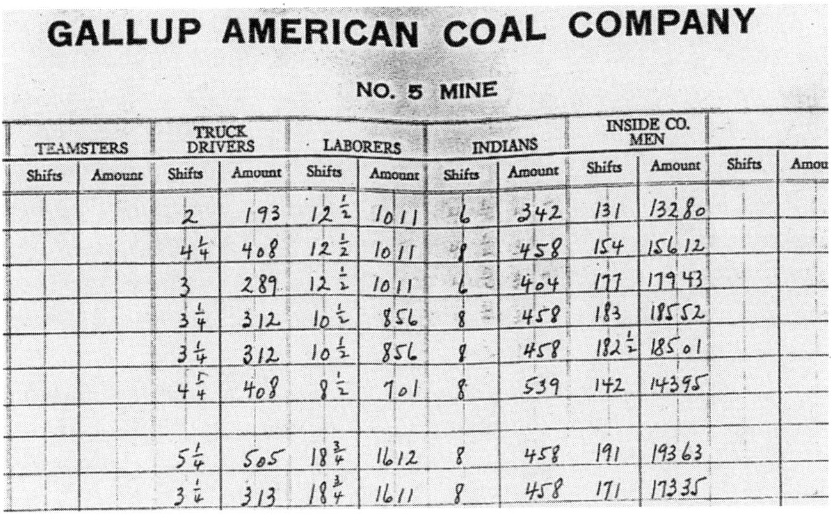

GALLUP AMERICAN COAL COMPANY

NO. 5 MINE

TEAMSTERS		TRUCK DRIVERS		LABORERS		INDIANS		INSIDE CO. MEN			
Shifts	Amount	Shifts	Amount	Shifts	Amount	Shifts	Amount	Shifts	Amount	Shifts	Amou
		2	193	12 1/2	1011	6	342	131	13280		
		4 1/4	408	12 1/2	1011	8	458	154	15612		
		3	289	12 1/2	1011	6	404	177	17943		
		3 1/4	312	10 1/2	856	8	458	183	18552		
		3 1/4	312	10 1/2	856	8	458	182 1/2	18501		
		4 5/4	408	8 1/2	701	8	539	142	14395		
		5 1/4	505	18 3/4	1612	8	458	191	19363		
		3 1/4	313	18 3/4	1611	8	458	171	17335		

Gallup American Coal Company Labor Compilation Record, January 1945. Gallup American Coal Company Records, Geological Information Center Archives, New Mexico State Bureau of Geology and Mineral Resources, New Mexico Institute of Mines and Technology, Socorro (unprocessed collection).

Indian work primarily consisted of marginal, surface labor and/or maintenance duties such as making repairs on company houses. The Gallup American Coal Company payroll records for 1945 show a breakdown of labor costs for various occupational titles, such as machinist, "inside men," weigh boss, shot firers, cagers, laborers, and so on. Beside those job titles is another column on the ledger titled "Indians" where payroll clerks recorded the total number of shifts worked. Yet, the "Indians" category was not broken down by the jobs performed. To the mining company officials, such work was obvious and did not merit specific description.[22]

When Kaseman worried about the union posting the Indian pay rates, he was not concerned that the union would disrupt the dual wage structure. He suspected, instead, that the union would exploit the wage differential between Indians and non-Indians to strengthen its membership among workers in the latter category. He had little reason to worry that the union would attempt to organize the Indians and advocate an end to the dual wage system. Nevertheless, he did not want to incite the workers' fears in Madrid, since he was facing union agitation there as well as at his operation in Gallup.[23]

In light of these conditions, the union's tactic of posting the wage rates paid for Indian work had explosive organizing potential. Although that strategy could be interpreted as advocating a pay increase for Indian workers, there is very little evidence to show that the unions were concerned about improving the working conditions for Native Americans. During the strike, the unions made little effort to address the needs of Navajo workers. Nor did they challenge the company's Indian work category. Struggles against racial discrimination focused primarily around the plight of Mexican immigrants and Mexican Americans who faced eviction and deportation at the hands of vigilantes, company thugs, and law enforcement officers.

Although Navajos did cross the unions' picket lines, they were not wholly responsible for breaking the strike. In the end, the NMU and UMWA's setback had more to do with vigilantism, violence, and a government that was less than sympathetic to their demands. In addition, the severe anti-Mexican backlash dished out by the mining companies and vigilante groups in Gallup polarized the conflict in racial terms. The union struggle became synonymous with the struggle for racial justice for Spanish-speaking people. Since the Navajos' actions during the strike did not endear them to labor leaders, they remained marginal to the movement that collapsed issues of racial and class solidarity.

Finding work in the Gallup coal mines after the strike was a delicate task for Navajo miners. The lingering resentment from union members must have made the Navajo mine workers terribly uncomfortable. Tsosie Blackgoat recalled that he and other Navajos were able to avoid problems with the union by making special arrangements with company officials to work for short amounts of time. Blackgoat remembered that the job "was just for a while, then we don't join the union. They don't say anything about it. . . . We knew the boss."[24] Navajo workers had to navigate this hostile terrain as they developed new strategies to ensure the survival of their reservation households. "Indian work" had survived the 1933 Gallup strike intact, ensuring Navajo workers with jobs that fit within their interest in seasonal wage work and their place on the margins of the capitalist wage labor market.

Contrary to Blackgoat's experience, some Navajo men worked in the Gallup mines for long periods and joined the union when the mines were eventually organized in the 1940s. Unlike their Anglo, "Mexican," and African American counterparts, the Navajos who worked in the Gallup mines year-round had not migrated to the area, nor did they live in one of the district's company towns. Instead, the mine owners came to them, locating their operations on the lands that had been part of Navajo traditional use areas for generations. Anthropologist Klara Kelley argued that from the earliest commercial development of coal in the region until approximately 1912, coal companies and Navajo families lived in "peaceful coexistence."[25] Navajo families continued to herd sheep, gather plants, and conduct ceremonials on the land before the mines opened and continued to do so when they were in operation. Klara Kelley's profiles of the families that lived in the vicinity of the Carbon City and Defiance mines demonstrated that those workers maintained mixed household economies. For example, Fred Tom, a Navajo man who grew up about 10 miles north of the mines in Rock Springs, traveled back and forth every day from his parents' home for Carbon City Mining Company. When he married the daughter of Bilii' Daalbahi ni' Biye' and moved in with her family, he continued to work at the mine while his wife and her family herded sheep on the surrounding mesas and flat lands.[26] That Tom was a proud member of the UMWA probably distinguished him from others who, like Blackgoat, were avoiding the unions and looking for occasional short-term jobs. Tom could incorporate the world of the Carbon City Mine without giving up his reservation household.

The relationship between Navajo workers and organized labor remained somewhat ambivalent throughout the 1930s and 1940s. Employed primarily in commercial agriculture, and on seasonal maintenance crews for railroad companies, Navajo workers may have seen unions as institutions that reinforced a labor force segmented along racial lines.[27] Union organizers did not do much to counter those impressions. They had been reluctant to reach out to Navajo workers, regarding them as potential strikebreakers who would undermine the wage rates of non-Navajos in the region. When the UMWA finally organized the Gallup coal mining district, a few Navajos joined the union; however, it seems that most others found short-term work that enabled them to avoid union membership.[28]

Organizing in Window Rock

Although Tsosie Blackgoat found short-term jobs at the Gamerco mine from time to time, like many Navajos employed as coal miners between the 1930s

Tsosie Blackgoat, former operator of the Window Rock mine,
left, with Lawrence Oliver, former president of the United Mine
Workers in Window Rock and president of the Naalnishí
labor federation. Photo by author, used by permission.

and the 1950s, he primarily worked in small mines operated by the BIA on the
reservation. These mines were larger than the kin-based operations I described in Chapter 2. Since 1912 a series of independent contractors, including one "unknown Anglo" and a "Mexican named One Eye" operated the Window Rock Mine. By the 1930s, it was one of the largest and most productive
mines operated by the Navajo Agency. Except for Tsosie Blackgoat, his brother,
Nahaya, and his father, Hastine Neez, few Navajos worked there in its first
years of operation.

The mine was located in the Blackgoat traditional use area where, until the
1930s, the family had grazed sheep and cattle.[29] Tsosie Blackgoat remembers,
"[t]hey used to have a lot of sheep at that time." But during the years of stock

Miner's cottage. Fort Defiance coal mine, 1929. Photo courtesy of the BLM.

reduction "they just sold most of it, to bring [the numbers] . . . back down. [My family] sold [the stock] at a real low price."[30] As they gave up their herds, the family relied more heavily on the wages earned by the men at the coal mine. More Navajos eventually joined the Blackgoats as the effects of stock reduction forced families with reduced herds to seek work in the mines.[31]

In 1932, geologists who had been frustrated by the unwillingness of independent contractors to conform to rationalized production methods convinced the BIA to take over the operation to ensure an inexpensive and reliable source of fuel for reservation day and boarding schools and other administrative facilities.[32] When the BIA reopened the mine, it employed primarily "white" miners and instituted what it considered more efficient mining methods.[33] By 1935 the BIA mining engineers started to replace the white miners with Navajos. Like soil conservation demonstration projects that taught Navajos new farming techniques, the BIA officials hoped to create a model that would teach the Navajos modern coal mining production methods. B. W. Dyer, the district mining supervisor who was responsible for inspecting mines throughout New Mexico, suggested to the BIA that "an Indian be employed as a helper or apprentice with each white miner in order that the Indian may learn the trade. As soon as he becomes qualified as a miner, he should be employed as a miner and paid accordingly."[34]

By 1937 the transition from white to Navajo miners was nearly complete. Mine inspector reports for that year show twelve Navajos and four white men employed at the Window Rock Mine, with the latter primarily in supervisory positions.[35] Although BIA mining personnel were pleased with the operation, they were not enthusiastic about the possibility of Navajos running the mine themselves. Dyer commented, "It will be many years before the Indian miners will have been sufficiently trained to mine this coal safely without the assistance of a white miner."[36]

A similar development at the Tohatchi Mine, 15 miles to the northeast of Window Rock, encouraged local BIA officials. According to E. R. Fryer, the general superintendent of the Navajo Service, this was no small feat. He boasted that "it required painstaking effort on the part of our mine foremen in providing the necessary training and safety features."[37] UMWA representatives did not share Fryer's enthusiasm. They were not pleased when the BIA replaced the white miners with newly trained Navajos.[38] But, since the mines were not organized, there was little the union could do to protest.[39]

In 1937, when Frank Hefferly, District 15 president of the UMWA, made an effort to organize the coal miners at the Window Rock Mine, he was primarily concerned with protecting the UMWA bargaining power in Gallup. He was worried that the coal companies in Gallup would hire Navajos at lower rates and thus depress the wages for other miners in the district.[40] That might blur the definition of "Indian work." He was also concerned that by producing coal so cheaply, the BIA mines would compel the Gallup district coal operators to lower their prices. Hefferly thought that the persistence of nonunion coal mining threatened the UMWA's efforts to organize the larger, commercial mines in Gallup.

But, to Hefferly's consternation, Bureau of Indian Affairs officials resisted the UMWA's efforts to organize their coal operations. In response to the union's initial request for recognition, Fryer abruptly refused to sign a collective bargaining agreement.[41] When union officials pursued the matter, they met even stiffer opposition from the BIA commissioner himself. John Collier asserted that since the agency was not producing coal for commercial purposes, the government-run mines were exempt from the Wagner Act, a recent piece of New Deal legislation that guaranteed workers the right to organize unions.[42] Collier's opposition to organized labor on the reservation seems a bit perplexing. In his early years as a reformer in New York, he had supported the struggles of working people, drawing inspiration from radical trade unionists and intellectuals who moved in and out of his Greenwich Village social network.[43] Perhaps he saw unions as a force of modernity that would corrupt Navajo culture; as a symptom of class antagonism that did not exist within his Indian ideal. Perhaps he recognized that the UMWA was not, at that time, interested in the welfare of the Navajo workers. It is difficult to know exactly what he thought. We do know that he continued to oppose the UMWA's efforts.

Hefferly complained that the BIA's intransigence on this issue undermined their organizing campaigns in the Gallup district. In a letter to Collier, Hefferly asked: "Just how we can ever negotiate wage contracts with these companies in face of the position taken by the United States Government . . . against collective bargaining is all beyond me, regardless of whether or not the coal produced in the Gallup mines comes in competition with coal mined at Fort Defiance at the Government mine."[44]

Hefferly hardly mentions the issues that concerned the Indian workers at the BIA mine. Judging from the mine inspector reports, the Navajo miners had plenty to complain about. He stressed instead how their nonunion status promised to undermine efforts to organize workers in Gallup. Even the powerful John L. Lewis, president of the UMWA, could not convince the BIA officials and their superiors at the Department of the Interior to support the union's efforts. Lewis found little sympathy from Secretary of the Interior Harold Ickes when pleading Hefferly's case in Washington. The mines remained nonunion until they closed in the 1950s.[45]

Hefferly's failed efforts would be the last attempt to organize Navajo workers for another thirteen years. World War II brought development programs on the reservation to a halt and pulled most able-bodied Navajos either into the military or into defense industries located in such cities as Phoenix, Los Angeles, and San Francisco. In the years following the war, money pouring into the reservation from the 1950 Navajo-Hopi Rehabilitation Act triggered a new era for Navajo workers. After 1950, permanent wage work would become part of the reservation landscape for a significant minority. And with the new jobs came challenges that required Navajo workers to renegotiate class and kin relationships.

El Paso Natural Gas Pipeline Campaign

In the 1950s, the BIA's opposition would no longer be the primary obstacle to organizing unions on the reservation. Instead, unions would have to confront a number of stumbling blocks that would make organizing extremely difficult into the 1970s. First, union organizers would have to face their own culturally bound assumptions about trade union behavior. Next, they would have to face a newly invigorated Navajo Tribal Council, which viewed unions as a threat to their sovereignty rights. And, finally, as a result of those struggles, Navajo workers would have to sort out the racialized landscape that framed the development of a Navajo-controlled labor movement on the reservation.

In the summer of 1950, Navajo workers got their first chance to sort out these issues approximately 125 miles north of Window Rock, near Farmington. On Monday, August 21, 1950, representatives from the Hod Carriers, Building, and Common Laborers Union launched a campaign to organize workers who were building the El Paso Natural Gas pipeline across the reservation.[46] This organizing effort was much different from earlier UMWA campaigns, where the union only sought to organize Navajos to protect its interests elsewhere. The Hod Carriers were there to organize Navajo workers for their own sake.

An Anglo organizer, to whom anthropologist Gorden Streib assigned the pseudonym "Harding," began the campaign by contacting potential workers at a community meeting assembled for other purposes. At first, he spoke in English without an interpreter, explaining the union's views on the pipeline project.[47] After he had addressed an audience made up of about sixty-seven Navajo men, women, and children for 30 minutes, a member of the community volunteered to interpret for him. The organizer outlined the union's point of view, arguing that the company was not complying with the lease agreement since it was not hiring Navajos for jobs they were qualified to perform. He also described the purpose of a union and what people gained when they went out on strike. Streib observed that the union representative recalled "previous union victories with other pipeline companies and stressed the union's support for equal pay for equal work and its opposition to racial or religious discrimination."[48] Apparently impressed by what the union proposed, twenty-

El Paso Natural Gas pipeline construction, no date. Photograph by Milton Snow, Courtesy of the Navajo Nation Museum, Window Rock, Arizona. Catalog # NO 16-462.

six Navajo men out of about thirty-five men and older boys present signed union cards.[49]

The next evening the organizer and "Charles Redhorse," a Navajo interpreter, went to a Nádaa dance to talk to community members about the union.[50] The organizer did not address the crowd directly as he had done the night before. Instead, Redhorse and the organizer mingled among the crowd, talking to members of the community and to a tribal council delegate. The next evening, when the dance moved to another location, the union organizer decided on a bolder approach. Harding was getting impatient with the slow-moving dynamics of speaking through an interpreter. To quicken the pace, he encouraged the interpreter to speak without his prompting. But Redhorse did more than deliver a strong pro-union plea. His criticism extended to the Navajo Tribal Council as well.

Harding's decision to let Redhorse speak freely was a serious, strategic blunder for the union. Redhorse was a Navajo, but he was not from the surrounding area, nor was he connected to the larger community through kin relations. Many of the workers drawn to the El Paso Natural Gas construction project came from Navajo families living in Fruitland, a farming community 18 miles southeast of Shiprock and 10 miles west of Farmington. In the 1950s, Fruitland was a small farming community of approximately 200 Navajo families who had settled on 10-acre plots of land allocated to them by the Bureau of Indian Affairs in exchange for giving up their livestock. Since the land allotments were so small, many family members were forced to seek out wage labor to contribute to the survival of their households. Complicating matters was the schism that had developed among the Fruitland households. People who had resided in the area for generations deeply resented other Navajos whom they termed as "outsiders" brought in to settle by the BIA.[51] Given these conditions, it is reasonable to assume that the community was predisposed to regard Redhorse with suspicion. He would have had very little status speaking out in a public forum.

Moreover, when Redhorse got up to speak, "Greyeyes," a respected elder and member of the tribal council, had just finished addressing the crowd about the merits of the company and the tribal council's position. This was a humiliating moment for the tribal elder, and the community blamed Redhorse for his bad manners. Redhorse had spoken directly after a respected elder and that was considered disrespectful. Streib explained that "[a]ccording to Navajo custom, it was considered in bad taste for a young man—a 'boy' as many men under forty are called by older people—to express opinions, and critical ones at that, at a large public gathering."[52] Streib's questioning of the participants revealed that although people in the community generally favored the union, many sided with Greyeyes because he had been treated so badly.

Unfortunately for the union, Harding's faux pas were not limited to the second night of the dance. He grew more frustrated as he tried to mobilize for a strike. He set up picket lines outside the pipeline operation and to encourage people to participate, he advertised that everyone who showed up for picket duty would be fed lunch. On the first day of the strike, Streib reported that four Navajo men and two Navajo women took their place alongside four white male union members on the picket line. But, by noon, the picket line had dissolved, and the Navajos were sitting on the ground holding their signs. At midday faithful picketers and curious observers gathered for lunch. Streib observed that the Navajos did not distinguish between union and nonunion people in the "chow line." According to Streib, Harding was beside himself. He was annoyed "that the union was feeding people who would readily take a job on the pipeline if offered one. He made a rule, which was unenforceable, that only those Navajos who worked with and for the union were to be fed."[53]

After that, fewer Navajos began to show up for picket duty. More were crossing the line and appearing at the traders to apply for work on the pipeline. In a desperate attempt to keep the strike going, Harding tried to convince the few pro-union Navajos to confront the strikebreakers by rushing up to the pick-up trucks and shouting, "Don't go to work." But they did not respond in the way Harding expected. For Harding, roughing up the scabs was, no doubt, well within the tactics commonly accepted of union activists. But, instead of rushing the trucks, the pro-union Navajos "walked very slowly. . . . By the time they reached it, the truck was already loaded and ready to leave. The new recruits departed without a murmur of protest on the part of union sympathizers."[54]

The organizer was growing increasingly fed up with what probably appeared to him as a lack of Navajo nerve and backbone. He was particularly disturbed when his interpreter refused to shout his commands. Redhorse spoke only in a conversational tone and was reluctant to teach Harding phrases that he could shout himself. Harding's own attempt to utter the Navajo words was met with silent stares from his audience. Streib noted that when "Redhorse tried to explain the retiring, shy behavior of his people, . . . Harding appeared unconvinced."[55] Harding did not quite appreciate the sensitive nature of Navajo relationships in this area of the reservation at the time. An unusually high number of witchcraft accusations in the Fruitland-Shiprock communities might have created some discomfort, and it is likely that as a result, Navajos would be highly conscious of how their behavior would be perceived by their neighbors.[56]

Although the organizer was astute enough to look for Navajo workers at community meetings and ceremonial gatherings, his understanding of Navajo ways did not extend much further. Streib reported that the organizer and the Navajo workers operated on very different sets of cultural assumptions about appropriate ways to behave in public and in situations that produced conflict. Harding was continuously frustrated by how the Navajos responded at critical moments in the union's struggle. In the end, his assumptions about how workers were supposed to behave undermined his organizing strategies. Navajos who were not generally acquainted with unions may have interpreted the Hod Carriers' organizing tactics as requiring them to behave in ways considered disrespectful by Navajo cultural traditions. Eventually, Navajo workers chose to work for El Paso Natural Gas rather than to participate in a strike. The campaign fizzled out, and the union lost the battle. But crossing the picket line and/or siding with Greyeyes at a public gathering did not necessarily mean that the community supported the tribal council. In fact, many of the workers hired by El Paso Natural Gas were from a section of Fruitland that had suffered the most from stock reduction. Historian Peter Iverson argued that many Navajos, especially in the Shiprock area, partly blamed the tribal council for the hardships they faced under the stock reduction program. At the time of the pipeline workers campaign, the tribal council was just beginning to assert its autonomy from the BIA.[57]

The union's failure cannot be simply summed up as a case of cultural misunderstanding. The white organizer's mistakes reveal that his strategies were deeply rooted in highly racialized assumptions of class identity and behavior. He did not realize how culturally bound trade union tactics were. He considered Indian behavior as "deviant." What Harding saw as a natural way to articulate class-based interests (therefore racially neutral as far as he was concerned) appeared to the Navajo as the "white man's way" of doing things. Navajo tribal leaders were quick to point out that the white man's way was inherently anti-Navajo. To the Navajos present at the Nádaa near Shiprock in August 1951, becoming a union member might have meant abandoning respect for elders in public. Denying food to one's kinsmen because they were anti-union could have been interpreted as placing the union's interests over the customary responsibilities associated with hospitality. Observers of Navajo society in the 1950s consistently commented that Navajo cultural practices generally discouraged belligerent behavior. Many Navajos equated such activity with drunken, irresponsible conduct.[58] For the Navajo workers, the traders seemed to offer the more familiar alternative. For as exploitative as that relationship could be, at least the trader accommodated Navajo ways of doing things.[59]

Texas-Zinc Campaign

Eight years later, the Hod Carriers tried again. This time they launched a campaign at the Texas-Zinc uranium processing mill 150 miles northwest of

Shiprock (or 75 miles as the crow flies), in Mexican Hat, Utah. Texas-Zinc had not been in business long. Three years earlier the company had acquired a contract from the Atomic Energy Commission to produce uranium concentrate, and the Navajo Tribal Council had agreed to lease them the land. The company wanted to locate its mill on Navajo land to be close to their mining operations in nearby Monument Valley. In 1957 they opened the mill.[60] What happened to the Navajo uranium workers is probably one of the most tragic events in U.S. working-class history. Workers employed in the uranium mills and mines throughout the reservation endured unsafe conditions, working without adequate ventilation or training. Many of them were completely ignorant of the dangers involved in uranium mining and processing. Over the years, many died from cancers they developed from exposure to toxic materials. Those who survive have been trying to gain compensation for their suffering under the provisions of the 1990 Radiation Exposure Compensation Act.[61]

Two years later, on May 12, 1959, accompanied by the United Steelworkers of America and the Operating Engineers, the Hod Carriers filed a petition with the NLRB requesting an election.[62] At the representation hearing, the Navajo Tribal Council objected to the petition on grounds that the NLRB had no jurisdiction on the reservation. On February 11, 1960, despite the tribal council's protests, the NLRB decided in favor of the unions and issued a direction of election. The board argued that since Texas-Zinc was engaged in interstate commerce, the NLRB had the right to regulate labor conditions.

One month later, the Navajo Tribal Council appealed the decision to the U.S. District Court. The tribal councilmen continued to insist on their sovereignty rights, arguing that the treaty of 1868 gave them "plenary authority of self-government" and the power to limit access of non-Indians to land within the reservation boundaries.[63] They also argued that the National Labor Relations Act did not apply to "commerce with an Indian Tribe or to interstate commerce resulting from business activities located on an Indian Reservation."[64]

The U.S. District Court confirmed the NLRB's decision, stating that federal law protecting workers' rights to organize superseded state and tribal laws to the contrary. They added that the treaty of 1868 was not intended to regulate labor-management relations and that "its provisions for preventing encroachment on tribal lands scarcely may be made the basis for vesting control of the problems of modern industrial relations in the Tribal Council."[65] More

important, the court stated that the federal government had the right to regulate Indians and that the "legal fiction of dealing with Indian Tribes through
treaties has long been ended."[66]

In addition to battling it out in the federal courts, the Navajo Tribal Council tried other tactics to defeat union organizing at the Texas-Zinc mill.[67] A
year before the campaign began, the Navajo Tribal Council had enacted a law
that prohibited trade union activity on reservation land.[68] When tribal councilors learned about the organizing campaign, they set out to enforce that policy and informed Navajo workers at Texas-Zinc that they would be subject
to six months hard labor for participating in union activities.[69]

The Navajo Tribal Council also prohibited white union representatives access to the reservation. On May 20, tribal police, acting on the authority of the
tribal council, evicted an Operating Engineers business agent, A. E. Jordan, from
reservation land. Two months later, Donald Wright, a Hod Carriers' representative, met a similar fate. In July 1960, he received word from Scott Preston,
vice chairman of the Navajo Tribal Council, that he was not permitted on
reservation land. Evoking the 1868 treaty and stressing their rights to govern,
the council charged Wright with violations of the Navajo tribal code, namely,
for "conducting unionization activities on Navajo Tribal land."[70] Preston instructed the Navajo police to escort Wright off the reservation if they encountered him. The tribal council president argued that he was forced to take
such drastic action "to protect the lives, health, morals and property of the
Navajo Tribe from possible damage." According to Preston and other tribal leaders, the council was predominantly concerned that unions contradicted tribal
customs.[71] Preston, a medicine man from Cameron, near Tuba City, assumed
that violence and moral decay would be the end result of the union's presence
on the reservation and that unions would "unsettle Indian relationships."[72]

Development efforts expanded greatly in the 1950s, and Paul Jones, who
was elected tribal chairman in 1955, in particular was instrumental in turn-
ing increasingly lucrative oil royalties into improvements in the physical and
political infrastructure on the reservation. It was a period when, as Peter Iverson has observed, the "Navajo Nation was born."[73] Flush with intense Navajo
nationalism, the tribal council was not inclined to take lightly any infringe-
ment on its power. Under the Jones administration, the Navajo Nation erected
new housing, established a scholarship fund, built chapter houses and new
electric power lines. Jones was particularly interested in protecting the ura-

nium mining and milling industry on reservation lands. He feared that closing off parts of the reservation to uranium development would have a disastrous effect on the Navajo economy. Writing to Arizona congressman John Rhodes in 1960, Jones even offered to urge the BIA to reduce royalty payments on low-grade ore, to stimulate production. "As you can see, we are extending every effort to assure the long range continuation of mining in Northern Arizona," Jones said.[74]

The Navajo Tribal Council also tried to discourage Texas-Zinc from recognizing the union.[75] The council argued that if Texas-Zinc agreed to collective bargaining, the company would be in violation of Navajo law and thus provide grounds for the council to cancel its lease. Evoking the part of the lease intended to prohibit the use of liquor or other "nuisances," the council argued that the company could "not use or permit to be used any part of said premises for any unlawful conduct or purpose whatsoever."[76]

Threatening to cancel Texas-Zinc's lease was also a veiled threat aimed at potentially pro-union Navajo workers. If Texas-Zinc lost its lease, fewer jobs would be available in a region where skilled, industrial work was relatively scarce. This fueled a rumor campaign that served an even more devastating blow to the union's efforts to organize. Apparently, the Navajo Tribal Council was spreading rumors that if a union were established at the mill, the company would hire white union members instead of Navajos.[77]

With the headline, "Unions to Invade Reservation Land," editors of the *Navajo Times* announced that the election vote would be held against the wishes of the tribal council. The paper exclaimed, "The way was clear today for the National Labor Relations Board to Invade the ancient tribal lands of the Navajo Indians." The paper described the Navajo Tribal Council's dissatisfaction with the ruling, indicating that the leadership was still on the "warpath." Characterizing the Navajo leadership in language that was strangely reminiscent of Hollywood images and stereotypes of American Indians, the paper reported that "the tribal chiefs would not be satisfied until the Supreme Court rules on what the Navajos consider an unwarranted application of *paleface* law."[78]

With a swift blow to the Navajo Tribal Council's claims to sovereignty, the unions were free to hold their election. But, fearing a loss, the Steelworkers withdrew their petition, leaving the Hod Carriers and the Operating Engineers to bring the struggle to its final conclusion. Evidently, the Navajos employed at Texas-Zinc either failed to see the union as their advocate, or they were unwilling to challenge the tribal council's position. On July 20, 1961, they voted 56 to 11 to remain nonunion.[79]

The union immediately protested the outcome of the election, charging the Navajo Tribal Council and Texas-Zinc with unfair labor practices. Both parties had conspired to create such a highly charged anti-union climate, they claimed, that a fair election was impossible. But the NLRB contended that the election was indeed fair and denied the union's charges. Even though the union lost the election, the Navajo Tribal Council could not exactly claim victory. Although they may have cheered the election results, the ultimate ruling of the federal courts seriously undermined their right to govern.

In the Texas-Zinc case, it is difficult to know what the Navajo workers thought about the conflict among the tribal leadership, the federal government, the unions, and company management. Although their unwillingness to endorse the union does not necessarily prove that they "sided" with the tribal council, it does show that their support for the union was not strong enough to enlist their loyalty in a long-drawn-out legal battle. Perhaps they too saw the union reps as "outsiders." Or they believed the rumors and propaganda circulated in Mexican Hat and Blanding, Utah, that assumed if the mill "went union," it would close and undermine the economy in the region.[80] Some Navajo workers did see unions as an avenue to better wages and working conditions. But those workers, caught in a web of conflicting loyalties, faced the difficult choice of identifying either with "the white man's way" that the unions, reinforced by U.S. federal law, represented or with the wishes of the Navajo tribal leadership. For Navajo tribal leaders, prohibiting trade unions on the reservation was an effort to assert their rights of self-governance and an attempt to garner legitimacy in the eyes of the Navajo people. The tribal council's construction of unions as white helped to cast organized labor as an "outsider," thus undermining its position in the changing economic climate. Doing this might then eliminate a possible contender in the struggle for the power to control economic development on the reservation. With their reputations still tarnished from the role they had played in stock reduction, Navajo tribal officials needed to stand up to the white man, to "Wááshindoon." In the wake of development brought by the Navajo-Hopi Rehabilitation Act, the Navajo Tribal Council needed to distinguish itself as a body with real power autonomous from the Bureau of Indian Affairs. The tribal government was not in a position to make that stand with the corporations they hoped to lure to the reservation. Thus opposing unions served a dual purpose. Tribal leaders could appear to be promoting the rights of Navajo workers while at the same time making reservation land more attractive to corporate developers.

Navajo Construction Workers Association

In the mid-1960s the relationship among the BIA, the Navajo Tribal Council, and organized labor improved significantly. Robert Bennett, the new commissioner of Indian affairs and the first American Indian to hold that position since the mid-nineteenth century, published an article in the *AFL-CIO Federationist* that seemed to indicate a new cooperative atmosphere. Using the *AFL-CIO Federationist* as a mouthpiece, Bennett announced a "a new era for American Indians." The article described the terrible poverty native peoples suffered throughout the United States and offered industrial development, an end to federal paternalism, and increasing self-sufficiency as solutions.[81] But Bennett failed to mention what role organized labor would have in that process. Although writing for an official publication of the American Federation of Labor–Congress of Industrial Organizations (AFL-CIO) hinted at better relations between unions and the BIA, Bennett did not endorse trade union organizing on reservations.

The election of Raymond Nakai in 1963 to the chair of the Navajo Tribal Council signified a change in Navajo labor relations. Nakai, unlike his predecessors Paul Jones and Scott Preston, assumed a rather pragmatic position on organized labor and did not use his position to discourage union membership among the Navajo people.[82] The tribal council's position remained consistent into the mid-1970s, even with the election of Peter MacDonald, who was notoriously anti-union.[83] Even though MacDonald was a firm supporter of the tribal "right-to-work" law, he eventually entered into a formal agreement with the AFL-CIO to ensure that Navajos would be hired at the Four Corners coal gasification plants near Shiprock.[84] Instead of viewing unions as a threat from "outsiders," BIA and Navajo tribal officials were beginning to see trade unions as vehicles for Navajo workers to use to gain access to skilled jobs.

At a hearing before the U.S. Commission on Civil Rights in Window Rock, Thomas Brose, director of the Office of Navajo Labor Relations, explained the tribal council's new, pragmatic labor policy. He told the commission that the tribal council did not enforce its "right to work policy."[85] Instead, the Office of Navajo Labor Relations worked with the unions to ensure that they included a Navajo preference clause in their collective bargaining agreements. These clauses were similar to those included in leasing agreements that were supposed to give Navajos priority access to jobs on the reservation. But, in the past, that protocol had not been enforced. In 1972 only 8 percent of the workers constructing the Four Corners project were Navajos. The situation was better at the Navajo Generating Plant, where Navajos made up 22 percent of the workforce.[86] Ideally, Brose explained, when jobs on the reservation were available, unions would first draw from a separate list of Navajo workers before they referred any non-Navajos to the employer.[87] Perhaps encouraging unions to adopt preference clauses was one way Navajo leaders could gain compliance from industries leasing reservation land.

Unlike their counterparts in Mexican Hat in 1961, Navajo workers in the new reservation industries did not completely reject unions. Prior to 1960 trade unions were largely superfluous to the experience of most Navajo workers, but by the 1970s that had changed. Unions were now a type of gatekeeper that allowed access to the best jobs that the reservation had to offer.

Despite the fact that Arizona was a "right-to-work" state, national labor agreements required contractors to hire union workers.[88] Union membership was required to get a job on most of the major construction projects on the reservation, including the Navajo Generating Station, near Page, Arizona, and the Four Corners Power Plant near Shiprock. Navajo workers at those plants as well as those working at Peabody Coal on Black Mesa and at the Pittsburgh and Midway Coal Company near Window Rock did join unions. As a result, Navajo membership in unions grew significantly in the 1970s. Lynn Robbins, an anthropologist who conducted the only study of Navajo union membership in that period, estimated that in 1950 there were only fifty Navajo union members on the reservation. By 1977 that number had increased to 6,000.[89]

Even with an improved relationship among the BIA, the Navajo Tribal Council, and organized labor, Navajo workers remained suspicious. The new industries that did hire Navajo workers did not retain them for long. "[T]he white man don't understand the way the Navajo lives," Navajo carpenter and labor activist Kenneth White explained at a hearing before the U.S. Civil Rights Commission in Window Rock in 1973. White, a member of Carpenters

Kenneth White, founder of the Navajo Construction Workers Association and first compliance officer for the Office of Navajo Labor
Relations. Used by permission.

Local 1100 and employed at the Navajo Power Plant near Page, Arizona, appeared before the commission to testify about the racial discrimination Navajos faced in the workplace and in the hiring hall.[90] But White was not there
to complain about legal barriers that undermined Navajo job opportunities.
Rather, White criticized the assumptions and practices that fundamentally
shaped the culture of the "White Man's" workplace. When commissioners
asked him to describe the "cultural problems that an employer has to be aware
of in dealing with Navajo workers," he challenged the underlying premise
implied in that question. Navajo culture was not an obstacle to economic
development. The problem was employers' ignorance about the Navajo way.

Refuting what many commissioners may have assumed was a universal truth that defined the American workplace, White explained that having a job was not the same as making a living. Navajos did not see their jobs at places like the Navajo Power Plant as central to their lives. What reservation households demanded from the Navajo workers was at least as important as, if not more important than, what employers wanted from them.

White then set out to outline what he thought the new Anglo-controlled industries on the reservation should accommodate. Navajo men needed to be free to attend to their household obligations on a seasonal basis. "A lot of people have cattle, sheep and horses," White explained, "especially in the wintertime they have to take care of their homes with hauling wood and water and stuff like that." In the summertime, Navajo men were needed less at home because "we do have school kids come home from schools and care for sheep and cattle and all that while we are working." But, when the children returned to school, Navajo men had to find ways to tend to the work of the household in their absence.

Yet, Navajo men were not solely responsible for the household's survival. Stressing the central role of women, White explained that "[t]he wife takes care of the daily chores of the livelihood." The Navajo labor leader's description of women's work as part of the "livelihood" is significant. Although wages were becoming more important, women's work was still central to the household's day-to-day survival. Herding sheep, weaving rugs, and maintaining Navajo traditions created the physical landscape from which Navajos defined their cultural identities.

Sometimes other responsibilities demanded the workers' attention. They often needed to stay at home to attend ceremonial functions. "[W]e do have culture that we respect very highly that still exists on this Navajo Reservation with the Navajo people," White declared. "[S]mall 1-night ceremonies to 5-night to 9-night ceremonies" required workers to miss work, particularly if a worker or someone in his household was ill. The workers would have to consult a "medicine man," White continued, and "these things have got to be respected. That's the way the feeling is by us Navajo people because a man might have gotten sick, got to be cared for, these things the white man's doctor can't cure," White explained.

According to White, Navajo workers tried to accommodate the employers' needs by asking for time off, instead of leaving without notifying them. He was particularly disturbed when employers were not sympathetic. Sometimes their household responsibilities required them to stay away longer than the workers originally intended.

> A lot of people do request for leave to take care of this, but when they overdo their leave—maybe they took off for 1 day and they had to go beyond that— they get fired for that, and this has got to be respected some way that we could understand each other. That's my feeling and we've been having a lot of problems with that and people have been fired for absenteeism lately.[91]

Navajo workers wanted employers to recognize the way wage work fit into their "livelihoods." Unions, too, needed to understand. They complained strongly about hiring procedures, charging that the unions did not refer Indians to jobs at the Navajo Power project. They claimed that Navajos had been excluded from referrals to jobs on or near the reservation because they were not union members. Navajo workers living near the Navajo Power Plant who tried to join the union had to make a 145-mile trip to Flagstaff, Arizona, to sign up at the union hall. Those workers who did travel to Flagstaff may not have been able to respond to referrals since most probably did not have telephones.[92] Dan Press, an attorney for the Diné Bee'iiná' Náhiilnah Bee Agha'diit'aahii (DNA), an independent Navajo civil rights and legal aid organization, told reporters that "[t]he union could care less about Navaho employment. They are using their regular hiring procedure [the white way]." The reporter added, "The hiring has been given to Mexican-Americans—to get the Navahos off."[93]

Before unions entered the scene, Navajos primarily found wage work through local networks. Navajos depended on relatives, friends, and other people they knew to get them jobs picking produce on commercial farms. They returned to work for farmers who they felt had treated them fairly in the past.[94] Or Navajo men relied on traders to refer them to local construction sites or for jobs on the railroad.[95] The union hiring hall threatened to replace the trading post and other familiar ways they had developed to dip into the waged economy.

For some unions, the building trades, the mine workers, and the longshoremen in particular, controlling the hiring process was a hard-won battle with management over the work process.[96] That type of class solidarity was not universally enjoyed by all workers, however. Historians studying the hiring hall and/or working-class institutions such as the neighborhood pub have shown that those settings could be highly gendered places that fostered an exclusively male atmosphere. The Navajo calls for access to that arena suggests that they were contending with a racialized arena as well.[97]

In their explanations and protests, Kenneth White and other Navajo workers who challenged management and union practices on the reservation articulated an alternative worldview that countered the model held by trade unionists and management. It was a world where responsibilities to one's kin and the work of the household were central. Less crucial were those relationships formed on the job, with coworkers and bosses, people not connected to the household through kinship lines.

Non-Navajo union members responded to the Navajo workers' demands in mixed ways. In May 1972, members of the Carpenters' Union launched a wildcat strike to protest the preferential hiring of Navajos at the Navajo project. The protest was inspired when the company laid off twenty-one non-Navajo carpenters and hired a Navajo apprentice on the same day. Since unions at the plant did not endorse the disgruntled workers' actions, the protest fizzled out after two days. In fact, members of the United Electrical Workers, a union that historically supported minority workers' rights, crossed the wildcat picket lines.[98]

In another incident almost a year later, Navajo workers once again felt at odds with their fellow union members. On March 22, 1973, Navajo employees of the Lee Long Construction Company in Montezuma Creek, Utah, walked off their jobs to protest racial discrimination. They contended that the construction company doing contract work for the Phillips Petroleum Company paid the Navajo workers $2.15 per hour, whereas the Phillips Petroleum Company employees, who were all Anglo, received a minimum of $4.00 an hour. Although some of the Navajo workers at the power plant and the construction company were union members, neither group looked to the union for relief. Instead they turned to the DNA to negotiate.[99]

Feeling besieged by both management and the unions, Navajo workers formed the Navajo Construction Workers Association (NCWA). It was not a union, designed to rival national labor organizations. Navajo workers did not want to give up the competitive edge that membership in unions like the UMWA gave them.[100] Rather, it functioned as an advocacy group aimed to fight discrimination against Navajos on and off the reservation. The organizers were experienced union members who worked in key reservation industries. Kenneth White, the founder of the NCWA, was a member of Local

1100 of the Carpenters' Union in Flagstaff and worked at the Navajo Power Plant near Page, Arizona.[101] Other leaders of the organization included a member of the UMWA who worked at the Peabody Coal Mine on Black Mesa and a member of the Operating Engineers who was a heavy equipment operator at the Morrison Knudsen Black Mesa and Lake Powell railroad construction project. Others who joined the NCWA were members of the Laborers Union in Flagstaff.[102] Kenneth White noted "we were told what we can't do against the monster—the Union. Now we are going to move in the direction to solve this problem."[103]

Kenneth White had traveled a great deal before he settled into working at the Navajo Generating Station in 1970. He was born into a large family in Wheatfields, Arizona, on the Navajo reservation in 1926 and was, as he explained, "raised raising sheep." At the age of ten he attended a BIA school 30 miles east of his home, in Toadlena, New Mexico. He stayed in school for six years until World War II drew him into the labor market. He worked on the railroad, in a munitions depot, and at an ice plant, jobs that took him to Nevada and California. After the war, he returned to school on the reservation and at Sherman Institute in Riverside, California. By then he was much older than the average student, too old, as he recalled, "to cut the mustard." In all, he attended school for a total of nine years. But he does not attribute his command of the English language to his formal education. He believes all those years he spent around white people, particularly when he was working in California, made him fluent.[104]

After he finished his schooling in Riverside, he returned to the reservation, where he married and started a family. Soon thereafter, he found out about the BIA's relocation program and decided to return to California. He filled out the forms, packed up his wife, son, and their belongings and headed for Los Angeles. When he arrived, the relocation office placed him in a job at the Chrysler manufacturing plant.

It was at that plant that White had his first experience with unions. He worked there for seven years and became an active member of the United Auto Workers. But, during a protracted strike, he left his job. He could not afford to wait it out since his growing family depended on him. He worried about raising his children in Los Angeles, a big city where they would grow up "wild" and isolated from the rest of his people. He was like other Navajos who took advantage of BIA relocation programs but did not behave in the way that the programs intended. He left the reservation, but he came back. He did not assimilate into the Los Angeles urban culture. His knowledge and experience off the reservation would inform not only his own future but the fate of all Navajo workers in the generation that followed.

By the time he started working for the Navajo Generating Station, he was no stranger to unions. His experience with the United Auto Workers convinced him of the importance of unions. He particularly appreciated how they protected workers' safety and improved wages. When he returned from California, he found a lot of construction jobs on the reservation, all union. So, he joined the Carpenters' Union and was soon the shop steward at the power plant.

But, for White, there seemed to be a limit to what unions could do. When I asked him if he had trouble organizing Navajos into a union, he said, "I had trouble with the union." They were good for safety and wages but not for protecting the rights of Indians. He had been working at the power plant, a facility operated by Arizona Public Service and California Edison, and subcontracted by the Bechtel Corporation, when he noticed a number of Navajos losing their jobs. He found out that Bechtel had fired a number of Navajos and had hired non-Indians, other union workers who had recently finished building a power plant in Nevada, to take their place. "It was disgraceful," Kenneth White remembered. "I had to stand up for my people." "I guess they called it prejudice, and at the same time it was an unfair labor practice," White continued.[105]

After that, White filed a complaint with the Navajo Tribal Council, contacted local community members in Page and lawyers from DNA legal services, whose name, translated into English, means "attorneys who contribute to the economic development of the people."[106] The tribal council responded to White's complaint by creating the Office of Navajo Labor Relations and appointing him its first compliance officer.[107] Thus started the struggle to create and enforce Navajo hiring preference clauses in leasing contracts. White continued to fight for the rights of Indians. He traveled to Washington, D.C., on a number of occasions; his most recent trip, in 1994, included testifying at a congressional hearing on an amendment to the Native American Religious Freedom Act. A roadman for the Native American Church, he continues to stand up for his people's rights. Reflecting on his broad experience that ranged from workers' rights to religious freedom, he said, "That's real interesting, I really stood up for the labor business and fought for the Religious Freedom Act, too." He summed up his comments at the end of our interview, taking stock in what he had done in the past thirty-four years: "As an Indian, as a Diné Indian, I look out for people. Mainly my children. They know it, too. At the same time too, I don't like to have anybody push my people around, you know? No matter where."[108]

Conclusion

Navajo workers and tribal authorities' association of trade unions with "white man's" ways was an articulation of Navajo identity in an economy where Diné households were becoming more dependent on wages to survive. By constructing trade unions as white, the Navajos were simultaneously contesting the racial hierarchy that they confronted off the reservation and creating a discursive foil against which to articulate "Navajoness."

But the complex racial geography of this part of the Southwest seemingly contradicts the Navajos' points of view. The Hod Carriers Union and the UMWA, central actors in these stories, were primarily made up of Mexican immigrants, native Hispanos, and other people of color, many of whom would have been surprised to discover that they were white. Navajo workers and tribal authorities were making a distinction that deemphasized skin color as a significant difference. For them, "white" was not a color, but a position of power in relation to the U.S. federal government. By defining unions as "white," the workers and the tribal council were naming what was *not* Navajo, thereby stressing their autonomy from the institutions that characterized U.S. culture.

Into the early 1970s, even with the prospects of relatively well-paid, union jobs, many Navajo workers did not see themselves as permanent wageworkers. Identifying primarily with a life centered around the reservation household, livestock raising, and farming, they existed on the margins of the capitalist wage economy, participating in it on a seasonal and occasional basis. Navajo workers supported union drives when their household-centered strategies benefited from organizing. When union practices and traditions threatened to undermine that way of life, Navajo workers condemned organized labor as white man's way. But, with the development of large industrial projects on reservation land, when new jobs offered the possibility of staying on the reservation, Navajos started to see unions differently. Joining a union became a way of gaining access to the resources that ensured the survival of their household economies.

Within that context, Navajos were contesting the terms of industrial development, but not development itself. Like their Anglo and Mexican American counterparts, they too needed jobs. As trade unions entered the scene and challenged the internal power structures on the reservation, including the authority of the Bureau of Indian Affairs, the traders, and the Navajo Tribal Council, the unions helped to create a discourse of class antagonism framed in racialized terms. The Navajo Tribal Council responded to unions' challenges by labeling their efforts as "white man's way." The interaction among the tribal council, trade unions, Navajo workers, and federal officials created part of a larger dynamic of "racial formation" in the southwestern United States.[109]

To create a Navajo labor movement, activists had to transform the unions and confront the discrimination of the companies. And it seems that they have been largely successful. Since the 1970s, and the enforcement of Navajo hiring preferences in labor contracts, the numbers of Navajos working in skilled, relatively well-paying jobs has grown tremendously. Kenneth White had a strong role to play in this transformation. His work opened the door for many Navajos to gain a foothold in the union training ladder that moves workers from an apprentice to journeyman status. He recalled to me that when he visits the Peabody mine on Black Mesa and sees fellow Navajos operating heavy machinery, he feels happy, because as he said, "I stood up for that! I fought for that!"[110]

With the advent of large-scale extractive industrial development on the reservation since the 1950s, unions such as the Laborers International, the United Mine Workers of America, the Operating Engineers, and the Carpenters' Union, to name just a few, have successfully organized Navajo workers. In the mid-1970s, the UMWA local in Window Rock elected its first Navajo president, Larson Manuelito. Navajos have served as presidents of that union ever since. In 1989, the Window Rock local elected Lawrence Oliver, a man who became a galvanizing force in the Navajo labor movement. He led the union through a difficult strike in 1994 and through complicated negotiations with the tribal government and the mining companies operating on the reservation. Oliver, fluent in Navajo and English and the son of one of the original code talkers, was instrumental in organizing and serving as the president of the Navajo Central Labor Council, called Naalnishí.[111] Now Navajo Nation leaders seem less worried about trade unions usurping their sovereignty rights. Since the mid-1990s, the Navajo Nation has developed labor laws that prohibit child labor and guarantee the right to organize and to engage in collective bargaining. In 2003, Lawrence Oliver resigned his leadership positions in the Navajo labor movement to assume a new role in the Navajo Nation government as the Division of Human Services director for the Navajo Nation. When asked whether he would support the unionization of Navajo Nation employees, he said diplomatically that he "had no position on the subject," but that unionization "was up to the employees under the laws passed by the council."[112] It appears that organized labor is no longer an imposition of the white man's world; it has become part of the Navajo way.

6

Rethinking Modernity and the Discourse of Development in American Indian History

A Navajo Example

I have been an independent farmer, raising abundant crops; and I have a good-sized alfalfa field for my horses. At school I had learned to read, write and speak English fluently, which helps me wherever I go. I have been successful, growing my own crops, which we live off of, and I have mutton on my table. I now receive my Social Security benefit, and that helps us.

    —Howard Bogoutin, from Mexican Water, Navajo Nation, Arizona[1]

One afternoon several years ago, I was browsing through the stacks in the library, and I stumbled upon a book entitled *Stories of Traditional Navajo Life and Culture.* That book, published in 1977 by the Navajo Community College Press and edited by its director, Broderick Johnson, included stories from twenty-two Navajo men and women about their "traditional culture."[2]

"Traditional culture?" My research was on twentieth-century labor and working-class history. I was interested in "the modern." So, the book sat on my desk for weeks while I tried to sort out the "modern" evidence I'd found in the archives, stories that were, at best, fragmented snapshots. Most troubling were the absences, the invisibility of Navajo workers in the documents. Where were the Navajo workers? Surely Navajo men worked in the coal mines in Gallup, one of the more industrialized towns bordering the reservation in the mid-twentieth century. I pored over payroll and company housing records, newspaper accounts as well as company correspondence, and found little evidence that could help me describe the experience or even the existence of Navajo workers in Gallup in the 1930s and 1940s.

When I finally opened the book on my desk that promised, at least in my imagination, sacred stories of emergence and fables that stressed values of pastoral traditions, I found something that made me reexamine my assumptions: workers. Almost every narrator in the book told a story about some sort of wage work; either working on the railroads, in the agriculture fields, for the Bureau of Indian Affairs, or at a trading post. They remembered the everyday struggles they faced in their jobs as well as their ongoing efforts to fulfill customary kinship and ceremonial obligations. For these Navajos, "modernity" and "tradition" were overlapping categories, not mutually exclusive. Navajo people met their sacred responsibilities as well as the demands of the capitalist workplace.

This research vignette illustrates how one's underlying assumptions about culture, tradition, and modernity shape modes of inquiry as well as the eventual narratives—large and small. The rigid modern/traditional dichotomy that too often marks historical writing is a byproduct of a larger problem that renders American Indians invisible within the broad narrative of American history. That narrative, steeped in positivist assumptions, tends to embrace and naturalize a universalized notion of modernity.[3]

Modernity, as a guiding social principle or state ideology, emerged during the eighteenth century. Enlightenment thinkers challenged the basic worldview and social structures of western European society, rejecting the absolute power of kings and the association of knowledge with the realm of Christianity. They advocated a rationalization of power, ideas, and social relationships. As geographer David Harvey explained, "It was, above all, a secular movement that sought the demystification and desacralization of knowledge and social organization in order to liberate human beings from their chains."[4] Part of that modernizing project involved seeking universal truths about human nature through scientific observation, logic, and reason. They were of course assuming that there was *a* universal humanity to be revealed. In the search for a singular truth, and the application of reason to political and economic realms, Enlightenment leaders generalized that which was "true" for western European societies to the rest of the world. As states contested for power in Europe and in their colonial holdings abroad, the "appeal to reason" increasingly informed expansionist ideology, justifying conquest of indigenous peoples as well as provoking opposition from nationalists throughout Europe in the mid-nineteenth century.[5] "Rule by reason" had its price. Its practitioners became the "apostles of modernity" and up to this day "readily tag others as opponents of progress." As Eric Wolf argued in his final book, "they have advocated industrialization, specialization, secularization, and rational bureaucratic allocation as reasoned options superior to unreasoned reliance on tradition."[6] Modernity has become synonymous with capitalism, and that narrative, a history where Indians are portrayed as irrelevant victims of military and economic conquest, pronounced the "cultural death" of indigenous peoples in twentieth-century America.[7] It seems that there is no room for tradition in a modern context, unless it is, of course, a highly circumscribed, museum-like arena that helps to justify the terms of modernity by comparison.[8]

Yet, the lived reality of American Indians in the twentieth century proved otherwise and makes us rethink the kinds of analytical categories that have for so long rendered them invisible. Like historian David Roediger, who helped us recognize whiteness, we need to lay bare the assumptions of what constitutes modernity.[9] This book examines examples that show where American Indians, the Navajos in particular, transcended these rigid categories and created alternative pathways of economic and cultural change that were not merely static renditions of some timeless past nor total acceptance of U.S. capitalist culture. Navajos in the twentieth century blended their modern and traditional worlds as a matter of course and in the process redefined those categories in ways that made sense to them.[10]

This final chapter is an attempt to rethink the modern/traditional dichotomy and to consider how that construct has informed ethnohistorical thinking about American Indian economic development. It is an effort to stimulate a conversation that examines the relationship between American Indian culture and capitalism by suggesting ways in which American Indian histories challenge the underlying assumptions about modernity itself. Revisiting the terms of the debate may inspire scholars and policy makers to see American Indian cultural and economic innovations as neither "modern," "premodern," nor even "antimodern." Instead, I am suggesting that American Indians have crafted alternative pathways of economic development that transcend linear analytical categories. This chapter explores that intellectual history and raises questions that complicate our notions of modernity to reveal a much more complicated past—a past revealed in the glimpse of Navajo labor history that this book unfolds.

Dependency and the Discourse of Development

The categories "modern" and "traditional" have survived a long and sordid history of draconian and paternalistic federal policies as well as internal debates among American Indian communities. Those categories describe a cultural position where American Indians define and are defined by their relationship to the U.S. capitalist economy, in all its political, cultural, and economic features. "Tradition" acquires meaning in relation to the "modern." The modern is the benchmark against which tradition is measured. And at least since the Enlightenment, the concept of the modern has been linked to the notion of "progress."[11]

The modern and traditional dichotomy is a product of modernization theory, a linear way of thinking about economic change that has shaped ideas about development as well as our understanding of dependency. Embraced by development "experts" in the post–World War II era, its underlying assumptions about culture and economic development date back to the mid-nineteenth century.[12] "Building on positivist notions of Western Enlightenment and 19th-century conceptions of evolution," according to Kathy Le Mons Walker, at the heart of modernization theory are the social evolutionary notions "that all cultures follow unilinear and evolutionary stages of development."[13] Infused with ideological notions of the "white man's burden," modernization theorists interpreted the expansion of capitalist relations into nonstate, indigenous societies as a sign of progress. It was a self-congratulatory embrace of capitalist values and logic that legitimized the expansion of Western imperialist powers worldwide.

Modernization theory has had a lasting impact on development policy, shaping intellectual paradigms and policy initiatives well into the twentieth century.[14] Scholars and policy makers concluded that the "neoclassic modeling of economic behavior that described the logic of incentive, disincentive, and growth in the advanced West could also describe the logic of economic backwardness and felicitous take-off in non-Western regions."[15] Developing countries would have everything to gain and nothing to lose from following the example of the West. In fact, these theorists argued that clinging to "archaic and outdated structures" kept American Indians poor and at the margins of the U.S. economy.[16] Clearly ethnocentric and at best paternalistic, modernization theory shaped the foundations of American Indian policy from the development of the first boarding schools and reservation land allotments to the Indian New Deal and termination.[17] The central thread that connected these sometimes-contradictory policies was that success, or for that matter, survival within the capitalist economic system required cultural change. Western society became synonymous with the "modern" and therefore not only desirable, but also the ultimate cultural destination on the road to economic development.

Dependency theory emerged as a counterbalance to modernization theory as the debates over development and modernization were taking shape in the midst of the decolonization struggles in Africa and Latin America.[18] Instead of viewing the inevitable capitalist transformation as a guarantee of prosperity, dependency theorists saw the extension of the capitalist economy to developing regions as one of the causes of poverty and cultural degradation.

Underdevelopment was more than an early stage of capitalist progress. Impoverished regions in the Third World were not just lagging behind the industrialized West. Borrowing from Latin American critics of dependency theory and incorporating the core-periphery concept, Andre Gunder Frank argued that capitalist development and underdevelopment were part of the same process. Coining the phrase *development of underdevelopment,* he called for a global analysis of the historical development of capitalism, suggesting that the success of capitalism hinged on the underdevelopment of peripheral countries. Feudal relationships in Latin America were a product of capitalist expansion, not a "backward" stage of economic development. Capitalist world markets had determined Latin American class relations ever since the Spanish arrived on American shores in the late fifteenth century.[19]

The use of dependency theory to explain Native American history in the United States has had extraordinary staying power for American scholars, activists, and officials.[20] Drawing on the work of Latin Americanists and African scholars, dependency theory offered intellectuals, policy experts, and community activists an explanatory model for understanding why Native Americans suffered such extreme poverty on Indian reservations in the United

States. They found that like African and Latin American peasants, American Indians suffered from a legacy of colonial exploitation. For example, dependency theorists argued that unequal trade restrictions between countries at the "core" and those in the "periphery" undermined the development of Latin American economies. Advanced capitalist countries siphoned the financial surplus from developing nations, preventing them from accumulating sufficient capital to develop an internal industrial base.

In 1971, anthropologist Joseph Jorgensen incorporated Frank's dependency model to show that incorporation into the U.S. political economy created desperate economic conditions on Indian reservations. Writing against the functionalist paradigm, an anthropological approach primarily concerned with American Indian assimilation, Jorgensen stated that "Indian poverty does not represent an evolutionary stage of acculturation." Contrary to what the functionalists assumed, incorporation into the U.S. market was not a solution. It was the root of the problem.[21]

Jorgensen described the relationship between the United States and American Indian communities as a history of superexploitation. Drawing from Frank's metropolis-satellite model, Jorgensen applied his analysis of the relationship between developing nations and advanced industrial states to the relationship between the United States and its Native American environs. He argued that "the conditions of the 'backward' modern American Indians are not due to rural isolation nor a tenacious hold on aboriginal ways, but result from the way in which United States urban centers of finance, political influence, and power have grown at the expense of rural areas." The growth of the metropolis, Jorgensen explained, depended largely on the wealth farmers, ranchers, and railroad and mining companies expropriated from Indian lands. Although rural people of all races suffered from the underdevelopment of the countryside, Indians remained formally disenfranchised, under the tutelage of a bureaucratic system, "special neocolonial institutions such as tribal governments which exercise[d] only a modicum of control over their affairs."[22]

Historian Richard White, in his examination of how U.S. policies undermined Native American subsistence strategies, not only incorporated the broad dependency frameworks suggested by Frank and Jorgenson but also examined how "underdevelopment" impacted the land and indigenous cultural practices. Drawing from the work of anthropologists and other social scientists who were thinking about capitalist development and underdevelopment in the Third World, his work showed the existence of similar types of historical dynamics in the United States. In the Navajo case, he argued that federal restrictions and non-Indian settlement patterns circumscribed Navajo land use methods. Confiscating livestock and enforcing strict grazing limits undermined the subsistence base for many Navajo families and forced them into the wage labor market, into a dependency relationship with the federal government, or both.[23]

Dependency theory supplied an emerging pan-Indian, nationalist movement with a fundamental explanation for what caused Native American impoverishment and connected that struggle with other liberation movements in the United States and abroad. But, like nationalist discourse in general, it was rife with internal tensions and contradictions. As Partha Chatterjee suggested, nationalist discourse both contests the "alleged inferiority of the colonized peoples" and asserts "that a backward nation could 'modernize' itself while retaining its cultural identity." The result, he said, is a discursive trap that "produced a discourse in which, even as it challenged the colonial claim to political domination, it also accepted the very intellectual premises of 'modernity' on which colonial domination was based."[24] By contesting the legitimacy of the BIA and demanding control over natural resources, the discourse of dependency and the discourse of development were two sides of the same coin. Activists and advocates demanded an end to superexploitation but did not challenge the goal of capitalist development. The dependency paradigm provided a compelling set of political objectives, including control over land, and political sovereignty, as well as a moral case for retribution, but it prohibited a discussion of alternative models of development. Scholars and activists then faced the prospect of choosing between "tradition," which relegated culture to a timeless past, or "modernity," a homogenous future within the dominant capitalist society. The dichotomy is preserved, only in reverse, as "romantic primitivism or crude nationalism."[25]

Scholars and policy specialists employing a dependency paradigm have revealed much about exploitation of indigenous people in the United States. Even though the dependency paradigm offered insight into the structural causes of poverty on Indian reservations, universal assumptions about the relationship between capitalism and Native American culture embedded in that framework obscured the role of indigenous people in crafting alternative strategies or pathways of development. If capitalism required a specific set of historical experiences, including alienation from the land, dependence on wage labor, and a culture that valued individualism, then how could a people like the Navajo create their own version of that system without losing all that was central to their cultural identity?

Even the noted anthropologist David Aberle, a strong advocate of Navajo rights and an expert in Navajo affairs, could not imagine alternatives that fell outside of the parameters of the dependency paradigm. In 1969 he explained to the Joint Economic Committee of the U.S. Congress that "Navajo country is an underdeveloped area." According to Aberle, "its historical and current relations with the larger polity, economy and society" caused such impoverishment. Like the dependency experts designing programs that would allow Latin American countries to "catch up" to the more industrialized world, Aberle argued that federal policies deprived the Navajo of capital and needed serious reform. With "a good deal of reflection on the condition of underdeveloped economies in the world today," he recounted how the BIA had underdeveloped the Navajo Reservation. First, and foremost, the Navajos did not have "the capital or the know-how to achieve development." Second, the Bureau of Indian Affairs was in no position to help, since Congress and the states were unwilling to supply the agency with adequate funds. Finally, private industry had expressed little interest in investing in industrial development on the reservation.[26] Like development experts who were fashioning programs for the Third World, Aberle saw the Navajo economy as something that could be fixed to follow the well-worn path toward capitalist development. But, much to his credit, Aberle knew that Navajos themselves determined the success of development efforts. Although he shared the view that the ultimate goal was industrialization, he did not advocate individualizing tribal lands, and he believed that the Navajos needed to be in control of their economy. Academics and specialists were there to offer the Navajo people their services, not to dictate policy. The Navajos should not be just part of a planning team, stressed Aberle. "The solution is for Navajos to plan for themselves, drawing on such advice as they wish, whether from the Bureau and other Federal agencies, Congressmen, universities, management consultants, private industry and whatever experts they need."[27]

Aberle's perspective, although sensitive to Navajo cultural imperatives, fell well within the development discourse of the post–World War II era. Latin American anthropologist Arturo Escobar argued that development experts of that generation conceived of Third World "problems" in ways that suggested a limited set of solutions. According to those scholars and policy specialists, Third World communities suffered from a lack of capital and insufficient industrialization. For these experts, "[t]he only things that counted," according to Escobar, "were increased savings, growth rates, attracting foreign capital, developing industrial capacity, and so on." This narrow discourse, then, prohibited alternative solutions that conceived of social change in egalitarian and culturally specific terms. Escobar concluded that this postwar climate preempted an analysis of economic development "as a whole life project, in which the material aspects would be not the goal and the limit but a space of possibilities for broader individual and collective endeavors, culturally defined."[28] Aberle's analysis and the solutions he proposed for improving the economic conditions on the Navajo reservation implied (like his counterparts devising plans for Latin America and Africa) a model of development measured by the "yardstick of Western progress."[29] That Aberle could at once critique the system that he found responsible for the impoverished status of Indian reservations, and yet find solutions for those problems within that same system, demonstrates how this paradigm prevented alternative ways of thinking about the past, understanding current problems, and planning for the future.

Since the 1970s, cultural anthropologists and other social scientists studying Africa and Latin America have generally rejected modernization frameworks, but they have yet to reexamine their assumptions about modernity.[30] As William Roseberry and Jay O'Brien suggested, even those scholars who are careful not to reproduce positivist paradigms still assign analytical categories that are only meaningful relative to a universal capitalist narrative. Thus, "traditional" only acquires meaning in relation to the modern; forms of exchange that do not conform to capitalist definitions are defined for what they are not. According to Roseberry and O'Brien, limiting an analysis of tradition to the realm of anticapitalist discourse "founders on the unrecognized use of capitalist categories or categories designed to illuminate Western capitalist life, to analyze non-Western economics and politics."[31] The traditional remains part of the unchanging past, and culture occupies a temporal space that exists outside of history. Modernity becomes the moment when history begins, and culture remains the product of precapitalist memory. Capitalist categories remain the historical benchmarks that define the significant moments, elements, and actors that bring about social change.

In the 1980s, Native American activists and scholars moved beyond the dependency paradigm to question the ultimate goal of development: Western-styled industrialization. At the heart of the problem, according to Ward Churchill, were the assumptions about modernization that Marxists as well as liberal scholars failed to examine. He argued that Marxists refused to consider issues that countered a positivist understanding of history, a perspective that saw industrialization as a necessary step toward human liberation.[32] Churchill's comments condemned leftist scholars in the United States for applying "European ideology" to American history. He argued that the inability of American Marxists to offer a satisfying analysis of Native American history centered on their refusal to accommodate questions of land, culture, and spirituality. Churchill found that a materialist approach, one that assumed a fundamental division between nature and culture, lacked explanatory depth for Native Americans. As he and other Native American leaders and scholars suggested, many Native Americans have historically articulated a more holistic and cyclical vision of human relationships to the land and to the past.[33] Churchill's critique echoed Escobar's analysis of the postwar development discourse. Because industrialization remained the final goal, among Marxists as well as more conservative agency officials, alternatives that did not embrace an industrial worldview were shut out of the debate.

Other critics of world systems and dependency analysis argue that these theories tend to minimize the historic specificity of capitalist development. More important, they suggest, are how local historical dynamics shaped incorporation into the capitalist market, from the development of commercial markets to the creation of colonial labor systems. The ensuing debates over dependency theory, world systems, and mode of production analysis moved the literature on the colonial and developing world beyond the mechanistic formulas that critics often characterized as teleological or economically deterministic.[34] Scholars influenced by social history and anthropological methodology stressed the importance of scrutinizing the historical specificity of colonial expansion and the internal dynamics of "receiving" societies.[35]

Modernity and Tradition

The problem is not necessarily with the concepts of the traditional and the modern but with the dichotomous manner with which they are employed.

That dichotomy paints a picture of American Indian history in polar extremes, leaving very little room to act in ways that defy the rigid and static construct.[36] It is a false dichotomy for American Indians. They exist in a world where the two cultural categories fold into each other. So, why not discard the categories once and for all? The notion of "tradition" as a cultural indicator of "difference" is primarily a Euro-American construct. Yet, it would be wrong to discard these terms altogether since the categories themselves have become important cultural markers for American Indians and have retained significant currency among native communities throughout the twentieth century. Asserting "traditional" rights has become a crucial strategy for American Indian communities in their struggle over decolonization. Navajos who have resisted relocation at Big Mountain, Arizona, since 1974 serve as a relatively recent example of American Indians' political use of "tradition." Their spiritual and cultural strategies powerfully frame their opposition to relocation in ways that endow them with moral authority and symbolize the essence of Navajoness. Their efforts have included documenting sacred places to support claims to the land under the 1978 American Indian Religious Freedom Act. Although Indian activists have insisted that this law is ineffective, it has provided the Big Mountain residents with some strategic advantage and postponed relocation, at least for the near future. Setting aside those terms ignores the ways American Indians have engaged those concepts, a process that at times amounts to a dynamic history of cultural reinvention.[37] Asserting the "traditional" as a political strategy or as an alternative way of living and seeing the world has had some measured success in forcing U.S. and Canadian governments to cede physical and epistemological terrain to native peoples. Native peoples are asserting the value of "local knowledge" in land use planning and decentering notions of conservation and other concepts about nature steeped in Western scientific tradition.[38]

Another, and perhaps more lighthearted, example of the Navajos' creative use of tradition is the Miss Navajo Nation pageant. The contest got its start at the Navajo Nation Fair in 1952 and has remained an important fixture of reservation culture ever since. For the first ten years of the pageant, judges selected two queens, Miss Modern Navajo Nation and Miss Traditional, assessing contestants' skills appropriate for each category. Judges, a panel usually made up of local dignitaries and tribal officials, awarded all contestants points on the "basis of beauty of feature and authenticity of clothing." Miss Traditional earned points for weaving, carding, spinning, making fry bread, or telling a Navajo story in Navajo. Miss Modern gained distinction for those skills pageant officials associated with the non-Navajo world, including sewing, public speaking, typing, job experience, and fluency in English.[39]

Throughout the 1950s, young Navajo women competed for the two distinct titles; each was supposed to bridge the gap between the Navajo Nation and the "outside" world, "using the tools of modern technology in practical ways, reflecting [Diné] traditional values."[40] In 1963 the two titles merged into the singular Miss Navajo. Each contestant had to demonstrate an ability to move between the two categories and "demonstrate the progress of the womanhood as well as the beauty of the Navajo people." Each contestant demonstrated her "modern" poise and typing skills alongside her "traditional" abilities of weaving, spinning, and making fry bread.[41]

Since the founding of the Miss Navajo pageant, officials have stressed the difference between this pageant and the beauty contests in the Anglo world. The former stressed internal beauty, whereas the latter celebrated superficial values. In 1960 one reporter from the *Navajo Times* stated that contestants would not be wearing bathing suits or low-cut gowns. Instead, the young women in the traditional category wore "the colorful velvet blouse and the long, gathered skirts associated with their people for over a century." And the modern contestants wore "simple daytime dress[es]." Reporters covering the Miss Navajo Nation pageant in recent years have continued to make this comparison. Gwen Florio, a *Denver Post* writer, noted that "[i]n the Miss America pageant, contestants tape their breasts to make them appear fuller. In the Miss Navajo Nation contest, they tape their feet." Crystal Chee, one of the contestants, explained that she did so to protect her white buckskin moccasins from blood when she and her fellow contestants butchered a sheep.[42] Today it seems that Miss Navajo Nation's public image largely reflects the legacy of tradition. As stated on the official Office of Miss Navajo Nation Web site, "Unlike most beauty pageants throughout the world, the Miss Navajo Nation pageant is of beauty 'within' one's self."[43]

The notion of change, or at least a dynamic interplay between the past and the demands of the present, is embedded in Navajo cultural definitions of tradition. With the concept of Hózhǫ́, Navajos are seeking harmony through a balance of conflicting forces, and that means finding ways to adjust to the transformation of their economy rather than either ignoring or resisting it.

But that adjustment did not mean full acceptance or assimilation of mass consumer culture or acquisitive individualism that characterize the "cultural economy" of the surrounding market.[44] It meant making changes, either working on the railroad, attending boarding schools, or accepting cures for "white man's" diseases; all of which would enable Navajos to remain on the reservation, continue attending ceremonies, and creating new ways of being Navajo in a world that has repeatedly tried to get them to abandon their cultural practices. Like contestants in the Miss Navajo Nation pageant, tradition and modernity sit side by side on the same stage, not in conflict with the other, but in harmonious conversation.

Despite the efforts of some American Indian communities to evoke "tradition" in their struggles to gain political rights, and power over land and resources, their frame of reference remains a kind of universalized modernity, a development discourse that emerged out of nineteenth-century economic theory and policy applications that were devastating to American Indian existence. Although evoking "tradition" may be a useful resistance strategy, a way to maintain cultural and economic sovereignty and to counterbalance the –impact of colonialism on American Indian culture, the modern/traditional dichotomy nonetheless remains problematic for those who are concerned about issues of culture and economic development. Some scholars have addressed this issue by examining how subaltern groups have evoked "imagined and archaic pasts" as a strategy to resist modernizing forces.[45] But is it enough to view indigenous cultures as socially constructed within modernizing contexts? Or to see cultural traditions as constituting "imagined communities"? William Roseberry and Jay O'Brien have argued that seeing the "natural as historical" or the "traditional as modern" merely preserved the dichotomous paradigm. Rather, they contended "that there have been a variety of modern tracks toward the traditional that with the construction of different household economies, different ethnicities, and so on, the (combined and uneven) development of the modern world has created worlds of social, economic, and cultural difference."[46]

Tradition and modernity are expressions of "difference" rather than historical benchmarks that distinguish a particular community's place in time. Indigenous peoples have developed new traditions in modernizing contexts, and in the process have contested the terms of modernity itself. These efforts are not necessarily conservative rejections of capitalist change. In some cases

American Indian communities embraced capitalist forms and did so in ways that cultivate and support their traditional practices, demonstrating that there might indeed be many paths of capitalist development.

Universalized Modernity

Modernity is a culturally specific, historic construct, yet the concept remains stubbornly reified as some sort of natural historical phenomenon. As Joseph Gusfield described in 1967, "We cannot easily separate modernity and tradition from some *specific* tradition and some *specific* modernity, some version which functions ideologically as a directive. The modern comes to the traditional society as a particular culture with its own traditions."[47]

Employing universal categories of capitalist development defines a particular kind of historical narrative. Theoretical paradigms that posit subsistence ways of life against proletarian experiences and the traditional versus the modern render historically invisible those economic systems that do not fit within those dualistic parameters. Recognizing the coexistence of modernity and tradition within the same historical time and space, and refusing to think of culture as purely a terrain of resistance, reveals a much more complicated and compelling story. As historian Kathy Walker suggested from her study of Chinese peasants, "[a]lternative pasts indicate a counter-appropriation of history that simply cannot be reduced to a logic of capitalist development or universalized modernity. They must be explained on their own terms."[48] Reaching for historic specificity does not mean ignoring the bigger picture or abandoning the work of capitalist theory. On the contrary, moving beyond the "discourse of development," to use Arturo Escobar's terms, means creating new theoretical models to help make sense out of the multiple histories that are bound to emerge once we remove the paradigmatic blinders.

American historians can learn a great deal from scholars studying the ways rural peoples in the Third World have shaped and have been shaped by capitalist development. Peasant and subaltern studies scholars have chipped away at assumptions that had previously characterized peasant societies as undifferentiated, or "traditional," and peasant uprisings as reactive and conservative. In effect, they opened Marx's "sack of potatoes" to look inside. What they found were complex societies divided along wealth, gender, and age hierarchies and united by kinship and other socially constructed identities. Third

World social scientists found that peasants, a social category once defined as "precapitalist," existed within capitalist structures as well as on the periphery of the world system. These scholars wondered how the internal dynamics of peasant cultures mediated their interactions with the world economy, how they resisted absorption into the capitalist market as well as how they accommodated to it. This type of scholarship produced a nuanced view that expanded definitions of resistance beyond collective uprising and revolution to oppositional popular culture, nationalism, gender antagonism, and subtle subversion encoded in "hidden transcripts."[49] Still, revealing the agency of historical actors does not necessarily shed light on the power structures within which they operate. These types of studies, however, revealed how complex a dance between power structures and historical agents can be.[50]

The history of American Indians' relationship to the developing capitalist market involves multiple strands of analysis. Even though it is important to think about how Indians responded to the cultural and economic demands of incorporation and how they fashioned strategies that rejected the incipient cultural logic of twentieth-century capitalism, the more compelling story involves the new institutions they created out of the conflict. Indeed, the capitalist market has taken its toll on American Indian communities, particularly since incorporation usually meant a devastating loss of land and other natural resources—elements of central economic and cultural significance. Yet, the ways indigenous communities recovered in the twentieth century showed a creative engagement with the market. By contesting the terms of incorporation, either as laborers or as tribal capitalists, American Indians are challenging the cultural assumptions of modernity itself.

Navajo Modernity

This book helps to flesh out what historian Florencia Mallon has described as "that skeleton historians call the 'development of capitalism.'" She examined how Andean peasants used "traditional relationships" to shape the transition of their villages to a capitalist economy and how, in the process, those "weapons of the weak" transformed the villagers and their communities.[51] Like members of the Navajo Tribal Council or other Navajo elites who utilized kinship networks and connections with traders to become the labor contractors that I described in previous chapters, wealthier peasants in the Yanamarca Valley drew on their influence at the village level to fashion a system of wage-based, commercial agriculture from a kinship-based system.[52]

The social transformations the Navajo experienced in the mid-twentieth century involved, to use William Roseberry and Jay O'Brien's words, "new expressions of cultural difference as well as fundamental redefinitions of old ones."[53] The battle over trade union organizing I described in Chapter 5 offers a glimpse of this dynamic at work. Defining what was Navajo in this context involved a larger fight over who would have the power to control the direction of economic development on the reservation. The Navajo Tribal Council saw trade union organizers as "outsiders" who were challenging the council's authority to rule. Rejecting trade unions as "white man's way," the council constructed a racialized definition of class that was difficult for Navajo workers to embrace. Navajo workers' previous experience with trade unions and conflicts with non-Navajo workers in border towns may have reinforced the Navajo Tribal Council's rhetoric. Trade unions seemed to them to operate within a cultural ethic that contradicted their own cultural values. Trade unions would unwittingly operate within a non-Navajo cultural framework until the Navajo workers directly challenged them in the early 1970s.

Prior to the formation of the Navajo Construction Workers Association, Navajo workers' relationship to trade unions may have been, at best, ambivalent. Their reluctance to support trade unions, however, did not mean that they passively participated in their own exploitation. As I explained in Chapter 4, Navajos devised wage work strategies that allowed them to retain their connections to the reservation household as well as ensure its continued survival. For the most part, they encountered great hardship and resisted the BIA's prodding to relocate.

Working for wages in the Navajo way was a form of contestation over the labor process itself. The Navajo workers defined the terms of employment by refusing to work longer than four months at a time and by leaving their jobs for ceremonials and to tend to familial obligations. Holding on to the land, and maintaining the reservation household, however symbolic, gave them a means to negotiate the terms of work. The Navajo example yields conclusions similar to what Keletso Atkins found in Natal, South Africa. In one rich case, she examined the stereotype of the "lazy Kafir" and found that, contrary to British colonial impressions, the Zulu had developed a strong work ethic. From their experience performing agricultural labor in their own village

communities, they defined a fair day's work as beginning at sunup and ending at sundown and kept track of their wages and workdays on a lunar cycle.
British officials who attempted to impose rationalized time regimes were dis-
mayed when the workers appeared before them and demanded: "The moon
is dead! Give us our money!" Those officials who did not conform or at least
adjust to the Zulu work ethic were subject to labor shortages.[54]

Like the British colonial officials who wanted to ensure their supply of laborers in Natal, South Africa, employers of Navajo labor have had to adjust to
their workers' cultural demands in order to get their crops picked, their railroads cleared, and their coal mined. As I described in Chapter 3, the BIA's failure to implement the Navajo colonization program is an example of how
Navajo priorities and southwestern employers' needs created a particular kind
of labor market, one that did not conform to federal policy goals. Railroad officials and commercial farmers refused to participate in that effort because it
was in their own economic interest to exploit the household-centered cultural
practices that the Navajo had developed in the post-stock-reduction period.

Those who managed to stay out of the wage labor market did so by utilizing their families' resources to develop new forms of household production.
Producing coal was a distinctly modern enterprise, its markets created by the
expansion of capitalist relations. As I show in Chapter 2, by reconfiguring their
cultural practices to shape that process, the Navajo coal miners created a new
system of coal mining that conformed to their pastoral lifeways. Those cultural ethics, specifically the concept of hózhǫ́, allowed them to construct a new
type of household, no less "Navajo" than the one it replaced.

This is not to say that wage work did not have a profound impact on
American Indian communities. The kinds of jobs available to American Indians, such as railroad work, agricultural labor, and domestic labor, usually
required them to leave their reservation communities for extended periods of
time. The absence of loved ones, the migration experience, and the dependence on wages rather than subsistence strategies influenced Indian communities in ways that we are just beginning to understand.[55]

Other lines of inquiry might explore the impact of wage work on American Indian ideas and social practices that define the gendered social worlds of
women and men. Yet, gendered relationships take on different meaning in
varying cultural and historical contexts. So, the gender impact of wage work
might mean something very different for American Indian households than

it does for non-Indian communities. For example, in the Navajo's "matricentric" culture, a man's identity may be closely linked to how well he attends to his mother's or his wife's needs, and as a result, he may remain somewhat ambivalent to the demands and rewards of the wage labor market. In this case, women retain a great deal of power and respect within their households, regardless of the increasing lure of the wage economy.

Navajo women and men, like other colonized peoples, experienced incorporation into the market economy in specifically gendered ways. A Navajo woman who worked at her loom was tied to the market economy through her relationship to the trader. Although she may have maintained some artistic autonomy and may have skillfully negotiated with the trader, she remained nonetheless in a state of dependency. Her husband may have also relied on the trader for referrals to railroad work or other seasonal jobs. Yet for the most part, for Navajo men, wage work allowed them more personal autonomy from the indebted nature of trader/Navajo relations. As a result, men and women participated in markets that were distinctly different, yet part of the same larger capitalist economy that was transforming their communities as a whole. Their combined efforts helped them weather such tremendous change and maintain their reservation households in ways that were no less Navajo than before.

I hope that the stories in this book about mining, weaving, agricultural work, and trade unions offer a more optimistic picture of Navajos than what worried the curio shop worker I met in Gallup. On one level these stories do help to undermine damaging stereotypes that have characterized Navajos, as she put it, as "silversmiths and drunks." On other levels, these stories demonstrate that American Indians, the Navajos in particular, have found creative ways to engage the "modern world" without abandoning their cultural values. Their history challenges us to rethink the terms of modernity itself in all its complex configurations. By working the Navajo way, the Diné were defying the static modern and traditional dichotomy that usually marginalized them within the larger narrative of U.S. economic development. They were clearing modern pathways with traditional tools and in the process redefining both.

NOTES

INTRODUCTION: NAVAJO HISTORY AND WESTERN CAPITALIST DEVELOPMENT

1. Quoted in Broderick H. Johnson, ed., *Stories of Traditional Navajo Life and Culture, Alk'idą́ą́' Yę́ę́k'ehgo Diné Kéédahat'íńę́ę Baa Nahane'* (Tsaile, Navajo Nation, AZ : Navajo Community College Press, 1977), 288.

2. David Hurst Thomas, *Skull Wars: Kennewick Man, Archaeology and the Battle for Native American Identity* (New York: Basic Books, 2000); Thomas C. Patterson, *A Social History of Anthropology in the United States* (New York: Berg, 2001); George W. Stocking Jr., ed., *Romantic Motives: Essays on Anthropological Sensibility* (Madison: University of Wisconsin Press, 1989); Thomas Biolsi and Larry J. Zimmerman, eds., *Indians and Anthropologists: Vine Deloria, Jr., and the Critique of Anthropology* (Tucson: University of Arizona Press, 1997).

3. This is an often-repeated saying among students of Navajo culture. See one example in John R. Farella, *The Main Stalk: A Synthesis of Navajo Philosophy* (Tucson: University of Arizona Press, 1984), 3.

4. Oral interview with Clarence and Margaret Kee by the author, interpreted by Juannita Brown (their daughter), at Tuller's Cafe, St. Michael's, AZ, May 18, 1995. Tape and transcript in author's possession.

5. Oral interview with Julia John by the author, interpreted by Paul George, Hogback Community on the Navajo Reservation, Hogback, NM, August 14, 2002. Tape and transcript in author's possession.

6. Rik Pinxten and Claire Farrer, "On Learning: A Comparative View," *Cultural Dynamics* 3, no. 3 (1990): 249.

7. Ethnographers have noted how Navajos adapted new technology and coped with the dramatic transformation of their economy and maintained their cultural identities and traditions. John R. Farella observed that "Navajos are not change oriented but rather . . . they are changing in order to remain 'traditional.' Specifically, they are altering their technology to maintain their epistemology." Farella, *The Main Stalk*, 190. In 1946, Clyde Kluckhohn and Dorothea Leighton observed that Navajos were successfully adapting "white" technology into their "preexistent design for living." Clyde Kluckhohn and Dorothea Leighton, *The Navaho* (Cambridge, MA: Harvard University Press, 1946), 28.

8. I am using the term *household* rather loosely here. As Louise Lamphere has pointed out, there is no Navajo term for household. Rather, Navajos describe living arrangements in terms of "spatial relationships." Lamphere described Navajos referring to their residential groups as "people who cook and eat together." She concluded that "nuclear family household is the smallest domestic unit and that the hoghan is the dwelling which defines its spatial boundaries." Louise Lamphere, *To Run after Them: Cultural and Social Bases of Cooperation in a Navajo Community* (Tucson: University of Arizona Press, 1977), 74–75.

9. David Aberle, "A Plan for Navajo Economic Development," in *Toward Economic Development for Native American Communities, Compendium of Papers Submitted to Subcommittee on Economy in Government,* vol. 1, pt. 1 (Washington, DC: Joint Economic Committee, 91st Cong., 1st sess., 1969), 223–276.

10. Examples of colonial Native American history that cast indigenous people as agents include William Cronon, *Changes in the Land* (New York: Hill and Wang, 1983); Richard White, *Middle Ground: Indians, Empires, and the Republic in the Great Lakes Region, 1650–1815* (New York: Cambridge University Press, 1991); Ramón Gutiérrez, *When Jesus Came, the Corn Mothers Went Away* (Stanford, CA: Stanford University Press, 1991); Eleanor Leacock and Mona Etienne, eds., *Women and Colonization: Anthropological Perspectives* (New York: Praeger, 1980); Sylvia Van Kirk, *Many Tender Ties: Women in Fur-Trade Society, 1670–1870* (Norman: University of Oklahoma Press, 1980); Elliott West, *Contested Plains: Indians, Goldseekers, and the Rush to Colorado* (Lawrence: University Press of Kansas, 1998); Susan Lee Johnson, *Roaring Camp: The Social World of the California Gold Rush* (New York: W. W. Norton, 2000); and Kevin Starr and Richard J. Orsi, eds., *Rooted in Barbarous Soil: People, Culture, and Community in Gold Rush California* (Berkeley: University of California Press, 2000).

11. Congress passed the IRA (or the Wheeler-Howard Act) in 1934. One aspect of the bill authorized reservations to set up tribal governments. For notable examples of twentieth-century Native American history, see Alice Littlefield and Martha Knack, eds., *Native Americans and Wage Labor: Ethnohistorical Perspectives* (Norman: University of Oklahoma Press, 1996); Brian C. Hosmer, *American Indians in the Marketplace: Persistence and Innovation among the Menominees and Metlakatlans, 1870–1920* (Lawrence: University Press of Kansas, 1999); Melissa L. Meyer, *The White Earth Tragedy: Ethnicity and Dispossession at a Minnesota Anishinaabe Reservation, 1889–1920* (Lincoln: University of Nebraska Press, 1994); Kathleen Ann Pickering, *Lakota Culture, World Economy* (Lincoln: University of Nebraska Press, 2000); Paul C. Rosier, *Rebirth of the Blackfeet Nation, 1912–1954* (Lincoln: University of Nebraska Press, 2001); Sarah H. Hill, *Weaving New Worlds: Southeastern Cherokee Women and Their Basketry* (Chapel Hill: University of North Carolina Press, 1997); Robert B. Campbell, "Newlands, Old Lands: Native American Labor, Agrarian Ideology, and the Progressive-Era State in the Making of the Reclamation Project, 1902–1926," *Pacific Historical Review* 71 (May 2002): 203–238; Kurt M. Peters, "Continuing Identity: Laguna Pueblo Railroaders in Richmond, California," *American Indian Culture and Research Journal* 22, no. 4 (1998): 187–198; Alexandra Harmon, *Indians in the Making: Ethnic Relations and Indian Identities around Puget Sound* (Berkeley: University of California Press, 1998); Frederick E. Hoxie, *Parading through History: The Making of the Crow Nation in America, 1805–1935* (New York: Cambridge University Press, 1995); Peter Iverson, *Diné: A History of the Navajos* (Albuquerque: University of New Mexico Press, 2002); Brian Hosmer and Colleen O'Neill, eds., *Native Pathways: American Indian Culture and Economic Development in the Twentieth Century* (Boulder: University Press of Colorado, 2004).

12. Although Richard White does not address the issue of Indian workers, he does exam-

ine how the encroaching capitalist market and federal policies undermined Indian self-sufficiency; see *The Roots of Dependency: Subsistence, Environment, and Social Change among the Choctaws, Pawnees, and Navajos* (Lincoln: University of Nebraska Press, 1983), 250–314. Other works look at underdevelopment of the Navajo Reservation in terms of market relationships; see, for example, Kent Gilbreath, *Red Capitalism: An Analysis of the Navajo Economy* (Norman: University of Oklahoma Press, 1973), and Lawrence Weiss, *The Development of Capitalism in the Navajo Nation* (Minneapolis: Marxist Educational Press, 1984).

13. U.S. labor and working-class historians have virtually ignored the significant body of anthropological literature on Native American workers, and as a result, they have minimized the roles of Native Americans as historical actors. For early anthropological studies, see Jack O. Waddell, *Papago Indians at Work* (Tucson: University of Arizona Press, 1969); William Y. Adams, "The Development of San Carlos Apache Wage Labor to 1954," in *Apachean Culture, History, and Ethnology,* University of Arizona Anthropological Papers, no. 21, ed. Keith H. Basso and Morris E. Opler (Tucson: University of Arizona Press, 1971), 116–128; Eric Henderson, "Skilled and Unskilled Blue Collar Navajo Workers: Occupational Diversity in a Native American Tribe," *Social Science Journal* 16 (1979): 63–80. For historical studies, see Rolf Knight, *Indians at Work: An Informal History of Native American Labour in British Columbia, 1858–1930* (Vancouver, BC: New Star Books, 1978); Daniel L. Boxberger, "In and Out of the Labor Force: The Lummi Indians and the Development of the Commercial Salmon Fishery of North Puget Sound, 1880–1900," *Ethnohistory* 35 (1988): 161–190; Albert Hurtado, "Hardly a Farmhouse or a Kitchen without Them: Indian and White Households on the California Borderland Frontier 1860," *Western Historical Quarterly* 13 (1982): 245–270; Joseph Mitchell, "Mohawks in High Steel," in *Apologies to the Iroquois,* ed. Edmund Wilson (New York: Farrar, Straus and Cudahy, 1959), 1–36.

14. Littlefield and Knack, *Native Americans and Wage Labor,* 4.

15. See, for example, William Robbins, *Colony and Empire: The Capitalist Transformation of the American West* (Lawrence: University Press of Kansas, 1994); Patricia Limerick, *The Legacy of Conquest: The Unbroken Past of the American West* (New York: W. W. Norton, 1987); Melvyn Dubofsky, "The Origins of Western Working Class Radicalism, 1890–1905," *Labor History* 7 (Spring 1966): 131–154.

16. Steve Stern, "Feudalism, Capitalism, and the World System in the Perspective of Latin America and the Caribbean," *American Historical Review* 93 (October 1988): 829–872. For a comprehensive review of Chicano historiography, see Alex M. Saragoza, "Recent Chicano Historiography: An Interpretive Essay," *Aztlán* 19 (Spring 1988–1990): 1–77. Richard White's work is a good example of the application of dependency theory to explain Native American history; see White, *The Roots of Dependency.* Eric Wolf used a mode-of-production framework to weave his narrative; see *Europe and the People without History* (Berkeley: University of California Press, 1982).

17. Rodolfo Acuña, *Occupied America: The Chicano's Struggle toward Liberation,* 1st ed. (San Francisco: Canfield Press, 1972), 4.

18. *Mutualistas* were mutual aid societies formed by Spanish-speaking populations in the U.S. Southwest to provide burial benefits to their members as well as other community services. In some communities they functioned like proto–civil rights organizations. Active in the late nineteenth century, Las Gorras Blancas was a militant organization, loosely affiliated with the Knights of Labor, that employed tactics such as fence cutting to resist the steady loss of their land to commercial ranching interests. Robert J. Rosenbaum, *Mexicano Resistance in the Southwest: "The Sacred Right of Self-Preservation"* (Austin: University of Texas Press, 1981), 102–139, 146–147; Mario T. García, *Mexican Americans: Leadership, Ideology, and Identity* (New Haven, CT: Yale University Press, 1989), 274–280; Arnoldo De León, *The Tejano Community, 1836–1900* (Albuquerque: University of New Mexico Press, 1982), 194–195.

19. Tomás Almaguer, "Interpreting Chicano History: The World System Approach to Nineteenth-Century California," *Review* 4 (Winter 1981): 498.

20. David Montejano, "Is Texas Bigger than the World System? A Critique from a Provincial Point of View," *Review* 4 (Winter 1981): 599; also see his monograph, *Anglos and Mexicans in the Making of Texas, 1836–1986* (Austin: University of Texas Press, 1987).

21. Rodolfo Acuña rejected his internal colonialism model in 1981 in the second edition of his book, *Occupied America*. Anthropologists continue to debate the use of world systems theory in their scholarship on the impact of capitalist incorporation on American Indian communities. See Kathleen Ann Pickering, *Lakota Culture, World Economy* (Lincoln: University of Nebraska Press, 2000), and Thomas Biolsi, *Organizing the Lakota: The Political Economy of the New Deal on the Pine Ridge and Rosebud Reservations* (Tucson: University of Arizona Press, 1993).

22. Deena González, *Refusing the Favor: The Spanish-Mexican Women of Santa Fe, 1820–1880* (New York: Oxford University Press, 1999); Tomás Almaguer, *Racial Fault Lines: The Historical Origins of White Supremacy in California* (Berkeley: University of California Press, 1994); Neil Foley, *The White Scourge: Mexicans, Blacks, and Poor Whites in Texas Cotton Culture* (Berkeley: University of California Press, 1997); Evelyn Nakano Glen, *Unequal Freedom: How Race and Gender Shaped American Citizenship and Labor* (Cambridge, MA: Harvard University Press, 2002); Vicki Ruiz, *From out of the Shadows, Mexican Women in Twentieth-Century America* (New York: Oxford University Press, 1999); David G. Gutiérrez, *Walls and Mirrors: Mexican Americans, Mexican Immigrants, and the Politics of Ethnicity* (Berkeley: University of California Press, 1995); Emma Pérez, *The Decolonial Imaginary: Writing Chicanas into History* (Bloomington: Indiana University Press, 1999); Matt García, *A World of Its Own: Race, Labor, and Citrus in the Making of Greater Los Angeles, 1900–1970* (Chapel Hill: University of North Carolina Press, 2001).

23. See, for example, Limerick, *The Legacy of Conflict*; Peggy Pascoe, *Relations of Rescue: The Search for Moral Authority in the American West, 1874–1939* (New York: Oxford University Press, 1990); Joan Jensen and Darlis Miller, *New Mexico Women: Intercultural Perspectives* (Albuquerque: University of New Mexico Press, 1986); and Vicki Ruiz and Susan Tiano, eds., *Women on the United States–Mexico Border: Responses to Change* (Boston: Allen and Unwin, 1987).

24. Patricia Nelson Limerick, "What on Earth Is the New Western History?" in *Trails: Toward A New Western History*, ed. Patricia Nelson Limerick, Clyde A. Milner II, and Charles E. Rankin (Lawrence: University Press of Kansas, 1991), 86.
25. Sara Deutsch, *No Separate Refuge: Culture, Class, and Gender on an Anglo-Hispanic Frontier in the American Southwest, 1880–1940* (New York: Oxford University Press, 1987), 160–161.
26. Linda Gordon, *Heroes of Their Own Lives: The Politics and History of Family Violence: Boston, 1880–1960* (New York: Viking Press, 1988); Pascoe, *Relations of Rescue.*
27. Philip J. Deloria, *Indians in Unexpected Places* (Lawrence: University Press of Kansas, 2004); Hosmer and O'Neill, *Native Pathways.*
28. See the Gutman/Montgomery debate derived from the classic works, Herbert Gutman, *Work, Culture, and Society in Industrializing America* (New York: Vintage Books, 1976), and David Montgomery, *The Fall of the House of Labor* (New York: Cambridge University Press, 1987).
29. Alice Kessler-Harris, "Treating the Male as 'Other': Redefining the Parameters of Labor History," *Labor History* 34 (Spring/Summer 1993): 195.
30. Earl Lewis, *In Their Own Interests: Race, Class, and Power in Twentieth-Century Norfolk, Virginia* (Berkeley: University of California Press, 1991), 5–6.
31. U.S. Commission on Civil Rights, *Hearing before the United States Commission on Civil Rights, Window Rock, Arizona, October 22–24, 1973,* Vol. 1: *Testimony* (Washington, DC: Government Printing Office, 1973), 119.
32. Susan E. Dawson, "Navajo Uranium Workers and the Effects of Occupational Illnesses," *Human Organization: Journal of the Society for Applied Anthropology* 51 (Winter 1992): 389–397; Peter H. Eichstaedt, *If You Poison Us: Uranium and Native Americans* (Santa Fe, NM: Red Crane Books, 1994); Doug Brugge, Timothy Benally, and Esther Yazzie-Lewis, "Uranium Mining on Navajo Indian Land," *Cultural Survival Quarterly* 25, no. 1 (2001):18–21; Ward Churchill and Winona LaDuke, "Native North America: The Political Economy of Radioactive Colonization," in *The State of Native America: Genocide, Colonization, and Resistance,* ed. M. Annette Jaimes (Boston: South End Press, 1992), 241–266; also see the film that documents the Cly family's struggle with effects of uranium mining, *The Return of Navajo Boy* (Jeff Spitz, *The Return of Navajo Boy* [Berkeley: University of California, Extension Center for Media and Independent Learning, 2000]).
33. Allan Richard Pred and Michael Watts, *Reworking Modernity: Capitalisms and Symbolic Discontent* (New Brunswick, NJ: Rutgers University Press, 1992), 107.

CHAPTER 1. THE DINÉ AND THE DINÉ BIKÉYAH: NAVAJO HISTORY AND NAVAJOLAND

1. Quoted in Broderick H. Johnson, ed., *Stories of Traditional Navajo Life and Culture Alk'idą́ą́' Yę́ę́k'ehgo Diné Kéédahat'íńę́ Baa Nahane'* (Tsaile, Navajo Nation, AZ : Navajo Community College Press, 1977), 253.
2. A mucker is a laborer who shovels rock or ore into mining cars inside the mine. Most Navajo laborers who worked at the Argentine Mining Company in the 1940s and 1950s

were classified as such even though they might perform work that required higher skill, such as setting charges and timbering.

3. Oral interview with Charlie Jones by the author, Farmington, NM, July 17, 2002. Tape and transcript in author's possession.

4. The origin story recounts a series of struggles among spirit people, holy people, insect people, and other beings. Conflict among them inspires migration from the first world (black) to the second world (blue), then to the third world (yellow), and finally to the fourth, glittering world. Each journey signifies an effort to restore balance and harmony to the people. Anthropologists and historians have recorded many versions of the creation story. See, for example, Paul G. Zolbrod, *Diné Bahane': The Navajo Creation Story* (Albuquerque: University of New Mexico Press, 1984); Leland C. Wyman, *Blessingway* (Tucson: University of Arizona Press, 1970); Ethelou Yazzie, ed., *Navajo History* (Chinle, AZ: Navajo Curriculum Center, Rough Rock Demonstration School, 1971); Peter Iverson, *Diné: A History of the Navajos* (Albuquerque: University of New Mexico Press, 2002), 8.

5. Sisnaajiní is also known as Jóhonaa'éí Dziil (Sun Mountain) and Yoołgaii Dziil (White Shell Mountain); Tsoodzil is also known as Niłtsá Dziil (Rain Mountain) and Dootł'izhii Dziil (Turquoise Mountain); Dook'o'oosłííd is also known as Dził Ghá'niłts'įįlii (Faultless Mountain) and Diichiłí Dziil (Abalone Shell Mountain); Dibé Ntsaa is also known as Dził Bíni'Hólóonii (the mountain with a mind) and Baashzhinii Dziil (Jet Mountain). Alan Wilson and Gene Dennison, *Navajo Place Names: An Observer's Guide* (Guilford, CT: Jeffrey Norton Publishers, 1995), 32, 38, 50, 54–55; Irvin Morris, *From the Glittering World: A Navajo Story* (Norman: University of Oklahoma Press, 1997), 12–13; Robert McPherson, *Sacred Lands, Sacred View* (Salt Lake City: Signature Books and Charles Redd Center for Western Studies, Brigham Young University, 1992), 15.

6. George Blueeyes, "Sacred Mountains," in *Between Sacred Mountains: Navajo Stories and Lessons from the Land,* comp. and ed. Rock Point Community School, vol. 11 of *Sun Tracks,* ed. Larry Evers (Tucson: University of Arizona Press, 1982), 2.

7. Denis Foster Johnston, *An Analysis of Sources of Information on the Population of the Navajo,* Smithsonian Institution Bureau of Ethnology, Bulletin 197 (Washington, DC: Government Printing Office, 1966), 137–138. Klara Bonsack Kelley and Peter M. Whitely estimated the resident population for 1960 to be 77,293 (see *Navajoland: Family Settlement and Land Use* [Tsaile, AZ: Navajo Community College Press, 1989], 207).

8. Clyde Kluckhohn and Dorothea Leighton, *The Navaho,* rev. ed. (Cambridge, MA: Harvard University Press, 1974), 45.

9. N. Scott Momaday, "Foreword," in *Between Sacred Mountains: Navajo Stories and Lessons from the Land,* comp. and ed. Rock Point Community School, vol. 11 of *Sun Tracks,* ed. Larry Evers (Tucson: University of Arizona Press, 1982), vii.

10. Kluckhohn and Leighton, *The Navaho,* 45.

11. Johnston, *An Analysis of Sources of Information on the Population of the Navajo,* 31; also see James M. Goodman, *The Navajo Atlas: Environments, Resources, People, and History of the Diné Bikéyah* (Norman: University of Oklahoma Press), 26–45.

12. Kluckhohn and Leighton, *The Navajo*, 45.

13. Ibid., 72.

14. The executive order that expanded the reservation in 1880 included an area originally granted to the Atlantic and Pacific Railroad that subsequently fell under the control of a variety of land speculation companies. Through a series of legislative measures, part of the land was returned to the Navajo Nation, whereas other tracts were allotted to individual Navajos and/or sold to private Navajo and non-Navajo citizens. As a result, jurisdictional boundaries vary by tract, creating a "checkerboard" of land use designated either as public domain, reservation land, or private. Lawrence C. Kelly, *The Navajo Indians and Federal Indian Policy, 1900–1935* (Tucson: University of Arizona Press, 1968), 20–21.

15. Willard Williams Hill, *The Agricultural and Hunting Methods of the Navajo Indians*, Yale University Publications in Anthropology, no. 18 (New Haven, CT: Department of Anthropology, Yale University, 1938), 15.

16. In their review of Navajo community studies conducted between 1936 and 1974, Eric Henderson and Jerrold Levy concluded that it was nearly impossible to generalize about Navajo culture and society and that methodological inconsistencies meant that comparisons could be, at best, impressionistic. Eric B. Henderson and Jerrold E. Levy, *Survey of Navajo Community Studies, 1936 –1974*, Lake Powell Research Bulletin, no. 6 (Los Angeles: University of California, Los Angeles, Institute of Geophysics and Planetary Physics, 1975), 4–5.

17. The higher concentration of wages in the Gallup area community in the 1930s reflected the jobs created by the Indian Civilian Conservation Corps. Kelley and Whitely, *Navajoland*, 228.

18. Thomas R. Berger, *Village Journey: The Report of the Alaska Native Review Commission* (New York: Hill and Wang, 1985), 51. Berger served as a justice on British Columbia's Supreme Court from 1971 to 1983. Following that service, Berger served as the head of the Alaska Native Review Commission, leading an effort to reexamine the Alaska Native Claims act. His report argued for retribalization and sovereignty for Alaskan natives.

19. Ibid., 52.

20. Ibid.

21. Ibid., 51.

22. Peter Iverson, *Diné: A History of the Navajos* (Albuquerque: University of New Mexico Press, 2002), 48–57.

23. Broderick Johnson, ed., *Navajo Stories of the Long Walk Period* (Tsaile, AZ: Navajo Community College Press, 1973), 23–24; Diné of the Eastern Region of the Navajo Reservation, *Oral History Stories of the Long Walk, Hwéeldi Baa Hané*, comp. and ed. Title VII Bilingual Staff (Crownpoint, NM: Lake Valley Navajo School, 1991); Morris, *From the Glittering World*, 17–30.

24. Garrick Bailey and Roberta Glenn Bailey, *A History of the Navajos* (Santa Fe, NM: School of American Research Press, 1986), 26–27; Robert A. Roessel Jr., "Navajo History, 1850–1923," in *Handbook of North American Indians*, vol. 10, ed. Alfonso Ortiz

(Washington, DC: Smithsonian Institution, 1983), 519–520; Goodman, *The Navajo Atlas*, 57; Kelly, *The Navajo Indians and Federal Indian Policy, 1900–1935*, 6–7.

25. The 1868 treaty included a central part of the land the Navajo had occupied prior to 1864, but it did not nearly encompass the areas where many Navajos lived and/or that they held sacred. Klara Bonsack Kelley and Harris Francis, *Navajo Sacred Places* (Bloomington: Indiana University Press, 1994), 114; Roessel, "Navajo History, 1850–1923," 520.

26. Francis Paul Prucha, *The Great Father: The United States Government and the American Indians*, abr. ed. (Lincoln: University of Nebraska Press, 1986), 317.

27. Lawrence C. Kelly, *The Assault on Assimilation: John Collier and the Origins of Indian Policy Reform* (Albuquerque: University of New Mexico Press, 1983), 273.

28. Introduced by Holm O. Bursum, a Republican from New Mexico, in 1921, this bill was designed to validate non-Indian claims to lands held by the Pueblos and to grant title of Pueblo lands. Ibid., 202–203.

29. Kathleen P. Chamberlain, *Under Sacred Ground: A History of Navajo Oil, 1922–1982* (Albuquerque: University of New Mexico Press, 2000), 39–40.

30. Donald L. Parman, *The Navajos and the New Deal* (New Haven, CT: Yale University Press, 1976), 27.

31. Richard White, *The Roots of Dependency: Subsistence, Environment and Social Change among the Choctaws, Pawnees, and Navajos* (Lincoln: University of Nebraska Press, 1983).

32. Ibid.; Marsha Weisiger, "Diné Bikéyah: Environment, Cultural Identity, and Gender in Navajo Country" (Ph.D. diss., University of Wisconsin, 2000); Iverson, *Diné*, 142; Robert Allan Young, "Regional Development and Rural Poverty in the Navajo Indian Area" (Ph.D. diss., University of Wisconsin, 1976).

33. Weisiger, "Diné Bikéyah," 19. See the voluminous collection of reports and data housed at the Center for Southwest Research at the University of New Mexico. For a concise analysis that links stock reduction to the encroaching capitalist market, see White, *The Roots of Dependency*. A classic study that explores the rise of the Native American Church as a response to stock reduction is David Aberle's *The Peyote Religion among the Navajos* (New York: Wenner Gren Foundation for Anthropological Research, 1966). To understand the impact of stock reduction on Navajo social/economic hierarchies and the redistribution of income on the reservation, see Eric Henderson, "Navajo Livestock Wealth and the Effects of the Stock Reduction Program of the 1930s," *Journal of Anthropological Research* 45 (Winter 1989): 379–403. For Navajo perspectives, see Ruth Roessel and Broderick Johnson, *Navajo Livestock Reduction: A National Disgrace* (Chinle, AZ: Navajo Community College, 1974).

34. A sheep unit was the standard of measurement developed by the Soil Conservation Service to assess the land's carrying capacity. One sheep unit is the equivalent of one sheep or goat grazing all year long. One head of cattle equaled four sheep units, and one horse equaled five sheep units. Aberle, *The Peyote Religion among the Navajos*, 67.

35. Kelley and Whitely, *Navajoland*, 111.

36. The flat 10 percent reduction was soon replaced with a system that issued permits for a specific number of stock based on the carrying capacity of the household's land use area.

37. U.S. Senate Subcommittee of Indian Affairs, *Survey of the Conditions of the Indians of the United States* (Washington, DC: Government Printing Office, 1937), 17446; Lawrence D. Weiss, *The Development of Capitalism in the Navajo Nation: A Political-Economic History* (Minneapolis: Marxist Educational Press Publications, 1984), 181; Henderson, "Navajo Livestock Wealth and the Effects of the Stock Reduction Program of the 1930s," 385. Kelley and Whitely pointed out that significant economic stratification was evident in the southern region of the reservation in the 1920s; "[s]tock reduction caused the rest of the reservation to catch up." Kelley and Whiteley, *Navajoland*, 112.

38. Gladys Reichard, "Another Look at the Navaho," unpublished manuscript, Gladys A. Reichard Papers, Museum of Northern Arizona, folder 32, p. 28.

39. White, *The Roots of Dependency*, 229.

40. Young, "Regional Development and Rural Poverty in the Navajo Indian Area," 230.

41. Aberle, *The Peyote Religion among the Navajos*, 87.

42. Collier was the commissioner of Indian affairs at the time of stock reduction. Deescheeny Nez Tracy, quoted in Johnson, *Stories of Traditional Navajo Life and Culture*, 161–162.

43. Iverson, *Diné*, 142.

44. Rose Mitchell, *Tall Woman: The Life Story of Rose Mitchell, a Navajo Woman, c. 1874–1977*, ed. Charlotte Johnson Frisbie (Albuquerque: University of New Mexico Press, 2001), 33.

45. Manuel Denetso, July 5, 1940, quoted in Peter Iverson and Monty Roessel, eds., *"For Our Navajo People": Diné Letters, Speeches, and Petitions, 1900–1960* (Albuquerque: University of New Mexico Press, 2002), 26.

46. U.S. Senate Subcommittee of Indian Affairs, *Survey of the Conditions of the Indians of the United States*, 17449–17450.

47. Letter from B. W. Dyer, district mining supervisor to E. R. Fryer, general superintendent, Navajo Service, Window Rock, May 10, 1939, U.S. Bureau of Land Management, Navajo, Tohatchi Mine Files, General Correspondence Files, Farmington, NM; Donald L. Parman, *The Navajos and the New Deal* (New Haven, CT: Yale University Press, 1976), 34–35.

48. A hogan is a "traditional" Navajo dwelling. It is usually a round, one-room structure and can be made from various materials, including rocks, mud, logs, and in some cases, cement. Styles have changed considerably over the last century. Gary Witherspoon, "Navajo Social Organization," in *Handbook of North American Indians*, vol. 10, ed. Alfonzo Ortiz (Washington, DC: Smithsonian Institution, 1983), 530–531.

49. *Albuquerque Journal*, May 30, 1996, p. A1.

50. *Healing v. Jones*, 373 U.S. 758 (1963).

51. Activists, journalists, and scholars have argued that corporate coal interests are behind the relocation orders. The disputed land is rich with coal deposits. Emily Benedek, *The Wind Won't Know Me: A History of the Navajo-Hopi Land Dispute* (New York: Alfred A. Knopf, 1992), 12–13, 133–142.

52. Enforcing those policies has at times meant bulldozing buildings and corrals built by the resident families. In May 1996, the tribal council and federal officials attempted to stop the Big Mountain residents from holding a Sun Dance, which had become an annual event that attracted Native American activists and non-Indian supporters to the area from all over the United States. Big Mountain residents used this event to mobilize support for their antirelocation efforts. *Navajo Times*, June 6, 1996. For more details on the history of the Navajo-Hopi land dispute, see Jerry Kammer, *The Second Long Walk: The Navajo-Hopi Land Dispute* (Albuquerque: University of New Mexico Press, 1980); Thayer Scudder, *No Place to Go: Effects of Compulsory Relocation on Navajos* (Philadelphia: Institute for the Study of Human Issues, 1982); Benedek, *The Wind Won't Know Me*; and David M. Brugge, *The Navajo-Hopi Land Dispute: An American Tragedy* (Albuquerque: University of New Mexico Press, 1994).

53. *Navajo Times*, February 6, 1997.

54. Navajo resisters at Big Mountain have evoked the sacredness of their land in their struggle against relocation. Kelley and Francis, *Navajo Sacred Places*, 54, 154–155.

55. Memo from Albert Hale to Navajo Nation employees, quoted in the *Albuquerque Journal*, May 30, 1996, p. A6.

56. Benedek, *The Wind Won't Know Me*, 383–386.

57. Personal conversation with Lavine Benally White, clan granddaughter of one of the Big Mountain elders, Highland Park, NJ, November 10, 1996.

58. *Albuquerque Journal*, May 30, 1996, p. A6.

59. This is not to suggest that other struggles articulated as "traditional" did not occur prior to the 1930s. The construction of the traditional before that date is beyond the scope of this study.

60. Kelley and Francis, *Navajo Sacred Places*, 46.

61. Emphasis in original. Mitchell, *Tall Woman*.

CHAPTER 2. MINING COAL LIKE HERDING SHEEP: NAVAJO COAL OPERATORS IN THE MID-TWENTIETH CENTURY

1. Oral interview with Evelyn John by the author, August 16, 2002, Hogback Senior Center, Hogback, NM. Tape and transcript in author's possession.

2. Oral interview with Burton Yazzie by the author, May 19, 1995, at Yazzie's home in Coyote Canyon, NM, on the Navajo Reservation. Tape and transcript in author's possession.

3. Abandoned Mines Reclamation Reports, Navajo Nation Historic Preservation Department, Window Rock, AZ.

4. Rena Martin, "Archaeological and Ethnographic Investigations at Four Coal Mine Areas South of Shiprock, San Juan County, New Mexico," Navajo Tribal Permit no.

NTC, BIA Use Authorization no. NNCRMP 0033–1, submitted November 12, 1986, on file at the Navajo Nation Historic Preservation Department, Window Rock, AZ. Other archaeological evidence shows coal piles replacing wood piles at Navajo homesites in the developed trading post era, in the 1920s, which corroborates Henna's memory and his statement linking coal with the acquisition of more consumer items from the traders. Lawrence Vogler, Dennis Gilpin, Joseph K. Anderson, et al., *Gallegos Mesa Settlement and Subsistence: A Set of Explanatory Models for Cultural Resources on Blocks VIII, IX, X, and XI, Navajo Indian Irrigation Project, Vol. 3,* Navajo Nation Papers in Anthropology, no. 12 (Window Rock, AZ: Navajo Nation Cultural Resource Management Program, 1982), 927. I owe thanks to Marsha Weisiger for pointing out this source to me.

5. By border towns I refer to towns that border the reservation, that is, Gallup, New Mexico; Farmington, New Mexico; and Flagstaff, Arizona.

6. See payroll records, Albuquerque and Cerrillos Coal Company Records, Center for Southwest Research, Zimmerman Library, University of New Mexico, Albuquerque, NM; Gallup American Coal Company Records, New Mexico State Bureau of Mines and Mineral Resources, New Mexico Institute of Mines and Technology, Socorro. (Neither collection had been processed at the time of this writing.)

7. F. W. Calhoun, "Engineer's Report regarding Coal Mines Operated by Individual Indians on the Northern Navajo Indian Reservation, New Mexico, October 1936," U.S. Bureau of Land Management, Miscellaneous Coal Mines, Northern Navajo Indian Reservation, General Correspondence, Farmington, NM (revised version).

8. F. W. Calhoun, mining engineer, U.S. Geological Survey, "Preliminary Report of Inspection. Navajo Reservation Coal Mines in New Mexico, November 6, 1936," U.S. Bureau of Land Management, Miscellaneous Coal Mines, Northern Navajo Indian Reservation, General Correspondence, Farmington, NM.

9. Ibid.

10. R. D. Reeder, "Engineer's Report of the Coal Mines Operated by the Shiprock Sub Agency and Schools on the Northern Navajo Indian Reservation in New Mexico, October 27, 1939"; R. H. Allport, district supervisor, "Inspection Report, North Hogback Agency and Individual Coal Mines, Northern Navajo Indian Reservation, January 5, 1943," U.S. Bureau of Land Management, Miscellaneous Coal Mines, Northern Navajo Indian Reservation, General Correspondence, expired, Farmington, NM.

11. Martin, "Archaeological and Ethnographic Investigations at Four Coal Mine Areas South of Shiprock, San Juan County, New Mexico."

12. Ibid.; letter from E. R. Fryer to Robert W. Knox, general counsel to National Bituminous Coal Commission, February 23, 1939, National Archives I, Record Group 75, Bureau of Indian Affairs, Classified Files, Navajo, Box 102, file 71392, Washington, DC; letter from E. R. Fryer, superintendent of the Navajo Agency, Window Rock, AZ, to commissioner of Indian affairs, January 24, 1939, National Archives I, Record Group 75, Bureau of Indian Affairs, Classified Files, Navajo, Box 102, File 71392–1938, Washington, DC.

13. Howard B. Nickelson, *One Hundred Years of Coal Mining in the San Juan Basin, New Mexico,* Bulletin 111, New Mexico Bureau of Mines and Mineral Resources (Socorro:

New Mexico Institute of Mining and Technology, 1988), 15; "Memorandum on Bituminous Coal Code Violations, in Certain Counties in Colorado and New Mexico,"
United Mine Workers' Papers, Historical Collections and Labor Archives, Box 21/5,
folder: District 15–1935-February-April, Pattee Library, Pennsylvania State University,
University Park.

14. Gladys A. Reichard, *Social Life of the Navajo Indians,* vol. 7 (New York: Columbia University Press, 1928), 93.

15. Ibid., 92.

16. B. W. Dyer, J. J. Bourquin, and C. L. Dyer, U.S. Geological Survey, "Engineers Report of
the Shiprock Coal Mines on the Northern Navajo Indian Reservation, New Mexico,
November 14, 1928," U.S. Bureau of Land Management, Miscellaneous Coal Mines,
Northern Navajo Indian Reservation, General Correspondence, Farmington, NM.

17. B. W. Dyer and J. J. Bourquin, U.S. Geological Survey, "Report on the Shiprock Coal
Mines on the Northern Navajo Indian Reservation, New Mexico, June 2, 1928," U.S.
Bureau of Land Management, Miscellaneous Coal Mines, Northern Navajo Indian
Reservation, General Correspondence, Farmington, NM.

18. Letter from E. R. Fryer, superintendent of the Navajo Agency, Window Rock, to the
commissioner of Indian affairs, Washington, DC, November 16, 1938, National Archives
I, Record Group 75, Bureau of Indian Affairs, Classified Files, Navajo, Box 102, File
71392–1938, Washington, DC.

19. Letter from E. R. Fryer to Robert W. Knox, general counsel to National Bituminous
Coal Commission, February 23, 1939, National Archives I, Record Group 75, Bureau
of Indian Affairs, Classified Files, Navajo, Box 102, file 71392, Washington, DC.

20. R. H. Allport, "Mine Inspector's Report, North Hogback Region, October 21, 1943,"
U.S. Bureau of Land Management, Miscellaneous Coal Mines, Northern Navajo Indian Reservation, Expired, Farmington, NM.

21. Martin, "Archaeological and Ethnographic Investigations at Four Coal Mine Areas
South of Shiprock, San Juan County, New Mexico."

22. Rosalie Fanale, "Navajo Land and Land Management: A Century of Change" (Ph.D.
diss., Catholic University, 1982), 144.

23. Helen Duncan, interview with the author, translated by Charlie Jones Jr., Hogback
Chapter House, Hogback, NM, July 15, 2002. Tape and transcript in author's possession.

24. Oral interview with Clarence and Margaret Kee by the author, interpreted by Juannita
Brown (their daughter), at Tuller's Cafe, St. Michael's, AZ, May 18, 1995. Tape and transcript in author's possession. The army did not create the Navajo sheep culture. Prior
to their incarceration at Ft. Sumner, the Navajo had developed a pastoral tradition
from their contact with their Spanish and Pueblo neighbors. In fact, part of the U.S.
army's tactics to subdue Navajo resistance in 1863 was to slaughter their livestock and
destroy their crops. But the Navajo economy did become more sheep centered when,
as a part of treaty negotiations, the Navajos agreed to curtail their raiding activities.
Ruth Underhill, *The Navajos* (Norman: University of Oklahoma Press, 1956), 118.

25. Oral interview with Clarence and Margaret Kee, May 18, 1995.
26. Nearly every miner I interviewed had a similar employment history. They all started working in small, underground mines and eventually found work in corporate uranium and coal mining operations, in the mid-1960s.
27. Oral interview with Burton Yazzie by the author, May 19, 1995, at Yazzie's home in Coyote Canyon, NM, on the Navajo Reservation. Tape and transcript in author's possession.
28. Personal communication with Lavine Bennally White, Highland Park, NJ, August 15, 1995.
29. Fanale, "Navajo Land and Land Management: A Century of Change," 142.
30. Klara Kelley, *Navajo Land Use: An Ethnoarchaeological Study* (Orlando, FL: Academic Press, 1983). Even though Kelley's evidence is for the Gallup–Window Rock area, it is reasonable to assume that since the Shiprock area was one of the hardest hit by stock reduction and, like Gallup, held considerable coal resources and bordered Anglo and Hispano/Mexican residential areas, Navajos living in the Shiprock area faced similar constraints. Fanale ("Navajo Land and Land Management") documented a similar settling pattern in the Shiprock area. Other than the archaeological surveys of abandoned mine lands, not a single published anthropological or historical study specifically mentions the land use of Navajo coal miners.
31. Dennis Gilpin, "The Navajo Coal Mines: Industrial Archaeology on the Navajo Indian Reservation"(paper presented at the 1987 Navajo Studies Conference, Northern Arizona University, Flagstaff, February 19–21, 1987), 18.
32. J. J. Bourquin, "Engineer's Report on Coal Mines of the Shiprock Agency on the Northern Navajo Indian Reservation, June 19, 1932," U.S. Bureau of Land Management, Miscellaneous Coal Mines, Northern Navajo Indian Reservation, General Correspondence, Farmington, NM; letter from Fryer to commissioner of Indian affairs, November 16, 1938, National Archives I.
33. Gary Witherspoon, *Navajo Weaving: Art in Its Cultural Context*, Mna Research Paper (Flagstaff: Museum of Northern Arizona, 1987), 100.
34. Milford Muskett, "Identity, *Hózhǫ́*, Change, and Land: Navajo Environmental Perspectives" (Ph.D. diss., University of Wisconsin–Madison, 2003), 186; Muskett quoted the term *dynamic beauty* from Gary Witherspoon, *Language and Art in the Navajo Universe* (Ann Arbor: University of Michigan Press, 1977), 91.
35. Although Joe and Lonewolf Miller drew their conclusions from research done in 1991, what they described seems to have informed the worldview of Navajos living in the mid-twentieth century as well. Writing from research done in the 1930s and 1940s, Gladys Reichard and Clyde Kluckhohn offered similar conclusions about how Navajos perceived their world and their place in it. Jennie R. Joe and Dorothy Lonewolf Miller, "The Dilemma of Navajo Industrial Workers," *Nature, Society, and Thought: A Journal of Dialectical and Historical Materialism* 4 (1991): 310. Also see Gladys Reichard, "Human Nature as Conceived by the Navajo," *Review of Religion* 6 (1943): 353–360, and *Navajo Religion* (Princeton, NJ: Princeton University Press, 1950); Clyde Kluckhohn, "The Philosophy of the Navajo Indians," in *Ideological Differences and World Order*, ed. F. S. C. Northrop (New Haven, CT: Yale University Press, 1949), 356–384.

36. This is not necessarily a practice embraced by all Navajos. It is particularly interesting, since in recent years "traditionals" have evoked the sacredness of the land in their efforts to resist strip-mining development in places such as Black Mesa. Klara Bonsack Kelley and Harris Francis, *Navajo Sacred Places* (Bloomington: Indiana University Press, 1994), 150–155. Oral interview with Burton Yazzie by the author, May 19, 1995, at Yazzie's home in Coyote Canyon, NM, on the Navajo Reservation. Tape and transcript in author's possession.

37. I use the terms *modern* and *traditional* with trepidation. Navajos use the English word *traditional* to describe cultural practices that they see as distinctly Navajo, and in the case of the current struggle at Big Mountain, some groups have deployed it as a form of resistance against relocation and of preservation of lands they consider sacred. The term *traditional* is not meant to imply that the "native ways" Burton Yazzie referred to are part of some pre-industrial and static past. In fact, the Yazzie coal operation shows the distinction between modern and traditional to be somewhat artificial.

38. Brian Jackson Morton, "Coal Leasing in the Fourth World: Hopi and Navajo Coal Leasing, 1954–1977" (Ph.D. diss., University of California, Berkeley, 1985), vii.

39. It is difficult to document exactly when the BIA started purchasing coal from the Navajo producers, since up until 1928 BIA and USGS officials did not record Navajo coal mining activity in any detail. But in 1938, BIA officials did remark that they had been purchasing coal from the Navajos for many years previous. Letter from "Dodd" (no first name noted) to William Zimmerman, assistant commissioner of Indian affairs, January 15, 1938; memo from Frederick L. Kirgis, acting solicitor, Office of the Solicitor, Washington, DC, to commissioner of Indian affairs, July 1, 1936, National Archives I, Record Group 75, Bureau of Indian Affairs, Classified Files, Navajo, Box 99, File 79478–1936, Washington, DC. Mines operated by the BIA did not open until 1936. Since archaeologists have dated the emergence of Navajo coal mining in the 1920s, it is possible to assume that BIA officials started purchasing coal from the Navajos then.

40. Dyer, Bourquin, and Dyer, "Engineers Report of the Shiprock Coal Mines on the Northern Navajo Indian Reservation, New Mexico, November 14, 1928," U.S. Bureau of Land Management.

41. For a discussion of the relationship among the BIA, oil development, and the formation of the Navajo Tribal Council, see Lawrence C. Kelly, *The Navajo Indians and Federal Indian Policy, 1900–1935* (Tucson: University of Arizona Press, 1968), 48–74; Kathleen Chamberlain, *Under Sacred Ground, A History of Navajo Oil* (Albuquerque: University of New Mexico Press, 2000), 29.

42. Dyer, Bourquin, and Dyer, "Engineers Report of the Shiprock Coal Mines on the Northern Navajo Indian Reservation, New Mexico, November 14, 1928," U.S. Bureau of Land Management. The first priority of these inspectors was to ensure a reliable source of cheap coal to heat the agency's offices and schools on the reservation. At $4.15 per ton for high quality coal delivered to the agency, they had a strong incentive for keeping the mines in good working order. Since Navajo coal was close by, they could save a lot of money compared to what it would cost to transport coal from Gallup.

43. Nickelson, *One Hundred Years of Coal Mining in the San Juan Basin, New Mexico,* 15; Clark C. Spence, *Mining Engineers and the American West: The Lace-Boot Brigade, 1849–1933* (Moscow: University of Idaho Press, 1993).

44. The term *slack* refers to coal that is too small to be used in boilers and stokers. Slack, especially fine coal dust, is highly flammable. Leaving it in the mines presented an extreme fire hazard.

45. B. W. Dyer, "Engineer's Report on the Shiprock Agency Coal Mines on the Northern Navajo Indian Reservation, August 13, 1931," U.S. Bureau of Land Management, Miscellaneous Coal Mines, Northern Navajo Indian Reservation, General Correspondence, Farmington, NM. Forking means sorting through the coal, separating it according to size.

46. Bourquin, "Engineer's Report on Coal Mines of the Shiprock Agency on the Northern Navajo Indian Reservation, June 19, 1932," U.S. Bureau of Land Management.

47. B. P. Six, superintendent, "Shiprock Inspection Notes, October 25, 1929," U.S. Bureau of Land Management, Miscellaneous Coal Mines, Northern Navajo Indian Reservation, General Correspondence, Farmington, NM; Dyer, Bourquin, and Dyer, "Engineers Report of the Shiprock Coal Mines on the Northern Navajo Indian Reservation, New Mexico, November 14, 1928," U.S. Bureau of Land Management.

48. Bourquin, "Engineer's Report on Coal Mines of the Shiprock Agency on the Northern Navajo Indian Reservation, June 19, 1932," U.S. Bureau of Land Management.

49. Bureau of Indian Affairs officials had also concluded that the Navajos had "too many sheep." See George A. Boyce, *When Navajos Had Too Many Sheep: The 1940's* (Albuquerque, NM: Indian Historical Press, Menaul Historical Library of the Southwest, 1974).

50. Calhoun, "Engineer's Report Regarding Coal Mines Operated by Individual Indians on the Northern Navajo Indian Reservation, New Mexico, October 1936," U.S. Bureau of Land Management.

51. Calhoun, "Preliminary Report of Inspection. Navajo Reservation Coal Mines in New Mexico, November 6, 1936," U.S. Bureau of Land Management.

52. Letter to Collier from director (signature not legible) of the USGS, May 21, 1937, National Archives I, Record Group 75, Bureau of Indian Affairs, Classified Files, Navajo, Box 101, File 32767, Washington, DC.

53. Calhoun, "Preliminary Report of Inspection. Navajo Reservation Coal Mines in New Mexico, November 6, 1936," U.S. Bureau of Land Management.

54. Ibid.

55. Letter to Collier from director, May 21, 1937, National Archives I.

56. Letter from John Collier, commissioner of Indian affairs, to E. R. Fryer, June 18, 1937, National Archives I, Record Group 75, Bureau of Indian Affairs, Classified Files, Navajo, Box 101, File 32767, Washington, DC.

57. Peter Iverson argued, however, that stock reduction stimulated Navajo nationalism. As a response to stock reduction, the Navajo Tribal Council asserted its identity as separate from the BIA. Peter Iverson, *The Navajo Nation* (Westport, CT: Greenwood Press, 1981), 30–34. Lawrence Kelly argued that the Navajo Tribal Council was not made up

of "yes men" for the BIA. Lawrence Kelly, *The Navajo Indians and Federal Indian Policy*, 190–194; Donald L. Parman, *The Navajos and the New Deal* (New Haven: Yale University Press, 1976), 76; *Navajo Nation v. United States*, 263 F.3d 1325, 150 Oil & Gas Rep. 28, 32 Envtl. L. Rep. 20,028. http://campus.westlaw.com/Welcome/WestlawCampus/default.wl?RS=imp1.0&VR=2.0&SP=usu–2000&FN=_top&MT=Westlaw&SV=Split (accessed August 8, 2004); Peter McDonald and Ted Schwarz, *The Last Warrior: Peter McDonald and the Navajo Nation* (New York: Orion Books, 1993), 210–213.

58. *Navajo Tribal Council Resolutions, 1922–1951* (Washington, DC: Department of the Interior, Office of Indian Affairs, 1952), 297.

59. Letter from E. R. Fryer, Navajo Service, Window Rock, to the commissioner of Indian affairs, July 26, 1937, National Archives I, Record Group 75, Bureau of Indian Affairs Classified Files, Box 101, File 32767, Navajo, Washington, DC.

60. Letter from Fryer to commissioner of Indian affairs, November 16, 1938, National Archives I.

61. Nearly every mine inspector report stressed the importance of having an Anglo, or white, foreman to supervise the Navajo workers.

62. Letter from E. R. Fryer, general superintendent, Navajo Service, to the commissioner of Indian affairs, June 16, 1936, National Archives I, Record Group 75, Bureau of Indian Affairs, Classified Files, Navajo, Box 99, File 79478–1936, Washington, DC.

63. Memo from Kirgis to commissioner of Indian affairs, July 1, 1936, National Archives I.

64. Letter from "Dodd" to Zimmerman, January 15, 1938, National Archives I.

65. Memorandum from William Zimmerman to Mr. Armstrong (no first name noted), January 4, 1938, National Archives I, Record Group 75, Bureau of Indian Affairs, Classified Files, Navajo, Box 99, File 79478–1936, Washington, DC.

66. Letter from J. M. Stewart, general superintendent of the Navajo Service, Window Rock, to Norman M. Littell, January 20, 1949, National Archives I, Record Group 75, Bureau of Indian Affairs Classified Files, Navajo, Box 104, File 1859–1949–232, Washington, DC. Stewart noted that the agency did not have records for the years prior to 1939.

67. The Bituminous Coal Act of 1937, also known as the Guffey-Vinson Act, established a new Bituminous Coal Commission made up of industry and labor representatives. It established minimum prices and assessed a one cent per ton tax on all coal sold in the United States and penalized those coal producers who were not members by levying a nineteen cents per ton penalty. The actions of the Bituminous Coal Commission were exempt from antitrust liability. James P. Johnson, *The Politics of Soft Coal: The Bituminous Industry from World War I through the New Deal* (Urbana: University of Illinois Press, 1979), 230–233.

68. R. D. Reeder, "Engineer's Report on the Coal Mines Operated by the Shiprock Sub-Agency and Schools of the Northern Navajo Indian Reservation in New Mexico, April 20 and 21, 1940," U.S. Bureau of Land Management, Miscellaneous Coal Mines, Northern Navajo Indian Reservation, General Correspondence, expired, Farmington, NM.

69. Johnson, *The Politics of Soft Coal*, 230–233.

70. Letter from Robert W. Knox, general counsel, Bituminous Coal Commission, Wash-

ington, DC, to E. R. Fryer, superintendent, Navajo Agency, February 1, 1939, National Archives I, Record Group 75, Bureau of Indian Affairs, Classified Files, Navajo, Box 102, File 71392, Washington, DC.

71. Reeder, "Engineer's Report of the Coal Mines Operated by the Shiprock Sub-Agency and Schools on the Northern Navajo Indian Reservation in New Mexico, October 27, 1939," U.S. Bureau of Land Management.

72. "Coal Mining Code for Hogback Coal Miners' Association, October 21, 1941," Thomas H. Dodge Collection, Box 5, folder 22, Arizona Collection, Hayden Library, Department of Manuscripts, Arizona State University, Tempe.

73. Ibid.

74. Resolution CM–13–39, May 18, 1939, *Navajo Tribal Council Resolutions, 1922–1951* (Washington, DC: U.S. Dept. of the Interior, Office of Indian Affairs, 1952), 271; Reeder, "Engineer's Report of the Coal Mines Operated by the Shiprock Sub-Agency and Schools on the Northern Navajo Indian Reservation in New Mexico, October 27, 1939," U.S. Bureau of Land Management.

75. Letter from Fryer to commissioner of Indian affairs, November 16, 1938, National Archives I.

76. Because of the dwindling market for coal, most of the major underground coal operations in New Mexico, including Gamerco in Gallup and the Albuquerque and Cerrillos Coal Company in Madrid, were forced to close their operations by 1955. The late 1950s marked a new phase of coal mining on the reservation. Large multinational companies started to open strip-mining operations on reservation land they leased from the Navajo Nation near Window Rock, Black Mesa, and Shiprock. Jeff Radford, *The Chaco Coal Scandal: The People's Victory over James Watt* (Corrales, NM: Rhombus Publishing Company, 1986), 25–26; Lorraine Turner Ruffing, "Navajo Mineral Development," *Indian Historian* 11 (Spring 1978): 28–29; Nickelson, *One Hundred Years of Coal Mining in the San Juan Basin*, 21.

77. David Brugge, "Navajo Land Usage: A Study in Progressive Diversification," in *Indian and Spanish American Adjustments to Arid and Semiarid Environments,* ed. C. S. Knowlton (Lubbock: Committee on Desert and Arid Zone Research, Texas Technological College, 1965), 23.

78. Brian Hosmer and Colleen O'Neill, eds., *Native Pathways: American Indian Culture and Economic Development in the Twentieth Century* (Boulder: University Press of Colorado, 2004).

CHAPTER 3. WEAVING A LIVING: NAVAJO WEAVERS AND THE
TRADING POST ECONOMY

1. Quoted in Broderick H. Johnson, ed., *Stories of Traditional Navajo Life and Culture, Alk'idą́ą́' Yéę́k'ehgo Diné Kéédahat'ínę́ę Baa Nahane'* (Tsaile, Navajo Nation, AZ: Navajo Community College Press, 1977), 185.

2. Oral interview with Betty Harvey by the author, interpreted by Minnie Hamstreet, Hogback, NM, on the Navajo Reservation, August 15, 2002 (tape and transcript in author's

possession); Garrick Alan Bailey and Roberta Glenn Bailey, *A History of the Navajos: The Reservation Years* (Santa Fe, NM: School of American Research Press, 1986), 175.

3. Oral interview with Betty Harvey by the author, August 15, 2002.

4. Harry John's original name in English was John Blueeyes. In our interview he described how he became "Harry John." When he was trying to get a job working for the CCC, his cousin suggested that he change his name to make it easier for the Anglo labor recruiters to understand. So, he inverted the order of his cousin's name, which was John Harry. He has gone by that name ever since. Oral interview of Harry John by the author, translated by Paul George, at John's home in the Hogback community on the Navajo Reservation, August 14, 2002. Tape and transcript in author's possession.

5. M-Z Employee Cards 1930–1942, from National Archives, Pacific Region, Record Group 75, Bureau of Indian Affairs, Classified Files, Navajos, Phoenix Area Office, box 224, Laguna Niguel, CA; Alice Littlefield, "Indian Education and the World of Work in Michigan, 1893–1933," in *Native Americans and Wage Labor: Ethnohistorical Perspectives,* ed. Alice Littlefield and Martha C. Knack (Norman: University of Oklahoma Press, 1996), 111; Robert A. Trennert Jr., *The Phoenix Indian School: Forced Assimilation in Arizona, 1891–1935* (Norman: University of Oklahoma Press, 1988), 73.

6. Ann Lane Hedlund, "'More of Survival than an Art,' Comparing Late-Nineteenth and Late-Twentieth-Century Lifeways and Weaving," in *Woven by the Grandmothers: Nineteenth-Century Navajo Textiles from the National Museum of the American Indian,* ed. Eulalie H. Bonar and National Museum of the American Indian (Washington, DC: Smithsonian Institution Press in association with the National Museum of the American Indian, Smithsonian Institution, 1996), 52–53; Frank McNitt, *The Indian Traders,* 1st ed. (Norman: University of Oklahoma Press, 1962), 10; Garrick Bailey and Roberta Glenn Bailey, *A History of the Navajos: The Reservation Years,* 1st ed. (Santa Fe, NM: School of American Research Press, distributed by University of Washington Press, 1986), 57; George Wharton James, *Indian Blankets and Their Makers* (1914; repr., New York: Dover, 1974), 20.

7. Gary Witherspoon, *Navajo Weaving: Art in Its Cultural Context,* Mna Research Paper 36 (Flagstaff: Museum of Northern Arizona, 1987), 60–68.

8. Bailey and Bailey, *A History of the Navajos,* 59.

9. McNitt, *The Indian Traders,* 46; Kathy M'Closkey, *Swept under the Rug: A Hidden History of Navajo Weaving* (Albuquerque: University of New Mexico Press, 2002), 45; Bailey and Bailey, *A History of the Navajos,* 50, 61.

10. Ken L. Bryant Jr., *History of the Atchison, Topeka, and Santa Fe Railway* (New York: Macmillan, 1974).

11. Simon Ortiz, "Grants to Gallup, New Mexico" in *Woven Stone,* vol. 21 in *Sun Tracks,* ed. by Larry Evers and Ofelia Zepeda (Tucson: University of Arizona Press, 1992), 242.

12. McNitt, *The Indian Traders,* 51; B. Youngblood, "Navajo Trading," in *Survey of Conditions of the Indians in the United States, Part 34: Navajo Boundary and Pueblos in New Mexico,* U.S. Senate, Subcommittee of the Committee on Indian Affairs, 75th Cong., 1st sess. (Washington, DC: Government Printing Office, 1937), 18043.

13. Richard White, *The Roots of Dependency: Subsistence and Social Change among the Choctaws, Pawnees, and Navajos* (Lincoln: University of Nebraska Press, 1983), 244.

14. Bailey and Bailey, *A History of the Navajos,* 57.

15. M'Closkey, *Swept under the Rug,* 57; Bailey and Bailey, *A History of the Navajos,* 152.

16. M'Closkey, *Swept under the Rug,* 60, 97.

17. There is a general consensus that traders had to adapt to Navajo cultural practices in order to be successful on the reservation. See the classic book on this subject, McNitt, *The Indian Traders.* For the later period, see Willow Roberts Powers, *Navajo Trading: The End of an Era* (Albuquerque: University of New Mexico Press, 2001) and her earlier book, *Stokes Carson: Twentieth-Century Trading on the Navajo Reservation* (Albuquerque: University of New Mexico Press, 1987). For a well-documented critique of the trading post system, see William Y. Adams, *Shonto: A Study of the Role of the Trader in a Modern Navaho Community,* Smithsonian Institution Bureau of American Ethnography, Bulletin 188 (Washington, DC: Government Printing Office, 1963). For a Marxist perspective, see Lawrence David Weiss, *The Development of Capitalism in the Navajo Nation: A Political-Economic History* (Minneapolis: Marxist Educational Press, 1984). A variety of biographies and autobiographies sheds considerable light on the role of traders in the Navajo economy. See, for example, Martha Blue, *Indian Trader: The Life and Times of J. L. Hubbell* (Walnut, CA: Kiva, 2000); Gladwell Richardson and Philip Reed Rulon, *Navajo Trader* (Tucson: University of Arizona Press, 1986); Sallie R. Wagner and Albuquerque Museum, *Wide Ruins: Memories from a Navajo Trading Post* (Albuquerque: University of New Mexico Press, 1997).

18. Interviews number 154 and 155, Hubbell Trading Post Ethnohistory Project, Hubbell Trading Post National Monument, Ganado, AZ. To protect the privacy of those Navajos who participated in the Hubbell ethnohistory project, I have omitted their names, and I will refer to their interviews by the transcript number. Blue, *Indian Trader.*

19. Indian correspondence, Hubbell Trading Post Records, Special Collections, University of Arizona, Box 125, Tucson, AZ.

20. Interviews number 1, 13, and 9, Hubbell Trading Post Ethnohistory Project.

21. McNitt, *The Indian Traders,* 46.

22. Teresa Jo Wilkins, "Producing Culture across the Colonial Divide: Navajo Reservation Trading Posts and Weaving" (Ph.D. diss., University of Colorado, 1999), iii; Laura Jane Moore, "The Navajo Rug Trade: Gender, Art, Work, and Modernity in the American Southwest, 1870s–1930s" (Ph.D. diss., University of North Carolina at Chapel Hill, 1999); Erika Marie Bsumek, "Making 'Indian-made': The Production, Consumption, and Construction of Navajo Ethnic Identity, 1880–1935" (Ph.D. diss., Rutgers University, 2000).

23. See interviews number 40, 12, and 1 for discussions of tin money, Hubbell Trading Post Ethnohistory Project.

24. Oral interview with Thomas Wheeler, June 26, 2001, at the Hogback Trading Post, in Waterflow, NM. Tape and transcript in author's possession. Tom Wheeler's family has operated the trading post for four generations.

25. Peter Iverson, *Diné: A History of the Navajos* (Albuquerque: University of New Mexico Press, 2002), 260.

26. Cited in Denis Foster Johnston, *An Analysis of Sources of Information on the Population of the Navaho*, Smithsonian Institution Bureau of American Ethnology, Bulletin 197 (Washington, DC: Government Printing Office, 1966), 36.

27. Betty J. Harris, "Ethnicity and Gender in the Global Periphery: A Comparison of Basotho and Navajo Women," *American Indian Culture and Research Journal* 14 (1990): 15–38; Florencia Mallon, "Gender and Class in the Transition to Capitalism: Household and the Mode of Production in Central Peru," *Latin American Perspectives* 13 (Winter 1986): 147–174.

28. Mallon, "Gender and Class in the Transition to Capitalism," 149.

29. John R. Farella, *The Main Stalk: A Synthesis of Navajo Philosophy* (Tucson: University of Arizona Press, 1984), 133; Maureen Trudelle Schwarz, *Molded in the Image of Changing Woman: Navajo Views on the Human Body and Personhood* (Tucson: University of Arizona Press, 1997), 93; Gary Witherspoon, *Navajo Kinship and Marriage* (Chicago: University of Chicago Press, 1975), 24.

30. For an excellent overview, see Malia B. Formes, "Beyond Complicity versus Resistance: Recent Work on Gender and European Imperialism," *Journal of Social History* 28 (1995): 629–641; Ann L. Stoler, "Making Empire Respectable: The Politics of Race and Sexual Morality in 20th-Century Colonial Cultures," *American Ethnologist* 16 (November 1989): 634–660; Karen Sacks, "State Bias and Women's Status," *American Anthropologist* 78 (September 1976): 565–569; Cherryl Walker, ed., *Women and Gender in Southern Africa to 1945* (London: J. Currey, 1990), 26.

31. Alice Kessler-Harris, *Out to Work: A History of Wage-Earning Women in the United States* (New York: Oxford University Press, 1982), 120; Jeanne Boydston, *Home and Work: Housework, Wages, and the Ideology of Labor in the Early Republic* (New York: Oxford University Press, 1994), 88–89; Linda Gordon, *Heroes of Their Own Lives: The Politics and History of Family Violence: Boston, 1880–1960* (New York: Viking, 1988), 96–97. Other important studies of industrial home workers include Christina E. Gringeri, *Getting By: Women Homeworkers and Rural Economic Development* (Lawrence: University Press of Kansas, 1994); Eileen Boris and Cynthia R. Daniels, *Homework: Historical and Contemporary Perspectives on Paid Labor at Home* (Urbana: University of Illinois Press, 1989).

32. Marsha Weisiger made this point in her insightful work, "Diné Bikéyah: Environment, Cultural Identity, and Gender in Navajo Country" (Ph.D. diss., University of Wisconsin, 2000), 97; also see Jennifer Denetdale's critique of feminist approaches to Navajo women's history, "Representing Changing Woman: A Review Essay on Navajo Women," *American Indian Culture and Research Journal* 25, Pt. 3 (2001): 1–26. For a discussion of the regional nature of Navajo gender relations, see Louise Lamphere, "Historical and Regional Variability in Navajo Women's Roles," *Journal of Anthropological Research* 45, no. 4 (1989): 453. And for the flexibility in Navajo division of labor, see Charlotte J. Frisbie, "Traditional Navajo Women: Ethnographic and Life History Por-

trayals, " *American Indian Quarterly* 6 (Spring/Summer 1982): 11–33; for a discussion of the private/public debate in feminist anthropology, see Henrietta L. Moore, *Feminism and Anthropology* (Minneapolis: University of Minnesota Press, 1988), 21–24; for a path-breaking critique of the separate spheres paradigm in women's history, see Linda K. Kerber, "Separate Spheres, Female Worlds, Woman's Place: The Rhetoric of Women's History," *Journal of American History* 75 (June 1988), 9–39.

33. Weisiger, "Diné Bikéyah," 95–96. See also Weisiger's book, *Sheep Dreams: Environment, Identity, and Gender in Navajo Country* (Seattle: University of Washington Press, forthcoming).

34. Rose Mitchell, *Tall Woman: The Life Story of Rose Mitchell, a Navajo Woman, c. 1874–1977*, ed. Charlotte Johnson Frisbie (Albuquerque: University of New Mexico Press, 2001), 296.

35. Ibid.

36. Denetdale, "Representing Changing Woman," 4; Gladys A. Reichard, "Position of Women," unpublished research notes, Gladys A. Reichard Papers, Museum of Northern Arizona, Flagstaff, 29–32.

37. For examples of male-dominated, matrilineal societies, see Beverly Grier, "Pawns, Porters, and Petty Traders: Women in the Transition to Cash Crop Agriculture in Colonial Ghana," *Signs: Journal of Women in Culture and Society* 17 (Winter 1992): 304–328; and Joan Bamberger's classic work, "The Myth of Matriarchy: Why Men Rule in Primitive Societies," in *Women, Culture, and Society*, ed. Michelle Zimbalist Rosaldo and Louise Lamphere (Stanford, CA: Stanford University Press, 1974), 263–280. There is considerable debate among anthropologists on the prevalence of matrilocal residence patterns in Navajo history. For an overview of the matrilocal and matrilineal debate, see Jerrold E. Levy, Eric Henderson, and Tracy J. Andrews, "The Effects of Regional Variation and Temporal Change on Matrilineal Elements of Navajo Social Organization," *Journal of Anthropological Research* 45, no. 4 (1989): 351; Lamphere, "Historical and Regional Variability in Navajo Women's Roles," 431–456; and Frisbie, "Traditional Navajo Women," 12.

38. Weisiger, "Diné Bikéyah," 95.

39. Hugh G. Calkins, "The Importance of Various Types of Income on the Navajo Reservation," U.S. Department of Agriculture, Soil Conservation Service, Region 8, Regional Bulletin no. 30, Conservation Economics Series no. 3, January 1935, Soil Conservation Service Records, Center for Southwest Research, Zimmerman Library, University of New Mexico, Albuquerque, A57, 16:30.

40. Karen Ritts Benally, "Thinking Good: The Teachings of Navajo Grandmothers," in *American Indian Grandmothers: Traditions and Transitions*, ed. Marjorie M. Schweitzer (Albuquerque: University of New Mexico Press, 1999), 26.

41. Oral interview with Julia John by the author, interpreted by Paul George, at Hogback Community on the Navajo Reservation, Hogback, NM, August 14, 2002. Tape and transcript in author's possession.

42. Ibid.

43. M'Closkey, *Swept under the Rug*, 84.

44. Helen Duncan, interview with the author, translated by Charlie Jones Jr., Hogback Chapter House, Hogback, NM, July 15, 2002; Julia John, interview with the author, translated by Paul George, John's home, in the Hogback Community, Navajo Reservation, August 14, 2002. In 1974, prior to its closing, Fairchild employed 922 Navajos, most of whom were women. Fairchild was one of the largest employers of Navajo labor on the reservation, second only to public sector employers, including the Bureau of Indian Affairs and the Navajo Nation. Office of Program Development, the Navajo Tribe, *The Navajo Nation: Overall Economic Development Program* (Window Rock, AZ: Navajo Nation, 1974), 24–25; Fairchild shut down its operations after American Indian Movement activists occupied the facility. The company cited the protest as the reason for closing the plant. Activists argued that the company closed down to thwart a union drive. Klara B. Kelley and Peter M. Whiteley, *Navajoland: Family Settlement and Land Use* (Tsaile, AZ: Navajo Community College Press, 1989), 143.

45. Margaret Kee, interview with the author, translated by Annita Fonseca, Navajo Nation Museum, Window Rock, AZ, June 29, 2001.

46. Rebecca Watson, interview with author, interpreted by Earl Watson, Coal Mine, AZ, on the Navajo Reservation, May 16, 1995. Tape and transcript in author's possession.

47. M'Closkey, *Swept under the Rug*, 4.

48. Kelley and Whiteley, *Navajoland*, 114. According to Kathy M'Closkey, even prior to 1928, the price of rugs had stagnated at 1902 prices, despite the fact that the cost of living for Navajos had quadrupled between 1895 and 1928. M'Closkey, *Swept under the Rug*, 249.

49. Soil Conservation Service Schedules, Areas 16–18, Combined, no. 1–49, Records of the Bureau of Indian Affairs, National Archives, Pacific Region, Record Group 75, Phoenix Area Office, Records Administration, Pacific Coast Branch, Laguna Niguel, CA, Box 1.

50. The high percentage of jewelry-making income (see Figure 3.1) is somewhat unique to this region. Silversmithing in the 1930s was concentrated around the Gallup area. Kelley and Whiteley, *Navajoland*, 114.

51. Seymour Parker, "Navaho Adjustment to Town Life: A Preliminary Report of the Navahos Residing in Farmington, 1954," 38, Leighton Papers, MS 216, Box 6, Folder 222, Special Collections, Cline Library, Northern Arizona University, Flagstaff.

52. Bailey and Bailey, *A History of the Navajos*, 250; Ruth M. Underhill, *The Navajos* (Norman: University of Oklahoma Press, 1956), 243.

53. Bailey and Bailey, *A History of the Navajos*, 260–261; Kelley and Whiteley, *Navajoland*, 223.

54. Helen Duncan, interview with the author, July 15, 2002.

55. M'Closkey, *Swept Under the Rug*, 63.

56. Kay Bennet, *Kaibah: Recollections of a Navajo Girlhood* (Los Angeles: Westernlore Press, 1964), 207.

57. Margaret Kee, interview with the author, June 29, 2001.

58. Helen Duncan, interview with the author, July 15, 2002.

59. Youngblood, "Navajo Trading," 18042.

60. D. Y. Begay, "*Shi' Sha' Hane',*" in *Woven by the Grandmothers: Nineteenth-Century Navajo Textiles from the National Museum of the American Indian,* ed. Eulalie H. Bonar (Washington, DC: Smithsonian Institution Press in association with the National Museum of the American Indian, Smithsonian Institution, 1996), 19.

61. Wesley Thomas, "*Shil Yóól T'ool:* Personification of Navajo Weaving" in *Woven by the Grandmothers: Nineteenth-Century Navajo Textiles from the National Museum of the American Indian,* ed. Eulalie H. Bonar (Washington, DC: Smithsonian Institution Press in association with the National Museum of the American Indian, Smithsonian Institution, 1996), 36.

62. Mitchell, *Tall Woman,* 65–66.

63. Ibid.

64. Bailey and Bailey, *A History of the Navajos,* 217.

65. Emma Reh, "Navajo Consumption Habits (for District 1) 1939," in *The University Museum of New Mexico State University Occasional Papers,* no. 9, ed. Terry R. Reynolds (Las Cruces: New Mexico State University, 1983), 5.

66. Interview number 16, Hubbell Trading Post Ethnohistory Project, Hubbell Trading Post National Monument Archives, Ganado, AZ.

67. Interviews number 1 and 9, Hubbell Trading Post Ethnohistory Project, Hubbell Trading Post National Monument Archives, Ganado, AZ.

68. Helen Duncan, interview with the author, July 15, 2002.

69. Margaret Kee, interview with the author, June 29, 2001.

70. Nancy Woodman, "The Story of an Orphan," in *Navajo Historical Selections,* ed. Robert Young and William Morgan (Phoenix, AZ: Phoenix Indian School Print Shop, 1954), 65.

71. Witherspoon, *Navajo Weaving,* 103.

72. Schwarz, *Molded in the Image of Changing Woman,* 111.

73. Tressa Berman, *Circle of Goods: Women, Work, and Welfare in a Reservation Community* (Albany: State University of New York Press, 2003); Witherspoon, *Navajo Weaving;* Denetdale, "Representing Changing Woman," 1–26; Sarah Hill, *Weaving New Worlds: Southeastern Cherokee Women and Their Basketry* (Chapel Hill: University of North Carolina Press, 1997); M'Closkey, *Swept under the Rug,* 205–252.

74. Tressa L. Berman, "Bringing It to the Center: Artistic Production as Economic Development among American Indian Women of Fort Berthold, North Dakota," *Research in Human Capital and Development* 10 (1996): 171–172.

75. M'Closkey, *Swept under the Rug,* 45; Bailey and Bailey, *A History of the Navajos,* 22.

76. Berman, *Circle of Goods,* 31; Kathy M'Closkey, "The Devil's in the Details: Tracing the Fingerprints of Free Trade and Its Effects on Navajo Weavers," in *Native Pathways: American Indian Culture and Development in the Twentieth Century,* ed. Brian Hosmer and Colleen O'Neill (Boulder: University Press of Colorado, 2004), 112–132.

77. Bennett, *Kaibah,* 96.

78. Wesley Thomas used the Navajo term *dah'iistł'ó* to describe a weaving. Dah'iistł'ó is a verb that describes the art of weaving; it "does not change even when the weaving is completed and removed from the loom." Thus the word embodies the process or act

of its creation. Wesley Thomas, "*Shił Yóół T'ool,* 34, 36; Gladys A. Reichard, *A Navajo Shepherd and Weaver* (New York: J. J. Augustin, 1936), 51. Although weaving was largely considered women's work, a small, yet significant number of men have been weavers since the development of the trading post economy. Johnston, *An Analysis of Sources of Information on the Population of the Navaho,* 36.

79. Witherspoon, *Navajo Weaving.*

80. Denetdale, "Representing Changing Woman," 12; Ann Lane Hedlund, "Give-And-Take: Navajo Grandmothers and the Role of Craftswomen," in *American Indian Grandmothers: Traditions and Transitions,* ed. Marjorie M. Schweitzer (Albuquerque: University of New Mexico Press, 1999).

81. Laurel Thatcher Ulrich, *A Midwife's Tale: The Life of Martha Ballard, Based on Her Diary, 1785–1812* (New York: Vintage Books, 1990); Joan M. Jensen, *Loosening the Bonds: Mid-Atlantic Farm Women, 1750–1850* (New Haven, CT: Yale University Press, 1986).

82. Hubbell Trading Post Records, Special Collections, University of Arizona, Box 45, Indians 1951–1966 and undated, Tucson, AZ.

83. Reh, "Navajo Consumption Habits (for District 1) 1939," 21.

84. "Red Lake Trading Notes," U.S. Soil Conservation Service Reports, MS 190, Box 32, folder 121.301, Rio Grande Historical Collections, New Mexico State University Library, Las Cruces. Thank you to Terry Reynolds for leading me to this source.

85. Parker, "Navaho Adjustment to Town Life: A Preliminary Report of the Navahos Residing in Farmington, 1954," 44–46.

86. Ibid.

87. Senate Committee on Indian Affairs, *Survey of Conditions of the Indians in the United States, Hearings before a Subcommittee of the Committee on Indian Affairs,* 75th Cong., 1st sess. (Washington, DC: Government Printing Office, 1937), 17479.

88. Tom T. Sasaki conducted the most comprehensive study of this community. His research was part of the larger Cornell University Southwest Project, a program that produced a number of important ethnographic works. Tom T. Sasaki, *Fruitland, New Mexico: A Navaho Community in Transition* (Ithaca, NY: Cornell University Press, 1960), 6–13.

89. Leila Shurkey's field notes, quoted in Lamphere, "Historical and Regional Variability in Navajo Women's Roles," 442.

90. Weisiger, "Diné Bikéyah," 95; Ruth Roessell, *Women in Navajo Society* (Rough Rock, AZ: Navajo Resource Center, Rough Rock Demonstration School, 1981); White, *The Roots of Dependency.*

CHAPTER 4. WORKING FOR WAGES THE NAVAJO WAY: NAVAJO HOUSEHOLDS AND OFF-RESERVATION WAGE WORK

1. Report from the Arizona State Employment Service, 1948, National Archives I, Record Group 75, Bureau of Indian Affairs, Classified Files [hereafter cited as BIACF], Navajos, box 498, file 5763-46-920, Washington, DC.

2. Clarence Kee and Margaret Kee, interview with author, interpreted by Juannita Brown, tape recording, Tuller's Cafe, St. Michaels, AZ, May 18, 1995.

3. David Aberle, *The Peyote Religion among the Navajos* (New York: Wenner Gren Foundation for Anthropological Research, 1966), 52; Richard White, *The Roots of Dependency: Subsistence, Environment, and Social Change among the Choctaws, Pawnees, and Navajos* (Lincoln: University of Nebraska Press, 1983), 310; Garrick Bailey and Roberta Glenn Bailey, *A History of the Navajos: The Reservation Years* (Santa Fe, NM: School of American Research, 1986), 182.

4. David Wallace Adams, *Education for Extinction: American Indians and the Boarding School Experience, 1875–1928* (Lawrence: University Press of Kansas, 1995), 162–163. Some schools, such as the Hampton Institute, included programs for American Indians in addition to providing "industrial" education for African Americans. Donald F. Lindsey, *Indians at the Hampton Institute, 1877–1923* (Urbana: University of Illinois Press, 1995), 19.

5. Meriam was a lead researcher from the Brookings Institution, a think tank commissioned by the Department of the Interior to conduct a review of Indian policy in the late 1920s. The resulting report, *The Problem of Indian Administration*, shaped James Collier's reform agenda in the 1930s. Lewis Meriam, *The Problem of Indian Administration* (Baltimore: Johns Hopkins Press, 1928), 14.

6. Ibid., 13.

7. Robert Trennert, *The Phoenix Indian School: Forced Assimilation in Arizona, 1891–1935* (Norman: University of Oklahoma Press, 1988), 69.

8. Meriam, *The Problem of Indian Administration*, 15.

9. Trennert, *The Phoenix Indian School*, 69.

10. Alice Littlefield, "Indian Education and the World of Work, 1893–1933," in *Native Americans and Wage Labor: Ethnohistorical Perspectives*, ed. Alice Littlefield and Martha Knack (Norman: University of Oklahoma Press, 1996), 102.

11. Bailey and Bailey, *A History of the Navajos*, 169.

12. George I. Sanchez, *"The People": A Study of the Navajo* (Lawrence, KS: U.S. Indian Service, 1948), 25.

13. Ibid.

14. Bailey and Bailey, *A History of the Navajos*, 156–157.

15. Between January 1 and April 29, 1950, 4,019 Navajo railroad workers applied for unemployment benefits. The Railroad Retirement Board paid out approximately $300,000 to those who qualified. Letter from F. H. Stapelton, regional director, Railroad Retirement Board, to Oscar L. Chapman, secretary of the interior, April 3, 1950, BIACF, Navajos, 57A-185-1948-52, box 109, file 5677-922; Stapelton to John H. Provinse, assistant commissioner of Indian affairs, November 19, 1947, BIACF, Navajos, 57A-185-1948-52, box 109, file 5677-922.

16. Minutes of Meeting to Discuss Off-Reservation Employment for Navajo and Hopi Indians, Westward Ho Hotel, Phoenix, Arizona, January 30, 1948, BIACF, Navajos, 57A 185(1948-52), box 109, file 57363 1948-920.

17. Letter from Lucy Adams to Provinse, March 25, 1948, BIACF, Navajos, 57A-185 box 109, file 57363-1948-920.

18. William Y. Adams, *Shonto: A Study of the Role of the Trader in a Modern Navaho Community*, Smithsonian Institution Bureau of American Ethnography, Bulletin 188 (Washington, DC: Government Printing Office, 1963), 51.

19. Peter Iverson, *The Navajo Nation* (Norman: University of Oklahoma Press, 1981), 51–52; Eric B. Henderson, "Navajo Livestock Wealth and the Effects of the Stock Reduction Program of the 1930s," *Journal of Anthropological Research* 45 (Winter 1989): 379–403; Eric B. Henderson, "Skilled and Unskilled Blue Collar Navajo Workers: Occupational Diversity in a Native American Tribe," *Social Science Journal* 16 (1979): 63–80.

20. Japanese Americans are a notable exception to the experience of minorities during wartime. For them, World War II did not bring about a weakening of racial and/or gender barriers in employment that many African Americans, Mexican Americans, and women of other ethnicities experienced. See Ronald T. Takaki, *Strangers from a Different Shore: A History of Asian Americans* (Boston: Little, Brown, 1989), 357–405.

21. Alison R. Bernstein, *American Indians and World War II: Toward a New Era in Indian Affairs* (Norman: University of Oklahoma Press, 1991), 74.

22. Ibid., 71.

23. The Navajo code talkers, the most notable group, were among 3,000 Navajos who saw military service in World War II. Regarded today as great war heroes, they were a select cadre of 450 Navajo men recruited by the Marines to develop and implement a communications code in Navajo for the Pacific theater. Doris A. Paul, *The Navajo Code Talkers* (Philadelphia: Dorrance and Company, 1973), 75; see Cozy Brown's account of his experience as a code talker in *Navajos and World War II*, ed. Broderick Johnson (Tsaile, AZ: Navajo Community College Press, 1977), 51–61.

24. Myrtle Waybenais, quoted in Johnson, *Navajos and World War II*, 132.

25. Minutes of the Farm Labor Advisory Committee Meeting, Arizona, BIACF, Navajos, box 109, file 57-363.

26. U.S. Department of the Interior, *Planning in Action on the Navajo-Hopi Indian Reservations: A Progress Report on the Land and Its People, the Long Range Program for Navajo-Hopi Rehabilitation as of March 31, 1952* (Window Rock, AZ: Navajo Service, 1953), 2. For a discussion of the impact of the legislation on Navajo economic and political institutions, see Iverson, *The Navajo Nation*, 47–82.

27. The ironic twist, as Iverson has noted, was that in the long run the legislation strengthened Navajo cultural and political identity and created conditions that made it possible for more people to stay on the reservation. Iverson, *The Navajo Nation*, 56. See the report that established the policy agenda for the Navajo-Hopi Rehabilitation Act, James A. Krug, *The Navajo: Report to the President by the Secretary of the Interior* (Washington, DC: Government Printing Office, 1948), x.

28. Employment Security Commission, Arizona State Employment Service, *State Information Bulletin no. 090, Supplement no. 6*, March 28, 1949, BIACF, Navajos, box 498 (916922), file 5763-46-920.

29. James M. Stewart, "The Problem of Instituting a Workable Off-Reservation Employment Program for the Navajo Indians," BIACF, Navajos, box 109, file 13590-1948-920, n.p.

30. Ibid. Apparently, Stewart was not aware that many Italian and some Asian immigrants did return home. Donna Gabaccia, *Militants and Migrants: Rural Sicilians Become American Workers* (New Brunswick, NJ: Rutgers University Press, 1988), and Suchen Chan, *Entry Denied: Exclusion and the Chinese Community in America, 1882–1943* (Philadelphia: Temple University Press, 1991).
31. Robert M. Kvasnicka and Herman J. Viola, eds., *The Commissioners of Indian Affairs, 1824–1977* (Lincoln: University of Nebraska Press, 1979), 283–292. For a detailed study of termination, see Donald Fixico, *Termination and Relocation: Federal Indian Policy, 1945–1960* (Albuquerque: University of New Mexico Press, 1986).
32. Stewart, "The Problem of Instituting a Workable Off-Reservation Employment Program for the Navajo Indians."
33. William H. Zeh, Office of Indian Affairs, "Report on the Meeting of January 30, 1948, at Phoenix Arizona with Prospective Employers of Indian Labor," BIACF, Navajos, 57A 185 (1948-52), box 109, file 57363 1948-920.
34. Minutes of the Farm Labor Advisory Committee Meeting.
35. Ibid.
36. In 1952, the BIA passed the responsibility of recruiting seasonal Navajo labor to the Railroad Retirement Board and the state employment services in Arizona, New Mexico, Colorado, and Utah. Leaving the recruiting and hiring of Navajo workers for seasonal labor to the states, the BIA focused specifically on trying to promote permanent relocation off the reservation. The Navajo Placement Office became the Navajo Agency Branch of Relocation. U.S. Department of the Interior, Bureau of Indian Affairs, *You Asked about the Navajo! Education, Health, and Economic Problems of the Navajo* (Washington, DC: Government Printing Office, 1957), 12.
37. Hugh G. Calkins, "The Importance of Various Types of Income on the Navajo Reservation," U.S. Department of Agriculture, Soil Conservation Service, Region 8, Regional Bulletin no. 30, Conservation Economics Series no. 3, January 1935, Soil Conservation Service Records, Center for Southwest Research, Zimmerman Library, University of New Mexico, Albuquerque, NM.
38. State of Colorado, Department of Employment Security, Colorado State Employment Service, "Recruitment of Navajo Indians for Colorado," BIACF, Navajos, box 498, file 5763-1946-920.
39. Minutes of Meeting to Discuss Off-Reservation Employment for Navajo and Hopi Indians, January 30, 1948.
40. Ibid.
41. Navajo Service Monthly Narrative Report, November 1948, 46, BIACF, Navajos, box 109, file 13590.
42. Ibid., 46.
43. Ibid., 37.
44. "Field Trips of Area Social Worker to Cotton Camps in Safford, Arizona below Globe (Solomon to Fort Thomas on Highway 70), November 1–2, 1950," National Archives, Pacific Region, Record Group 75, Phoenix Area Office, file 721, Laguna Niguel, CA.

45. Lucy Adams to Provinse, March 25, 1948.

46. William Y. Adams, "Early Navajo Experiences in Seasonal Wage Work" (paper delivered at the 14th Annual Navajo Studies Conference, Diné College, Tsaile, Arizona, April 2–5, 2003), 7.

47. Julia John, interview with the author, interpreted by Paul George, Hogback Community on the Navajo Reservation, Hogback, NM, August 14, 2002. Tape recording.

48. Simon J. Ortiz, *Fight Back: For the Sake of the People, for the Sake of the Land* (Albuquerque, NM: Institute for Native American Development, 1980), 54.

49. Simon Ortiz, "Starting at the Bottom," in *Woven Stone*, vol. 21 in *Sun Tracks*, ed. Larry Evers and Ofelia Zepeda (Tucson: University of Arizona Press, 1992), 298.

50. Minutes of Meeting to Discuss Off-Reservation Employment for Navajo and Hopi Indians, January 30, 1948.

51. Ibid.

52. Kitty Calavita, *Inside the State: The Bracero Program, Immigration and the I.N.S.* (New York: Routledge Books, 1992), 18–41.

53. Minutes of the Farm Labor Advisory Committee Meeting.

54. Sara Deutsch, *No Separate Refuge: Culture, Class, and Gender on an Anglo-Hispanic Frontier in the American Southwest, 1880–1940* (New York: Oxford University Press, 1987), 202–203.

55. Minutes of the Farm Labor Advisory Committee Meeting.

56. Clyde Kluckhohn and Dorothea Leighton, *The Navaho*, rev. ed. (Cambridge, MA: Harvard University Press, 1974), 77–80; Adams, *Shonto*, 69; Iverson, *The Navajo Nation*, 168–169; Meriam, *The Problem of Indian Administration*, 76.

57. Frank E. Richter, placement assistant, Phoenix Office, to Lucy Adams, memorandum for the Monthly Narrative Report, Phoenix, Arizona, January 30, 1948, BIACF, Navajos, box 109, file 13590, 1948-920.

58. Ibid.

59. Robert W. Young, "A Report on Off Reservation Employment in Utah and Colorado, Especially with References to the Railroad and Mine Work," Window Rock, August 29, 1949, 13; Phoenix, Arizona, January 30, 1948, BIACF (916-922), box 56A-588, file 5763-46-920.

60. In 1951, compilers of the progress report on the 1950 Navajo-Hopi Relocation Act noted that Navajos had settled in towns that bordered the reservation such as Gallup, Holbrook, Winslow, Flagstaff, Farmington, and Cortez. Others settled in Albuquerque, Phoenix, Salt Lake City, and Los Angeles as well as at section points along the Santa Fe railroad. U.S. Department of the Interior, *Planning In Action on the Navajo-Hopi Indian Reservations*, 33.

61. Young, "A Report on Off Reservation Employment," 13.

62. Robert W. Young, *The Navajo Yearbook of Planning in Action* (Window Rock, AZ: Navajo Agency, 1955), 76.

63. Ralph A. Luebben, "A Study of Some Off-Reservation Navaho Miners" (Ph.D. diss., Cornell University, 1955), 116. Although he was mainly concerned with how well Navajos functioned in a modern industrial workplace and was informed by the assimila-

tionist spirit of the 1950s, Luebben's accounts provide an unusual glimpse into the work life and living conditions of Navajos.

64. Clarence Kee and Margaret Kee, interview with author, May 18, 1995; George T. Barrett, "Report of a Survey of Working Conditions in Agriculture and Industry in Utah and Idaho by the Tribal Advisory Committee Conducted by the Placement Division of the Navajo Service," Phoenix, Arizona, January 30, 1948, Navajos, box 109, file 57363-1948-920.

65. Luebben, "A Study of Some Off-Reservation Navajo Miners," 169, 324.

66. Ibid., 46.

67. Ibid., 117.

68. Ibid., 139.

69. Ibid., 150.

70. Ibid., 153.

71. Ibid., 311.

72. Navajo Service Monthly Narrative Report, August 1949, 12, BIACF, Navajos, box 109, file 13590.

73. Clarence Kee and Margaret Kee, interview with author, May 18, 1995.

74. U.S. Department of the Interior, *You Asked about the Navajo!* 13.

75. U.S. Department of the Interior, *Planning in Action on the Navajo-Hopi Indian Reservations: A Progress Report on the Land and Its People. The Long Range Program for Navajo-Hopi Rehabilitation as of December 31, 1953* (Window Rock, AZ: U.S. Bureau of Indian Affairs, Navajo Agency, 1954), 42–43.

76. U.S. House of Representatives, Committee on Interior and Insular Affairs, *Indian Unemployment Survey: Part I, Questionnaire Returns* (Washington, DC: Government Printing Office, July 1963), 210.

CHAPTER 5. NAVAJO WORKERS AND WHITE MAN'S WAYS:
RACE, SOVEREIGNTY, AND ORGANIZED LABOR ON THE
NAVAJO RESERVATION

1. Kenneth White, interview with author, Fort Defiance, AZ, April 4, 2003. Tape and transcript in author's possession.

2. Letter from Charles E. Minton, executive director of the New Mexico Commission on Indian Affairs, to Paul Jones, chairman of the Navajo Tribal Council, September 15, 1958, New Mexico Commission on Indian Affairs Papers [hereafter cited as NM Indian Affairs Papers], Navajo–General, State Records Center and Archives, Santa Fe, NM. Violent racial incidents of this kind continued to occur in Farmington until as late as 1974, when a group of white teenage boys killed a number of Navajos for "fun." See M. Annette Jaimes, "American Racism: The Impact on American-Indian Identity and Survival," in *Race,* ed. Steven Gregory and Roger Sanjek (New Brunswick, NJ: Rutgers University Press, 1994), 41, and Rodney Barker, *The Broken Circle* (New York: Simon and Schuster, 1992).

3. Letter from Minton to Jones, October 28, 1957, NM Indian Affairs Papers. The event

involving Pinto and John was preceded by a series of violent racial incidents in the Farmington area. Between 1953 and 1958, the FBI and the Department of Justice had investigated the following incidents: the shooting death of Willie Ahkeah, a Navajo miner, at the hands of a white store owner in Rico, Colorado; police brutality by the Utah State Police; "unlawful shooting of Navajos" by the San Juan County sheriff; and the "unlawful dispossession on an Indian, Peshlakai Atsibi of certain land to which [he] had a clear right of occupancy and use" by the Bureau of Land Management. Local officials charged the Rico store owner with involuntary manslaughter, a misdemeanor. Mark Reno, a lawyer representing the Navajo Tribal Council, was convinced that the "prosecuting attorney was quite frank about wishing to secure an acquittal." Letter from Mark C. Reno, legal adviser to the Navajo Tribal Council, to Senator Carl T. Hayden, February 28, 1955; letter from J. Edgar Hoover to Senator Carl Hayden, March 2, 1955; letter from Warren Olney III, U.S. attorney general to Mark Reno, legal adviser to the Navajo Tribal Council, March 11, 1955; letter from Warren Olney to Douglas McKay, secretary of the interior, March 22, 1955, Carl T. Hayden Papers, FBI Files, Navajo Abuse, Box 195, file 31, Department of Archives and Manuscripts, University Libraries, Arizona State University, Tempe.

4. It is not clear if the firemen were Texans. And this quote might be read as indicative of Minton's own class perspective, since at the time of his writing, a flood of workers from Texas had migrated to Farmington to look for work in the growing extractive industries in the area, namely oil and natural gas. Letter from Minton to Jones, October 28, 1957, NM Indian Affairs Papers.

5. In a review article, Herbert Hill argued that labor historians have "failed to confront the fundamental issue: the historical development of working class identity as racial identity." Frustrated with labor historians' persistent view of race as derivative of class dynamics, Hill suggested that a better model would conceptualize race as "not a fixed entity, but rather a cluster of meanings and that the process of racialization confers racial meaning on identities, practices and institutions." Herbert Hill, "The Problem of Race in American History," *Reviews in American History* 24 (June 1996): 192. For a critique of how the "new" labor history glossed over white working-class racism, see Nell Irvin Painter, "The New Labor History and the Historical Moment," *International Journal of Politics, Culture, and Society* 2 (Spring 1989): 369. Earl Lewis's work on African American workers in Norfolk, Virginia, provided a good example of how labor historians were beginning to address the problems raised by Hill and Painter. Lewis moved beyond the shop-floor/ethnocultural dichotomy that had dominated the field. Earl Lewis, *In Their Own Interests: Race, Class, and Power in Twentieth-Century Norfolk, Virginia* (Berkeley: University of California Press, 1991), 6.

6. Charles Mattox, interview by the author, at Mattox's home in Albuquerque, NM, May 27, 1994. Tape and transcript in author's possession.

7. The National Miners' Union was the largest member of the Trade Union Unity League, a popular front organization mobilized by the Communist Party. Although the American Communist Party was involved in organizing the NMU, it is a mistake to believe

that the party controlled the direction and the politics of the union in Gallup and Madrid. Mexican members of the NMU came to those communities with a legacy of radical politics born out of their experience in the Mexican Revolution. It is likely that the American communists and the Mexican communists cooperated to organize the NMU, but as Charles Mattox said, "they didn't want the gringos to run things." Mattox, who had been a member of the Communist Party in the 1930s, left the party in the 1940s over disagreements about artistic expression. One of the issues in the strike included a complaint about management's tampering with weights used to measure the tonnage of coal the workers mined and the heavy fines levied against them for loading dirty coal (rock mixed with coal). They demanded an end to payment in scrip as well as just treatment for minorities in the assignment of work areas. Most of all, they wanted wage cuts halted and higher pay for dead work (the maintenance work that did not involve mining that management required them to perform). Charles Mattox, interview by the author, May 27, 1994. See also Harry R. Rubenstein, "Political Repression in New Mexico: The Destruction of the National Miners' Union in Gallup," in *Labor in New Mexico: Unions, Strikes, and Social History since 1881*, ed. Robert Kern (Albuquerque: University of New Mexico Press, 1983), 94–96.

8. Dead work is the labor not directly related to removing coal from the mines. It often involved a variety of maintenance duties. Rubenstein, "Political Repression in New Mexico," 96.

9. Ibid., 97.

10. Ibid., 100.

11. Ibid., 104.

12. Workers who lived in Chihuahuaita, the largely Mexican part of town, were facing mass eviction. The Gallup American Coal Company sold that land to Senator Clarence F. Vogel, and he did not want to continue collecting ground rents from the miners. Union leaders saw it as a front for the Gallup American Coal Company's efforts to remove union activists. Ibid., 107.

13. Ibid., 132–133.

14. Frank Hefferly, "Statement to the United Mine Workers Journal," April 12, 1943, United Mine Workers' Papers, Box 21/6, folder D15-1943-April-May, Historical Collection and Labor Archives, Pattee Library, Pennsylvania State University, University Park.

15. Telegram to Governor Seligman from Sub District Board, National Miners' Union, Gallup, September 11, 1933, Governor Arthur Seligman Papers, Special Reports: Labor, State Records Center and Archives, Santa Fe, NM.

16. Letter to Governor Seligman from Warren Bracewell, state inspector of mines, New Mexico, September 15, 1933, Albuquerque, Governor Arthur Seligman Papers, Special Reports: Labor, State Records Center and Archives, Santa Fe, NM.

17. Harry R. Rubenstein, "The Great Gallup Coal Strike of 1933," *New Mexico Historical Review* 52 (July 1977): 173–192.

18. Transcript of hearing held by the Coal Labor Board, January 30–31, 1934, p. 6, National Archives II, Record Group 9, National Recovery Administration Entry 25, Consolidated

Files on Industries Governed by Approved Codes, Code no. 24: Bituminous Coal, Folder: Division V, Code Authority Box 1000, College Park, MD. Thanks to Zaragosa Vargas for locating this document for me.

19. Memo to Oscar Huber from George Kaseman, Albuquerque, May 17, 1934, Albuquerque and Cerrillos Coal Company Records, Center for Southwest Research, Zimmerman Library, University of New Mexico, Albuquerque (unprocessed collection).

20. When Kaseman said "Old Mexicans," he was referring to recent migrants from Mexico. "New Mexicans" were people from the northern New Mexico villages who were often identified as Hispanos, tracing their heritage back to the original Spanish settlers.

21. Nelson Lichtenstein, *Labor's War at Home: The CIO in World War II* (New York: Cambridge University Press, 1982), 34; James P. Johnson, *The Politics of Soft Coal: The Bituminous Industry from World War I through the New Deal* (Urbana: University of Illinois Press, 1979), 171.

22. Although the company may have extended the term *Indians* to a variety of Native Americans living in the area, such as the Zuni, it is likely that "Indian work" primarily referred to jobs performed by Navajos. Gallup American Coal Company labor compilation records, January 1945, Gallup American Coal Company Records, Geological Information Center Archives, New Mexico State Bureau of Geology and Mineral Resources, New Mexico Institute of Mines and Technology, Socorro (unprocessed collection).

23. George Kaseman was obsessed with keeping track of union activities. He kept special records on labor called "X-files" and employed spies to keep him informed about the day-to-day actions of pro-union workers. See Albuquerque and Cerrillos Coal Company Records, Center for Southwest Research, Zimmerman Library, University of New Mexico, Albuquerque, folder "X" files: Labor Situation.

24. Oral interview with Tsosie Blackgoat by author, interpreted by Lawrence Oliver, at Blackgoat's home in Coal Mine, NM, on the Navajo Reservation, May 26, 1995. Tape and transcript in author's possession.

25. Klara B. Kelley, "Ethnohistory: Navajos and the Coal Mines around Gallup," in *The Gamerco Project: Flexibility as an Adaptive Response,* Report no. 071, comp. Cherie Scheick, prepared for Carbon Coal, Inc., Albuquerque, NM, September 13, 1983, 572, on file at the Navajo Nation Historic Preservation Department, Window Rock, AZ. Also see Frederick F. York and Joseph C. Winter, *Report of An Ethnographic Study and Archeological Review of Proposed Coal Lease Tracts in Northwestern New Mexico* (Albuquerque: Office of Contract Archeology, University of New Mexico, 1988), and James L. Moore, *An Archaeological Study of the Catulpa Mine, and an Ethnographic Profile of the Catulpa Canyon Navajo* (Albuquerque: Office of Contract Archaeology, University of New Mexico, 1981).

26. Kelley, "Ethnohistory," 585.

27. Union members in New Mexico and Arizona were a racially diverse group, representing various European, Euro-American, and African American ethnic groups as well as recent Mexican immigrants and Hispanos who had moved to mining and railroad towns in search of work. Unions organized railroad workers in the 1890s but excluded

extra-gang track labor from their ranks until the 1960s. Jeffrey Marcos Garcilazo, "Traqueros: Mexican Railroad Workers in the United States, 1870–1930" (Ph.D. diss., University of California, Santa Barbara, 1995). Even though Navajos seemed to offer the large commercial operations in reservation border towns an obvious source of labor, they did not occupy a significant place within that multiracial, industrial workforce in the 1950s (except briefly during World War II, after which many returned to the reservation). Mexicans, Hispanos, Anglos, and blacks got the relatively skilled and higher-paying union jobs. Unskilled, stoop labor, jobs, which up to that time were not organized, were reserved for Indians. No studies on Navajo railroad workers have been written, but it is reasonable to assume that their experience might be similar to workers from Laguna Pueblo. See Kurt M. Peters, "Watering the Flower: Laguna Pueblo and the Santa Fe Railroad, 1880–1943," in *Native Americans and Wage Labor: Ethnohistorical Perspectives,* ed. Alice Littlefield and Martha Knack (Norman: University of Oklahoma Press, 1996), 177–197. For a general historical overview of labor in New Mexico, see Robert Kern, ed., *Labor in New Mexico: Unions, Strikes, and Social History since 1881* (Albuquerque: University of New Mexico Press, 1983).

28. Lynn Robbins, *Navajo Participation in Labor Unions,* Lake Powell Research Project Bulletin (Los Angeles: University of California, Los Angeles, Institute of Geophysics and Planetary Physics, 1975), 11; also see his article "Navajo Labor and the Establishment of a Voluntary Workers Association," *Journal of Ethnic Studies* 6 (Fall 1978): 97–112. Oral interview with Tsosie Blackgoat by author, interpreted by Lawrence Oliver, at Blackgoat's home in Coal Mine, NM, on the Navajo Reservation, May 26, 1995; tape and transcript in author's possession. Klara B. Kelley, "Ethnohistory," 585; Gallup American Coal Company labor compilation records.

29. The name of the mine changed in 1937 from the Fort Defiance Mine to the Window Rock Mine. B. W. Dyer, "Inspection Report for the Window Rock Coal Mine, September 27, 1938," U.S. Bureau of Land Management, Navajo Agency, Inspection Reports, Farmington, NM. Ronald P. Maldonado, "Window Rock Coal Mine Archaeological Survey, CRMP-81-014, March 6, 1981," on file in the Navajo Nation Historic Preservation Department, Window Rock, AZ. A "Mexican" contractor named One Eye took over the operation from the "unknown Anglo" and primarily employed Mexican, Italian, and Slavic immigrants as miners. Klara B. Kelley, "Archaeological Surveys of the Blackgoat and Window Rock AML Areas, McKinley County, New Mexico (project number) NNCRMP-86-304; BIA NAO-NTM-86-315," submitted by Anthony Klesert, director, Navajo Nation Archaeology Department, prepared for Martin Begaye, director, Abandoned Mine Lands Department, October 1988, on file in the Navajo Nation Historic Preservation Department, Window Rock, AZ.

30. Oral interview with Tsosie Blackgoat by author, May 26, 1995.

31. Klara B. Kelley and Teddy James, "Window Rock Coal Mine Survey—Pittsburgh and Midway Coal Mining Company, NTM-81-116," on file in the Navajo Nation Historic Preservation Department, Window Rock, AZ.

32. Letter from John Collier, commissioner of the Office of Indian Affairs, to E. R. Fryer,

superintendent, Navajo Agency, June 29, 1936, National Archives I, Record Group 75, Bureau of Indian Affairs, Classified Files, Navajo, Box 99, File 79478-1936, Washington, DC.

33. The mine inspector reports noted the use of white miners, but local residents interviewed by anthropologists remembered primarily Mexicans working in the mine at that time. B. W. Dyer, district mining supervisor, U.S. Department of the Interior, Geological Survey, "District Mining Supervisor's Report on Navajo Indian Reservations July 24–August 1, 1935," U.S. Bureau of Land Management, Miscellaneous Coal Mines, Northern Navajo Indian Reservation, General Correspondence, Farmington, NM.

34. Ibid.

35. B. W. Dyer, "Engineer's Report on the Fort Defiance Coal Mine on the Southern Navajo Indian Reservation, May 19, 1937," U.S. Bureau of Land Management, Window Rock Coal Mine Inspection Reports, Farmington, NM.

36. Ibid.

37. Letter from E. R. Fryer to commissioner of Indian affairs, Washington, DC, December 8, 1937, U.S. Bureau of Land Management, Navajo, Tohatchi Mine Files, General Correspondence Files, Farmington, NM.

38. Ibid.

39. Ibid.

40. Letter from Frank Hefferly to John Collier, commissioner of Indian affairs, March 2, 1937, United Mine Workers' Papers, Box 21/5, folder: District 15-1937-Jan-March, Historical Collections and Labor Archives, Pattee Library, Pennsylvania State University, University Park, PA.

41. Letter from E. R. Fryer, general superintendent of the Navajo Service, to Bozo Damich, UMWA representative, May 9, 1936, United Mine Workers' Papers, Box 21/5, folder: District 15-1937-Jan-March, Historical Collections and Labor Archives, Pattee Library, Pennsylvania State University, University Park, PA.

42. Letter from John Collier to Frank Hefferly, February 15, 1937, United Mine Workers' Papers, Box 21/5, folder: District 15-1937-Jan-March, Historical Collections and Labor Archives, Pattee Library, Pennsylvania State University, University Park.

43. Collier was particularly impressed with the Paterson strike pageant organized by Mabel Dodge and John Reed to publicize the plight of the 1913 Paterson, New Jersey, textile strikers. Lawrence Kelly, *The Assault on Assimilation: John Collier and the Origins of Indian Policy Reform* (Albuquerque: University of New Mexico Press, 1983), 41–42.

44. Letter from Frank Hefferly to John Collier, March 2, 1937.

45. Hefferly mentioned that the Navajos employed at the Window Rock Mine complained about the BIA's paying them only once a month. Although Hefferly did not mention any other problems, it is likely that some Navajo workers were not happy with housing facilities. In 1935, housing conditions were so bad that mine inspectors worried that they would be unable to retain a "better class of miner." B. W. Dyer, "Engineer's Report on the Fort Defiance Coal Mine on the Southern Navajo Indian Reservation, November 1935," U.S. Bureau of Land Management, Window Rock Coal Mine Inspection reports, Farmington, NM.

46. Information on efforts to organize the El Paso Natural Gas pipeline workers is drawn largely from anthropologist Gordon F. Streib's participant observer study, "An Attempt to Unionize a Semi-Literate Navajo Group," *Human Organization* 11 (Spring 1952): 23–31.
47. Gordon Streib assigned pseudonyms to all the participants in this campaign.
48. Streib, "An Attempt to Unionize a Semi-Literate Navajo Group," 25.
49. The organizer said he could have signed up more, but he ran out of cards. Ibid., 25, 27.
50. A Nádaa, (also referred to as a squaw dance) is part of the three-day-long Enemy Way ceremony. Louise Lamphere described the purpose of the Enemy Way as "curing illness caused by a ghost, an alien or an enemy." Louise Lamphere, *To Run after Them: Cultural and Social Bases of Cooperation in a Navajo Community* (Tucson: University of Arizona Press, 1977), 160. The Nádaa is the most public part of the ceremony, attracting many onlookers who are not directly involved, either as kin or clan relatives. Kluckhohn and Leighton stressed the secondary social function of this event. They suggested that the "rite offers a chance to see and be seen. . . ." At one part of the ceremony, young, single women ask young, single men to dance. Writing in 1946, Kluckhohn and Leighton noted that this practice was once only a minor element of the Enemy Way, but "today it is the chief attraction for the great crowds that invariably attend." Clyde Kluckhohn and Dorothea Leighton, *The Navaho*, rev. ed. (Cambridge, MA: Harvard University Press, 1974), 228.
51. Tom T. Sasaki, *Fruitland, New Mexico: A Navajo Community in Transition* (Ithaca, NY: Cornell University Press, 1960), 11.
52. Streib, "An Attempt to Unionize a Semi-Literate Navajo Group," 25.
53. Ibid., 26.
54. Ibid., 28.
55. Ibid.
56. Sasaki, *Fruitland*, 24, 55; and Clyde Kluckhohn, *Navaho Witchcraft* (Cambridge, MA: Peabody Museum, 1944), 63.
57. Peter Iverson, *The Navajo Nation* (Norman: University of Oklahoma Press, 1982), 67–82.
58. Clyde Kluckhohn observed that Navajo cultural traditions functioned to discourage "agitators" in favor of "social cooperation." Kluckhohn argued that witchcraft accusations functioned to maintain social control and that Navajo values generally discouraged aggressive behavior. Kluckhohn and Leighton also claimed that in Navajo culture, "Generosity is uniformly praised and stinginess despised." They explained further that "one must keep one's temper; one must warmly and cheerfully do one's part in the system of reciprocal rights and obligations, notably those which prevail between kinfolk." Kluckhohn and Leighton, *The Navaho*, 249, 298–299.
59. For a contemporary account of traders serving as labor contractors on the Navajo Reservation, see William Y. Adams, *Shonto: A Study of the Role of the Trader in a Modern Navajo Community*, Smithsonian Institution, Bureau of American Ethnology, Bulletin 188 (Washington, DC: Government Printing Office, 1963), 130–131, 218–219.

60. The Mexican Hat processing plant is no longer operating, but its radioactive waste byproducts continue to threaten the health and safety of Navajo communities who live in the region. Peter Eichstaedt, *If You Poison Us: Uranium and Native Americans* (Santa Fe, NM: Red Crane Books, 1994), 129. For a brief history of the Mexican Hat operation, see the Energy Information Administration Web site: www.eia.doe.gov/cneaf/ nuclear/page/umtra/mexican_hat_title1.html (accessed August 14, 2004).

61. Stuart Udall was instrumental in getting the bill passed in Congress. Eichstaedt, *If You Poison Us,* 118–125. Later, President Clinton issued a formal apology to the Navajo miners, but the process of obtaining relief is often prohibitive. The Office of Navajo Uranium Miners continues to advocate for these miners and offers assistance to those who want to file claims for compensation. I did not set out to write about uranium workers' history, since at the time I was doing research, other scholars and activists were working on documenting their experience. Since their work was aimed at helping the miners gain compensation, I did not want to interfere. See, for example, Doug Brugge, Timothy Benally, Phil Harrison, and Chenoa Bah Stilwell, *Memories Come To Us in the Rain and the Wind: Oral Histories and Photographs of Navajo Uranium Miners and Their Families* (Boston: Navajo Uranium Miner Oral History and Photography Project, 2000).

62. Texas-Zinc operated the mill on reservation land leased from the Navajo Nation. The plant shipped materials that amounted to more than 5 million dollars annually to the Atomic Energy Commission's receiving station in Colorado and employed eighty-seven persons, forty-seven of whom were Navajo. "*Navajo Tribe v. N.L.R.B.,* 288 F.2d 162 (C.A.D.C)," in *Court Decisions Relating to the National Labor Relations Act, Volume XII. January 1, 1961 through February 28, 1962* (Washington, DC: National Labor Relations Board, Government Printing Office, 1968), 171; Bureau of National Affairs, *Labor Relations Reference Manual* 47 (1961): 2645–2647.

63. "Memorandum in Support of Motion of Defendants National Labor Relations Board, Its Chairman and Members, to Dismiss the Complaint or in the Alternative for Summary Judgment," in *The Navajo Tribe, et al. v. The National Labor Relations Board, et al.* [hereafter cited as *NLRB v. The Navajo Tribe,* case files], U.S. District Court for the District of Columbia, Civil Action No. 867-60, National Archives II, Record Group 25, National Labor Relations Board, Selected Taft-Hartley Case Files, Closed 1961, Case no. 27-RC-2034, Box 1208, College Park, MD.

64. "*Navajo Tribe v. N.L.R.B.,* 288 F.2d 162 (C.A.D.C)," 171.

65. Memorandum in Support of Motion of Defendants, *NLRB v. The Navajo Tribe,* case files.

66. Ibid.

67. The tribal council's use of the federal legal system to argue for sovereignty rights in an effort to establish their power outside that system, and to assert social control over its constituents, is similar to what Martin Charnock observed in Central Africa. See, for example, his discussion of marriage and sexuality. Martin Charnock, *Law, Custom, and Social Order: The Colonial Experience in Malawi and Zambia* (Cambridge: Cambridge University Press, 1985), 192–216.

68. Tribal Council Resolution CA-54-58, *Navajo Tribal Code*, vol. 3 (Oxford, NH: Publishing Corporation, 1977), 415.

69. Telegram from Joseph M. Stone, Esq., et al., attorneys for the International Hod Carriers, Building, and Common Laborers Union, and the International Operating Engineers, to Clyde Waer, NLRB regional director, July 27, 1961, *NLRB v. The Navajo Tribe*, case files.

70. Motion for Stay of Election, Texas-Zinc Minerals Corporation and United Steelworkers of America, AFL-CIO, *NLRB v. The Navajo Tribe*, case files.

71. Affidavit of Robert B. Sheets, in *The Navajo Indian Tribe, et al. vs. The National Labor Relations Board, et al., NLRB v. The Navajo Tribe*, case files.

72. Vincent F. Morreale and Robert J. Connerton, Memorandum in Opposition to Motion for a Stay Pending Determination on Appeal, *NLRB v. The Navajo Tribe*, case files.

73. Peter Iverson, *The Navajo Nation* (Westport, CT: Greenwood Press, 1981), 68–69.

74. Paul Jones, Navajo Tribal Council chairman, to Honorable John J. Rhodes, U.S. representative from the First Congressional District, Arizona, June 24, 1960, John Rhodes Collection, Department of Archives and Manuscripts, Arizona State University, box 86, folder 23.

75. Affidavit of Robert B. Sheets.

76. Memorandum in Support of Motion of Defendants, *NLRB v. The Navajo Tribe*, case files.

77. There is no direct evidence that confirms the Navajo workers' fears that the Hod Carriers would have replaced them with white workers. It is more likely that Texas-Zinc officials would fail to honor the Navajo preference clause in their lease agreement. In similar industries operating on the reservation at that time, companies initially hired a large percentage of Navajos but quickly replaced them with Anglo or Hispano workers. In industries where unions controlled hiring practices, however, unions may have substantiated Navajo workers' fears. Although the Navajo Power Plant case antedates the Texas-Zinc campaign by twelve years, it is possible that such discrimination could have occurred earlier, considering the general legacy of tense relations between Navajos and trade unions prior to 1950. Telegram from Stone to Waer, July 27, 1961; *Dine' Baa-Hani*, January 1972, p. 1; testimony of Kenneth White, in U.S. Commission on Civil Rights, *Hearing before the United States Commission on Civil Rights, Window Rock, Arizona, October 22–24, 1973*, vol. 1: *Testimony* (Washington, DC: Government Printing Office, 1973), 125–126.

78. *Navajo Times*, March 1961, p. 6, emphasis added. The *Navajo Times* was founded in 1958 by Anglos, who served as its editors throughout this period. The *Navajo Times* was the official newspaper of the Navajo Nation. Since the paper served as a mouthpiece for the Navajo Tribal Council, its editorial practices often reflected the perspective of the political faction in power. Iverson, *The Navajo Nation*, xxvi, 95.

79. Telegram from Stone to Waer, July 27, 1961; *Navajo Times*, October 25, 1961, p. 1.

80. The mayor of Blanding published an editorial in the *Blanding Outlook* on July 14, 1961,

just prior to the vote, in which he speculated that unionization would close the mill, thereby undermining the entire uranium mining–related industry around Mexican Hat.

81. Robert Bennett, "A New Era for American Indians," *AFL-CIO American Federationist* 73 (December 1966): 14–17.

82. Lynn A. Robbins, "Navajo Labor and the Establishment of a Navajo Voluntary Workers Association," *Journal of Ethnic Studies* 6 (Fall 1978): 100.

83. Robbins, *Navajo Participation in Labor Unions*, 17.

84. Iverson, *The Navajo Nation*, 173. This was not the first attempt to involve organized labor in training Navajo workers. On January 10, 1951, at a meeting in Gallup, New Mexico, representatives of organized labor, Indian Service officials, Native American leaders, apprenticeship training representatives from the federal Department of Labor, and others from the U.S. and state employment service bureaus met to work out a process to train Indians for work in various crafts. Letter from Howard A. Clements, business manager of United Association of Journeymen and Apprentices of the Plumbing Pipe Fitting Industry, Local 469, to Carl Hayden, U.S. senator from Arizona, January 22, 1951, Carl T. Hayden Papers, Indian affairs subseries, Box 140, folder 21, Department of Archives and Manuscripts, University Libraries, Arizona State University, Tempe.

85. Testimony of Thomas H. Brose, in *Hearing before the United States Commission on Civil Rights, Window Rock, Arizona, October 22–24, 1973*, vol. 1: *Testimony* (Washington, DC: Government Printing Office, 1973), 140.

86. Ibid., 125.

87. Ibid., 139.

88. U.S. Commission on Civil Rights, *Southwest Indian Report* (Washington, DC: Government Printing Office, 1973), 59.

89. Robbins drew from figures supplied by the Office of Navajo Labor Relations. He noted that this number was nearly 25 percent of the employed Navajos on the Reservation, but this figure accounted for off-reservation workers as well. Robbins, "Navajo Labor and the Establishment of a Voluntary Workers Association," 96.

90. In 1973 White became the contract compliance officer, Office of Navajo Labor Relations. Quoted in U.S. Commission on Civil Rights, *Hearing before the United States Commission on Civil Rights, Window Rock, Arizona, October 22–24, 1973*, vol. 1: *Testimony* (Washington, DC: Government Printing Office, 1973), 119.

91. Ibid., 125–126.

92. *Dine' Baa-Hani*, January 1972, 1. This paper was a mouthpiece for "Navajo power" activists in the 1970s. Garrick Bailey and Roberta Glenn Bailey, *A History of the Navajos* (Santa Fe, NM: School of American Research Press, 1986), 285.

93. *Dine' Baa-Hani*, January 1972, p. 5. Brackets in original.

94. Victor Uchendu, "Seasonal Agricultural Labor among the Navaho Indians: A Study in Socio-Economic Transition" (Ph.D. diss., Northwestern University, 1966), 173.

95. In 1952, Evon Z. Vogt reported in his field notes that the local trader "recruits for railroad and is usually waiting for them, bill in hand, when they get back." Evon Z. Vogt Field Notes, 1952, Laboratory of Anthropology, Santa Fe, NM. William Adams observed a similar role of the trader in Shonto, Arizona. Adams, *Shonto*, 217.

96. David Montgomery, *Workers' Control in America: Studies in the History of Work, Technology, and Labor Struggles* (New York: Cambridge University Press, 1979). In the struggle to control hiring, some unions, primarily in the AFL, barred African Americans and other people of color from union membership. This practice was particularly common in the Longshoreman's union and in the building trades. Joe William Trotter Jr., *Black Milwaukee: The Making of an Industrial Proletariat, 1915–45* (Urbana: University of Illinois Press, 1985), 156; Richard Boyden, "Breaking the Color Bar in Wartime Bay Area Shipyards, 1941–1942" (unpublished paper, February 1994), 7; see also the struggle against race and gender bias in hiring on the Seattle docks, *Seattle Times*, March 23, 1997, p. 1.

97. Roy Rosensweig, *Eight Hours for What We Will: Workers and Leisure in an Industrial City, 1870–1920* (New York: Cambridge University Press, 1983), 63.

98. Robbins, *Navajo Participation in Labor Unions*, 7–8.

99. *Diné Baa-Hani*, December 1972, p. 18.

100. Robbins, *Navajo Participation in Labor Unions*, 11.

101. U.S. Commission on Civil Rights, *Hearing before the United States Commission on Civil Rights, Window Rock, Arizona, October 22–24, 1973*, vol. 1: *Testimony* (Washington, DC: Government Printing Office, 1973), 119.

102. Robbins, *Navajo Participation in Labor Unions*, 8.

103. *Diné Baa-Hani*, January 1972, p. 5.

104. Kenneth White, interview with author, Fort Defiance, AZ, April 4, 2003. Tape and transcript in author's possession.

105. Ibid.

106. Peter Iverson, *Diné: A History of the Navajos* (Albuquerque: University of New Mexico Press, 2002), 238.

107. Lynn Robbins, *Navajo Participation in Labor Unions*, 10.

108. Kenneth White, interview with author, April 4, 2003.

109. I am using the term *racial formation* as defined by Michael Omni and Howard Winant: "the process by which social, economic and political forces determine the content and importance of racial categories, and by which they are in turn shaped by racial meanings." Michael Omni and Howard Winant, *Racial Formation in the United States, from the 1960s to the 1980s* (New York: Routledge and Kegan Paul, 1986), 61–62.

110. Kenneth White, interview with author, April 4, 2004.

111. Lawrence Oliver, conversation with author, July 11, 2002, Gallup, NM.

112. *Gallup Independent*, July 24, 2003.

CHAPTER 6. RETHINKING MODERNITY AND THE DISCOURSE OF
DEVELOPMENT IN AMERICAN INDIAN HISTORY: A NAVAJO EXAMPLE

1. Quoted in Broderick H. Johnson, ed., *Stories of Traditional Navajo Life and Culture, Ałk'idą́ą́' Yę́ę́k'ehgo Diné Kéédahat'íńę́ę́ Baa Nahane'* (Tsaile, Navajo Nation, AZ: Navajo Community College Press, 1977).

2. Johnson, *Stories of Traditional Navajo Life and Culture.*

3. A full discussion of modernity, including its numerous manifestations in art, litera-ture, and architecture, is beyond the scope of this book. In this chapter I am primar-ily concerned with how the social, economic, and political assumptions of the concept have shaped the underlying notions about American Indian history and the implica-tions of that thinking for federal Indian policy.

4. David Harvey, *The Condition of Postmodernity: An Enquiry into the Origins of Cultural Change* (Oxford: Blackwell, 1989), 12–13.

5. Eric R. Wolf, *Envisioning Power: Ideologies of Dominance and Crisis* (Berkeley: Uni-versity of California Press, 1999), 25–28.

6. Ibid., 25.

7. Edward W. Soja, *Postmodern Geographies: The Reassertion of Space in Critical Social Theory* (London and New York: Verso, 1989); Frederick E. Hoxie, *Parading through His-tory: The Making of the Crow Nation, 1805–1935* (New York: Cambridge University Press, 1995), 2.

8. Philip J. Deloria, *Playing Indian* (New Haven, CT: Yale University Press, 1998), 100; Ger-ald Vizenor, "Ishi Obscura," *Hastings West-Northwest Journal of Environmental Law and Policy* 7 (Spring 2001): 302. The place where "modernity" and "tradition" most dra-matically overlap is in the commodification of American Indian culture. Much has been written about the exploitive relationship between non-Indian consumers and In-dian producers, including studies that explore the impact of tourism on American In-dian cultural expressions and the creation and consumption of the colonial "exotic." Sherry L. Smith, *Reimagining Indians: Native Americans through Anglo Eyes, 1880–1940* (New York: Oxford University Press, 2000); Molly H. Mullin, *Culture in the Market-place: Gender, Art, and Value in the American Southwest* (Durham, NC: Duke Univer-sity Press, 2001); Laurie Ann Whitt, "Cultural Imperialism and the Marketing of Na-tive America", in *Contemporary Native American Cultural Issues*, ed. Duane Champagne (Walnut Creek, CA: AltaMira Press, 1999), 169–192; L. G. Moses, *Wild West Shows* (Al-buquerque: University of New Mexico Press, 1996); Erika Marie Bsumek, "Making 'Indian-made': The Production, Consumption, and Construction of Navajo Ethnic Identity, 1880–1935" (Ph.D. diss., Rutgers University, 2000).

9. David R. Roediger, *The Wages of Whiteness: Race and the Making of the American Work-ing Class* (New York: Verso, 1991).

10. Brian Hosmer and Colleen O'Neill, eds., *Native Pathways: American Indian Culture and Development in the Twentieth Century* (Boulder: University Press of Colorado, 2004).

11. David Harvey, *The Condition of Postmodernity*, 12.

12. Examples of modernization theorists who significantly shaped social science research in the postwar era include W. W. Rostow, *The Stages of Economic Growth: A Non Com-munist Manifesto* (New York: Cambridge University Press, 1960), and Talcott Parsons and Neil J. Smelser, *Economy and Society: A Study in the Integration of Economic and Social Theory* (Glencoe, IL: Free Press, 1956). For an insightful analysis of the politics of anthropology and anthropologists' involvement in development policy in the post-war era, see Thomas C. Patterson, *A Social History of Anthropology in the United States*

(New York: Berg, 2001), 105–123; for a gender analysis of modernization and dependency theories, see Catherine Scott, *Gender and Development: Rethinking Modernization and Dependency Theory* (Boulder, CO: Lynne Rienner Publishers, 1995).

13. Kathy Le Mons Walker, *Chinese Modernity and the Peasant Path: Semicolonialism in the Northern Yangzhi Delta* (Stanford, CA: Stanford University Press, 1999), 255.

14. Brian C. Hosmer, *American Indians in the Marketplace: Persistence and Innovation among the Menominees and Metlakatlans, 1870–1920* (Lawrence: University Press of Kansas, 1999), 7–9; Thomas D. Hall, "Patterns of Native American Incorporation into State Societies," in *Public Policy Impacts on American Indian Economic Development,* ed. C. Matthew Snipe (Albuquerque: Native American Studies, Institute for Native American Development, University of New Mexico, 1988), 23–38; David E. Wilkins, "Modernization, Colonialism, Dependency: How Appropriate Are These Models for Providing an Explanation of North American Indian 'Underdevelopment,'" *Ethnic and Racial Studies* 16 (July 1993): 390–419.

15. Steve Stern et al., *Confronting Historical Paradigms: Peasants, Labor, and the Capitalist World System in Africa and Latin America* (Madison: University of Wisconsin Press, 1993), 12. See also Walker, *Chinese Modernity and the Peasant Path,* 255.

16. Hosmer, *American Indians in the Marketplace,* 8.

17. Ibid. Scholars such as Robert Berkhofer and Frederick Hoxie, who have done extensive studies on the impact of federal assimilationist efforts on American Indians, have made similar points about Eurocentric notions of progress and civilization. Robert Berkhofer, *The White Man's Indian Images of the American Indian from Columbus to the Present* (New York: Knopf, 1978); Frederick Hoxie, *The Final Promise: The Campaign to Assimilate the Indians, 1880–1920* (Lincoln: University of Nebraska Press, 1984). For an overview of modernization theory and American Indians, see Wilkins, "Modernization, Colonialism, Dependency," 390–419, and Hosmer, *American Indians in the Marketplace,* 8–13.

18. Stern et al., *Confronting Historical Paradigms,* 12.

19. Andre Gunder Frank, "The Development of Underdevelopment," *Monthly Review* 18 (1966): 17–31. For an intellectual history of the dependency theory debates, see David Goodman and Michael Redclift, *From Peasant to Proletarian: Capitalist Development and Agrarian Transitions* (New York: St. Martin's Press, 1982), 24–67; for a critical appraisal of these theories for the U.S. West, see Thomas D. Hall, *Social Change in the Southwest, 1350–1880* (Lawrence: University Press of Kansas, 1989), 8–32.

20. One of the most notable uses of dependency theory in American Indian history is Richard White's *The Roots of Dependency: Subsistence, Environment, and Social Change among the Choctaws, Pawnees, and Navajos* (Lincoln: University of Nebraska Press, 1983). For policy applications, see, for example, U.S. Commission on Civil Rights, *The Navajo Nation: An American Colony* (Washington, DC: U.S. Commission on Civil Rights, 1975). Other writers who have examined how colonial models apply to Native American history include Vicki Page, "Reservation Development in the U.S.: Peripherality in the Core," in *Native American Resurgence and Renewal: A Reader and Bibliography,* ed. Robert N. Wells Jr. (Metuchen, NJ: Scarecrow Press, 1994), 354–388;

Lawrence D. Weiss, *The Development of Capitalism in the Navajo Nation: A Political-Economic History* (Minneapolis: Marxist Education Press, 1984); Cardell K. Jacobson, "Internal Colonialism and Native Americans: Indian Labor in the United States from 1871 to World War II," *Social Science Quarterly* 65 (1984): 158–171; Gary C. Anders, "Theories of Underdevelopment and the American Indian," *Journal of Economic Issues* 14 (September 1980): 681–701; Joseph Jorgensen, Richard O. Clemmer, et al., *Native Americans and Energy Development* (Cambridge, MA: Anthropology Resource Center, 1978); Joseph Jorgensen, "Indians and the Metropolis," in *The American Indian in Urban Society*, ed. Jack O. Waddell and O. Michael Wilson (Boston: Little, Brown, 1971), 66–113; Joseph Jorgensen, *Oil Age Eskimos* (Berkeley: University of California Press, 1990).

21. Functionalism dominated anthropological research on Native Americans in the 1950s and 1960s and tended to reinforce federal policy that favored the termination of Indian reservations. Anthropologists employing this paradigm generally favored Native American acculturation of dominant American values and behavior. They conducted various studies that explored Native American adaptations to urban contexts, including how they transcended cultural "obstacles" that prevented their full incorporation into non-Indian communities. Quote is from Jorgensen's critique, "Indians and the Metropolis," 84. See also Brian C. Hosmer's explanation of functionalism in his Ph.D. dissertation, "Experiments in Capitalism: Market Economics, Wage Labor, and Social Change among the Menominees and Metlakahtlans, 1860–1920" (University of Texas at Austin, 1993), 14.

22. Jorgensen, "Indians and the Metropolis," 85.

23. White, *The Roots of Dependency;* geographer Robert Allen Young made a similar case for the impact of stock reduction. He demonstrated how federal policies since the mid-nineteenth century underdeveloped the Navajo reservation. Robert Allan Young, "Regional Development and Rural Poverty in the Navajo Indian Area" (Ph.D. diss., University of Wisconsin, Madison, 1976), 46.

24. Partha Chatterjee, *Nationalist Thought and the Colonial World—A Derivative Discourse* (London: Zed Books, 1986), 30. Thank you to Kathy Le Mons Walker for leading me back to Partha Chatterjee's work.

25. William Roseberry and Jay O'Brien, *Golden Ages/Dark Ages: Reimagining the Past in Anthropology and History* (Berkeley: University of California Press, 1991), 10.

26. David Aberle, "A Plan for Navajo Economic Development" in *Toward Economic Development for Native American Communities: A Compendium of Papers Submitted to the Subcommittee on Economy in Government of the Joint Economic Committee Congress of the United States* (Washington, DC: Government Printing Office, 91st Cong., 1st sess., 1969), 237.

27. Ibid., 250.

28. Arturo Escobar, *Encountering Development: The Making and Unmaking of the Third World* (Princeton, NJ: Princeton University Press, 1995), 83.

29. Ibid.

30. For a brief description of modernization theory, see Stern et al., *Confronting Historical Paradigms,* 11.

31. Roseberry and O'Brien, *Golden Ages/Dark Ages,* 3.

32. Ward Churchill, "Introduction: Journeying toward a Debate," *in Marxism and Native Americans,* ed. Ward Churchill (Boston: South End Press, 1983), 14.

33. George Cornell, "Native American Perceptions of the Environment," in *Buried Roots and Indestructible Seeds: The Survival of American Indian Life in Story, History, and Spirit,* ed. Mark A. Lindquist and Martin Zanger (Madison: University of Wisconsin Press, 1993), 21–41; Winona LaDuke, "Natural and Synthetic and Back Again," in *Marxism and Native Americans,* ed. Ward Churchill (Boston: South End Press, 1983), i–iix; Russel Lawrence Barsh, "Contemporary Marxist Theory and Native American Reality," *American Indian Quarterly* 12 (Summer 1988): 205.

34. Stern et al., *Confronting Historical Paradigms.*

35. Steve Stern, "Feudalism, Capitalism, and the World System in the Perspective of Latin America and the Caribbean," *American Historical Review* 93 (October 1988): 829–872.

36. David Rich Lewis, "Reservation Leadership and the Progressive-Traditional Dichotomy: William Wash and the Northern Utes, 1865–1928," *Ethnohistory* 38 (Spring 1991): 141.

37. James Treat, "Intertribal Traditionalism and the Religious Roots of Red Power," in *Native American Spirituality: A Critical Reader,* ed. Lee Irwin (Lincoln: University of Nebraska Press, 2000), 270–294.

38. Contemporary American Indian activists have often framed their struggles over fishing rights, against relocation, and for the preservation of sacred landscapes in terms of "tradition." See, for example, Hopi, Lakota, and Wintu efforts to preserve sacred lands chronicled in the film by Christopher McLeod and presented by the Independent Television Service and Native American Public Telecommunications, *In the Light of Reverence* (Oley, PA: Bullfrog Films, 2001); also see Winona LaDuke, *All Our Relations: Native Struggles for Land and Life* (Cambridge, MA: South End Press, 1999), and C. D. James Paci and Lisa Krebs, "Local Knowledge as Traditional Ecological Knowledge: Definition and Ownership," in Brian Hosmer and Colleen O'Neill, eds., *Native Pathways: Economic Development and American Indian Culture in the Twentieth Century* (Boulder: University Press of Colorado, 2004), 259–280.

39. *Navajo Times,* August 4, 1960, p. 1.

40. Office of Miss Navajo Nation official Web site: http://www.missnavajo.navajo.org/history.html (accessed August 4, 2004).

41. *Navajo Times,* September 5, 1963, p. 1.

42. *The Denver Post,* September 9, 2001, p. 1.

43. Office of Miss Navajo Nation official Web site.

44. I am using Paul Rosier's term that he used to describe the Blackfeet and applying the term to describe American mass consumer culture. Paul Rosier, "Searching for Salvation and Sovereignty: Blackfeet Oil Leasing and the Reconstruction of the Tribe," in Brian Hosmer and Colleen O'Neill, *Native Pathways: American Indian Culture and Economic Development in the Twentieth Century* (Boulder: University Press of Colorado, 2004), 45.

45. Benedict Anderson, *Imagined Communities: Reflections on the Origin and Spread of Nationalism* (London: Verso, 1983); Eric Hobsbawm and Terence Ranger, eds., *The Invention of Tradition* (New York: Cambridge University Press, 1983).

46. Roseberry and O'Brien, *Golden Ages/Dark Ages*, 11.

47. Joseph R. Gusfield, "Tradition and Modernity: Misplaced Polarities in the Study of Social Change," *American Journal of Sociology* 72 (January 1967): 361.

48. Walker, *Chinese Modernity and the Peasant Path*, 4.

49. Drawing from Marx's treatment of the French peasantry in *The Eighteenth Brumaire of Louis Bonaparte*, Marxists have often portrayed peasants as conservative or backward, without revolutionary potential. But with the renewed interest in peasants kindled by the Vietnam War, Third World scholars consistently challenged that characterization. For example, see the body of literature inspired by Eric Wolf's *Peasants* (Englewood Cliffs, NJ: Prentice Hall, 1966) and his *Peasant Wars of the Twentieth Century* (New York: Harper and Row, 1969) as well as Teodor Shanin, ed., *Peasant and Peasant Societies* (New York: Basil Blackwell, 1987) and James Scott, *Domination and the Arts of Resistance: Hidden Transcripts* (New Haven, CT: Yale University Press, 1990). See, for example, Stephen Vlastos's treatment of ideology and popular culture of Japanese peasants in *Peasant Protests and Uprisings in Tokugawa Japan* (Berkeley: University of California Press, 1986), and the writings of the "subaltern group," in particular, Partha Chatterjee, "More on Modes of Power and the Peasantry," in *Selected Subaltern Studies,* ed. Ranagit Guha and Gayatri C. Spivak (New York: Oxford University Press, 1988), 351–390.

50. See Wolf, *Envisioning Power,* 1–15; Richard G. Fox and Orin Starn, *Between Resistance and Revolution: Cultural Politics and Social Protest* (New Brunswick, NJ: Rutgers University Press, 1997).

51. Florencia Mallon, *The Defense of Community in Peru's Central Highlands: Peasant Struggle and Capitalist Transformation, 1860–1940* (Princeton, NJ: Princeton University Press, 1983), xi.

52. Ibid.

53. Roseberry and O'Brien, *Golden Ages/Dark Ages,* 1.

54. Keletso Atkins, *The Moon Is Dead! Give Us Our Money! The Cultural Origins of an African Work Ethic, Natal South Africa, 1843–1900* (Portsmouth, NH: Heinemann, 1993), 78–98; Atkins's approach is reminiscent of June Nash's work on Bolivian tin miners. See June Nash, *We Eat the Mines, and the Mines Eat Us: Dependency and Exploitation in Bolivian Tin Mines* (New York: Columbia University Press, 1979).

55. Alice Littlefield and Martha Knack, eds., *Native Americans and Wage Labor: Ethnohistorical Perspectives* (Norman: University of Oklahoma Press, 1996).

BIBLIOGRAPHY

MANUSCRIPT COLLECTIONS

Abandoned Mine Reclamation Lands Reports. Navajo Nation Historic Preservation Department. Navajo Nation. Window Rock, AZ.

Albuquerque and Cerrillos Coal Company Records. Center for Southwest Research. Zimmerman Library. University of New Mexico. Albuquerque.

Dodge, Thomas H., Collection. Arizona Collection. Arizona State University. Department of Archives and Manuscripts. Tempe.

Gallup American Coal Company Records. Geological Information Center Archives, New Mexico State Bureau of Geology and Mineral Resources. New Mexico Institute of Geology and Technology. Socorro.

Hayden, Carl T., Papers. Arizona Collection. Arizona State University. Department of Archives and Manuscripts. Tempe.

Hubbell Trading Post Ethnohistory Project. Hubbell Trading Post National Monument. Ganado, AZ.

Hubbell Trading Post Records. Special Collections. University of Arizona. Tucson.

Leighton Papers. Special Collections. Cline Library. Northern Arizona University. Flagstaff.

National Archives I. Record Group 75. Bureau of Indian Affairs. Classified Files, Navajo. Washington, DC.

National Archives II. Record Group 9. National Recovery Administration Entry 25. Consolidated Files on Industries Governed by Approved Codes. College Park, MD.

National Archives II. Record Group 25. National Labor Relations Board. Selected Taft-Hartley Case Files. Closed 1961. College Park, MD.

National Archives, Pacific Region. Record Group 75. Phoenix Area Office. Laguna Niguel, CA.

National Archives, Rocky Mountain Regional Branch. Record Group 75. Navajo Service. Denver, CO.

New Mexico Commission on Indian Affairs Papers. Navajo—General. State Records Center and Archives. Santa Fe.

Reichard, Gladys A., Papers. Museum of Northern Arizona. Flagstaff.

Rhodes, John, Papers. Arizona Collection. Department of Archives and Manuscripts. Arizona State University. Tempe.

Seligman, Governor Arthur, Papers. Special Reports: Labor. State Records Center and Archives. Santa Fe, NM.

Soil Conservation Service Records. Center for Southwest Research. Zimmerman Library. University of New Mexico. Albuquerque.

United Mine Workers' Papers. Historical Collections and Labor Archives. Pattee Library. Pennsylvania State University. University Park.

U.S. Bureau of Land Management. Miscellaneous Coal Mines. Northern Navajo Indian Reservation. General Correspondence. Farmington, NM.

U.S. Bureau of Land Management. Navajo Agency. Inspection Reports. Farmington, NM.
U.S. Bureau of Land Management. Navajo, Tohatchi Mine Files. Farmington, NM.
U.S. Bureau of Land Management. Window Rock Coal Mine Inspection Reports. Farmington, NM.
U.S. Soil Conservation Service Reports. Rio Grande Historical Collections. New Mexico State University Library. Las Cruces.
Vogt, Evon Z. Field Notes. Laboratory of Anthropology. Santa Fe, NM.

ORAL INTERVIEWS CONDUCTED BY THE AUTHOR
Tapes and transcripts of all interviews conducted by the author are in the author's possession.
Blackgoat, Tsosie. Interview with author. Interpreted by Lawrence Oliver. Coal Mine, NM, on the Navajo Reservation. May 26, 1995.
Cambridge, Harris. Interview with author. Interpreted by Minnie Hamstreet and Paul George. Hogback, NM, on the Navajo Reservation. August 13, 2002.
Duncan, Helen. Interview with author. Interpreted by Charlie Jones Jr. Hogback Chapter House on the Navajo Reservation. Hogback, NM. July 15, 2002.
Harvey, Betty. Interview with author. Interpreted by Minnie Hamstreet. Hogback, NM, on the Navajo Reservation. August 15, 2002.
John, Evelyn. Interview with author. Hogback Senior Center on the Navajo Reservation. Hogback, NM. August 16, 2002.
John, Harry, and Julia John. Interview with author. Interpreted by Paul George. Hogback Community on the Navajo Reservation. Hogback, NM. August 14, 2002.
Jones, Charlie, Sr., and Juanita Jones. Interview with author. Farmington, NM. July 17, 2002.
Jones, Tom, Jr., and Alice Jones. Interview with author. Hogback Chapter House on the Navajo Reservation. Hogback, NM. August 16, 2002.
Kee, Clarence, and Margaret Kee. Interview with author. Interpreted by Juannita Brown. St. Michael's, AZ. May 18, 1995.
Kee, Margaret. Interview with author. Interpreted by Annita Fonseca. Navajo Nation Museum. Window Rock, AZ. June 29, 2001.
Mattox, Charles. Interview with author. Albuquerque, NM. May 27, 1994.
Oliver, Lawrence. Personal conversation with author. July 11, 2002. Gallup, NM.
Watson, Joe Lee, and Rebecca Watson. Interview with author. Interpreted by Earl Watson. Coal Mine, AZ, on the Navajo Reservation. May 16, 1995.
Wheeler, Thomas. Interview with author. Hogback Trading Post. Waterflow, NM. June 26, 2001.
White, Kenneth. Interview with author. Fort Defiance, AZ. April 4, 2003.
White, Lavine Bennally. Personal conversation with author. August 15, 1995. Highland Park, NJ.
Yazzie, Burton. Interview with author. Coyote Canyon, NM, on the Navajo Reservation. May 19, 1995.

ARCHAEOLOGICAL REPORTS

Kelley, Klara B. "Archaeological Surveys of the Blackgoat and Window Rock AML Areas, McKinley County, New Mexico, NNCRMP-86-304; BIA NAO-NTM-86-315." Submitted by Anthony Klesert, director, Navajo Nation Archaeology Department. Prepared for Martin Begaye, director, Abandoned Mine Lands Department. October 1988. On file at the Navajo Nation Historic Preservation Department, Window Rock, AZ.

—————. "Ethnohistory: Navajos and the Coal Mines around Gallup." In *The Gamerco Project: Flexibility as an Adaptive Response*. Report no. 071. Compiled by Cherie Scheick. Prepared for Carbon Coal, Inc., Albuquerque, New Mexico, September 13, 1983. On file at the Navajo Nation Historic Preservation Department, Window Rock, AZ.

Kelley, Klara B., and Teddy James. "Window Rock Coal Mine Survey—Pittsburgh and Midway Coal Mining Company, NTM-81-116." On file at the Navajo Nation Historic Preservation Department, Window Rock, AZ.

Maldonado, Ronald P. "Window Rock Coal Mine Archaeological Survey, CRMP-81-014, March 6, 1981." On file in the Navajo Nation Historic Preservation Department, Window Rock, AZ.

Martin, Rena. "Archaeological and Ethnographic Investigations at Four Coal Mine Areas South of Shiprock, San Juan County, New Mexico." Navajo Tribal Permit no. NTC, BIA Use Authorization no. NNCRMP 0033-1. Submitted November 12, 1986. On file at the Navajo Nation Historic Preservation Department, Window Rock, AZ.

Moore, James L. *An Archaeological Study of the Catulpa Mine and an Ethnographic Profile of the Catulpa Canyon Navajo*. Albuquerque: Office of Contract Archaeology, University of New Mexico, 1981.

York, Frederick F., and Joseph C. Winter. *Report of An Ethnographic Study and Archeological Review of Proposed Coal Lease Tracts in Northwestern New Mexico*. Albuquerque: Office of Contract Archeology, University of New Mexico, 1988.

GOVERNMENT DOCUMENTS

Aberle, David. "A Plan for Navajo Economic Development." In *Toward Economic Development for Native American Communities: A Compendium of Papers Submitted to Subcommittee on Economy in Government of the Joint Economic Congress of the United States*. Vol. 1, pt. 1. Washington, DC: Government Printing Office, 91st Cong., 1st sess., 1969.

Adams, William Y. *Shonto: A Study of the Role of the Trader in a Modern Navaho Community*. Smithsonian Institution Bureau of American Ethnography, Bulletin 188. Washington, DC: Government Printing Office, 1963.

Bureau of National Affairs. *Labor Relations Reference Manual* 47 (1961): 2645–2647.

Healing v. Jones, 373 U.S. 758 (1963).

Johnston, Denis Foster. *An Analysis of Sources of Information on the Population of the Navaho*. Smithsonian Institution Bureau of Ethnology, Bulletin 197. Washington DC: Government Printing Office, 1966.

Krug, James A. *The Navajo: Report to the President by the Secretary of the Interior.* Washington, DC: Government Printing Office, 1948.

Navajo Nation v. United States, 263 F.3d 1325, 150 Oil and Gas Rep. 28, 32 Envtl. L. Rep. 20,028. http://campus.westlaw.com/Welcome/WestlawCampus/default.wl?RS=imp1.0&VR=2. 0&SP=usu–000&FN=_top&MT=Westlaw&SV=Split (accessed August 8, 2004).

Navajo Tribal Code. Vol. 3. Oxford, NH: Publishing Corporation, 1977.

Navajo Tribal Council Resolutions, 1922–1951. Washington, DC: Department of the Interior, Office of Indian Affairs, 1952.

"*Navajo Tribe v. N.L.R.B.,* 288 F.2d 162 (C.A.D.C)." In *Court Decisions Relating to the National Labor Relations Act, Volume XII. January 1, 1961 through February 28, 1962.* Washington, DC: National Labor Relations Board, Government Printing Office, 1968.

Office of Program Development, The Navajo Tribe. *The Navajo Nation: Overall Economic Development Program.* Window Rock, AZ: Navajo Nation, 1974.

Sanchez, George I. *"The People": A Study of the Navajo.* Lawrence, KS: U.S. Indian Service, 1948.

U.S. Commission on Civil Rights. *Hearing before the United States Commission on Civil Rights, Window Rock, Arizona, October 22–24, 1973.* Vol. 1: *Testimony.* Washington, DC: Government Printing Office, 1973.

———. *The Navajo Nation: An American Colony.* Washington, DC: U.S. Commission on Civil Rights, 1975.

———. *Southwest Indian Report.* Washington, DC: Government Printing Office, 1973.

U.S. Department of the Interior. *Planning in Action on the Navajo-Hopi Indian Reservations: A Progress Report on the Land and Its People. The Long Range Program for Navajo-Hopi Rehabilitation as of March 31, 1952.* Window Rock, AZ: U.S. Bureau of Indian Affairs, Navajo Agency, 1953.

———. *Planning in Action on the Navajo-Hopi Indian Reservations: A Progress Report on the Land and Its People. The Long Range Program for Navajo-Hopi Rehabilitation as of December 31, 1953.* Report no. 3. 81st Cong. Window Rock, AZ: Navajo Service, 1954.

U.S. Department of the Interior. Bureau of Indian Affairs. *You Asked about the Navajo! Education, Health and Economic Problems of the Navajo.* Washington, DC: Government Printing Office, 1957.

U.S. House of Representatives. Committee on Interior and Insular Affairs. *Indian Unemployment Survey: Part I, Questionnaire Returns.* Washington, DC: Government Printing Office, 1963.

U.S. Senate. Subcommittee of Indian Affairs. *Survey of the Conditions of the Indians of the United States.* Washington, DC: Government Printing Office, 1937.

Writers' Program of the Works Projects Administration in the State of New Mexico. *New Mexico: A Guide to the Colorful State.* New York: Hastings House, 1940.

Youngblood, B. "Navajo Trading." In *Survey of Conditions of the Indians in the United States, part 34: Navajo Boundary and Pueblos in New Mexico.* U.S. Senate, Subcommittee of the Committee on Indian Affairs, 75th Cong., 1st sess. Washington, DC: Government Printing Office, 1937.

NEWSPAPERS
Albuquerque Journal
Blanding Outlook
Denver Post
Diné Baa-Hani
Gallup Independent
Navajo Times
Seattle Times

PUBLISHED SOURCES
Aberle, David. *The Peyote Religion among the Navajos.* New York: Wenner Gren Foundation for Anthropological Research, 1966.
Acuña, Rodolfo. *Occupied America: The Chicano's Struggle toward Liberation.* 1st ed. San Francisco: Canfield Press, 1972.
Adams, David Wallace. *Education for Extinction: American Indians and the Boarding School Experience, 1875–1928.* Lawrence: University Press of Kansas, 1995.
Adams, William Y. "The Development of San Carlos Apache Wage Labor to 1954." In *Apachean Culture, History, and Ethnology,* edited by Keith H. Basso and Morris E. Opler, 116–128. University of Arizona Anthropological Papers, no. 21. Tucson: University of Arizona Press, 1971.
Albers, Patricia. "From Legend to Land to Labor: Changing Perspectives on Native American Work." In *Native Americans and Wage Labor: Ethnohistorical Perspectives,* edited by Alice Littlefield and Martha C. Knack, 245–273. Norman: University of Oklahoma Press, 1996.
Almaguer, Tomás. "Interpreting Chicano History: The World System Approach to Nineteenth-Century California." *Review* 4 (Winter 1981): 490–525.
———. *Racial Fault Lines: The Historical Origins of White Supremacy in California.* Berkeley: University of California Press, 1994.
Anders, Gary C. "Theories of Underdevelopment and the American Indian." *Journal of Economic Issues* 14 (September 1980): 681–701.
Anderson, Benedict. *Imagined Communities: Reflections on the Origin and Spread of Nationalism.* London: Verso, 1991.
Atkins, Keletso. *The Moon Is Dead! Give Us Our Money! The Cultural Origins of an African Work Ethic, Natal, South Africa, 1843–1900.* Portsmouth, NH: Heinemann, 1993.
Bailey, Garrick, and Roberta Glenn Bailey. *A History of the Navajos: The Reservation Years.* 1st ed. Santa Fe, NM: School of American Research Press, 1986; distributed by the University of Washington Press.
Bamberger, Joan. "The Myth of Matriarchy: Why Men Rule in Primitive Societies." In *Women, Culture, and Society,* edited by Michelle Zimbalist Rosaldo and Louise Lamphere, 263–280. Stanford, CA: Stanford University Press, 1974.

Barker, Rodney. *The Broken Circle.* New York: Simon and Schuster, 1992.

Barsh, Russel Lawrence. "Contemporary Marxist Theory and Native American Reality." *American Indian Quarterly* 12 (Summer 1988): 187–211.

Bee, Robert, and Ronald Gingerich. "Colonialism, Classes, and Ethnic Identity: Native Americans and the National Political Economy." *Studies in Comparative International Development* 12 (1977): 70–93.

Begay, D. Y. "*Shi' Sha' Hane'.*" In *Woven by the Grandmothers: Nineteenth-Century Navajo Textiles from the National Museum of the American Indian,* edited by Eulalie H. Bonar, 13–27. Washington, DC: Smithsonian Institution Press in association with the National Museum of the American Indian, Smithsonian Institution, 1996.

Benally, Karen Ritts. "Thinking Good: The Teachings of Navajo Grandmothers." In *American Indian Grandmothers: Traditions and Transitions,* edited by Marjorie M. Schweitzer, 25–52. Albuquerque: University of New Mexico Press, 1999.

Benedek, Emily. *The Wind Won't Know Me: A History of the Navajo-Hopi Land Dispute.* New York: Alfred A. Knopf, 1992.

Bennet, Kay. *Kaibah: Recollections of a Navajo Girlhood.* Los Angeles: Westernlore Press, 1964.

Bennett, Robert. "A New Era for American Indians." *AFL-CIO American Federationist* 73 (December 1966): 14–17.

Berger, Thomas R. *Village Journey: The Report of the Alaska Native Review Commission.* New York: Hill and Wang, 1985.

Berkhofer, Robert. *The White Man's Indian: Images of the American Indian from Columbus to the Present.* New York: Knopf, 1978.

Berman, Tressa L. "Bringing It to the Center: Artistic Production as Economic Development among American Indian Women of Fort Berthold, North Dakota." *Research in Human Capital and Development* 10 (1996): 171–189.

———. *Circle of Goods: Women, Work, and Welfare in a Reservation Community.* Albany: State University of New York Press, 2003.

Bernstein, Alison R. *American Indians and World War II: Toward a New Era in Indian Affairs.* Norman: University of Oklahoma Press, 1991.

Biolsi, Thomas. *Organizing the Lakota: The Political Economy of the New Deal on the Pine Ridge and Rosebud Reservations.* Tucson: University of Arizona Press, 1993.

Biolsi, Thomas, and Larry J. Zimmerman, eds. *Indians and Anthropologists: Vine Deloria, Jr., and the Critique of Anthropology.* Tucson: University of Arizona Press, 1997.

Blanchard, Kendall A. *The Economics of Sainthood: Religious Change among the Rimrock Navajos.* Rutherford, NJ: Fairleigh Dickinson University Press, 1977.

Blue, Martha. *Indian Trader: The Life and Times of J. L. Hubbell.* Walnut, CA: Kiva, 2000.

Blueeyes, George. "Sacred Mountains." In *Between Sacred Mountains: Navajo Stories and Lessons from the Land,* compiled and edited by Rock Point Community School, vol. 11 of *Sun Tracks,* edited by Larry Evers, 2–3. Tucson: University of Arizona Press, 1982.

Boris, Eileen, and Cynthia R. Daniels. *Homework: Historical and Contemporary Perspectives on Paid Labor at Home.* Urbana: University of Illinois Press, 1989.

Boxberger, Daniel L. "In and Out of the Labor Force: The Lummi Indians and the Development of the Commercial Salmon Fishery of North Puget Sound, 1880–1900." *Ethnohistory* 35 (1988): 161–190.

Boyce, George A. *When Navajos Had Too Many Sheep: The 1940's*. Albuquerque, NM: Indian Historical Press, Menaul Historical Library of the Southwest, 1974.

Boydston, Jeanne. *Home and Work: Housework, Wages, and the Ideology of Labor in the Early Republic*. New York: Oxford University Press, 1994.

Brenner, Robert. "Agrarian Class Structure and Economic Development in Pre-Industrial Europe." In *The Brenner Debate: Agrarian Class Structure and Economic Development in Pre-Industrial Europe*, edited by T. H. Aston and C. H. E. Philpin, 10–63. New York: Cambridge University Press, 1985.

———. "The Origins of Capitalist Development: A Critique of Neo-Smithian Marxism." *New Left Review* 104 (July–August 1977): 25–92.

Brugge, David M. *The Navajo-Hopi Land Dispute: An American Tragedy*. Albuquerque: University of New Mexico Press, 1994.

———. "Navajo Land Usage: A Study in Progressive Diversification." In *Indian and Spanish American Adjustments to Arid and Semiarid Environments*, edited by C. S. Knowlton, 16–26. Contribution no. 7. Lubbock: Committee on Desert and Arid Zone Research, Texas Technological College, 1965.

Brugge, Doug, Timothy Benally, Phil Harrison, and Chenoa Bah Stilwell. *Memories Come to Us in the Rain and the Wind: Oral Histories and Photographs of Navajo Uranium Miners and Their Families*. Boston: Navajo Uranium Miner Oral History and Photography Project, 2000.

Brugge, Doug, Timothy Benally, and Esther Yazzie-Lewis. "Uranium Mining on Navajo Indian Land." *Cultural Survival Quarterly* 25, no. 1 (2001): 18–21.

Bryant, Ken L., Jr. *History of the Atchison, Topeka, and Santa Fe Railway*. New York: Macmillan, 1974.

Calavita, Kitty. *Inside the State: The Bracero Program, Immigration, and the I.N.S.* New York: Routledge Books, 1992.

Camacho, David E. *Environmental Injustices, Political Struggles: Race, Class, and the Environment*. Durham, NC: Duke University Press, 1998.

Campbell, Robert B. "Newlands, Old Lands: Native American Labor, Agrarian Ideology, and the Progressive-Era State in the Making of the Newlands Reclamation Project, 1902–1926." *Pacific Historical Review* 71 (May 2002): 203–238.

Chamberlain, Kathleen. *Under Sacred Ground, a History of Navajo Oil*. Albuquerque: University of New Mexico Press, 2000.

Chan, Suchen. *Entry Denied: Exclusion and the Chinese Community in America, 1882–1943*. Philadelphia: Temple University Press, 1991.

Charnock, Martin. *Law, Custom and Social Order: The Colonial Experience in Malawi and Zambia*. Cambridge: Cambridge University Press, 1985.

Chatterjee, Partha. "More on Modes of Power and the Peasantry." In *Selected Subaltern Studies*, edited by Ranagit Guha and Gayatri C. Spivak, 351–390. New York: Oxford University Press, 1988.

————. *Nationalist Thought and the Colonial World—A Derivative Discourse.* London: Zed Books, 1986.

Churchill, Ward. "Introduction: Journeying toward a Debate." In *Marxism and Native Americans,* edited by Ward Churchill, 1–18. Boston: South End Press, 1983.

Churchill, Ward, and Winona LaDuke. "Native North America: The Political Economy of Radioactive Colonization." In *The State of Native America: Genocide, Colonization and Resistance,* edited by M. Annette Jaimes, 241–266. Boston: South End Press, 1992.

Cooper, Frederick, Allen Isaacman, Florencia Mallon, William Roseberry, and Steve J. Stern, eds. *Confronting Historical Paradigms: Peasants, Labor, and the Capitalist World System in Africa and Latin America.* Madison: University of Wisconsin Press, 1993.

Cornell, George. "Native American Perceptions of the Environment." In *Buried Roots and Indestructible Seeds: The Survival of American Indian Life in Story, History, and Spirit,* edited by Mark A. Lindquist and Martin Zanger, 21–41. Madison: University of Wisconsin Press, 1993.

Cronon, William. *Changes in the Land: Indians, Colonists, and the Ecology of New England.* New York: Hill and Wang, 1983.

Dawson, Susan E. "Navajo Uranium Workers and the Effects of Occupational Illnesses." *Human Organization: Journal of the Society for Applied Anthropology* 51 (Winter 1992): 389–397.

De León, Arnoldo. *The Tejano Community, 1836–1900.* Albuquerque: University of New Mexico Press, 1982.

Deloria, Philip J. *Indians in Unexpected Places.* Lawrence: University Press of Kansas, 2004.

————. *Playing Indian.* New Haven, CT: Yale University Press, 1998.

Denetdale, Jennifer. "Representing Changing Woman: A Review Essay on Navajo Women." *American Indian Culture and Research Journal* 25, no. 3 (2001): 1–26.

Deutsch, Sara. *No Separate Refuge: Culture, Class, and Gender on an Anglo-Hispanic Frontier in the American Southwest, 1880–1940.* New York: Oxford University Press, 1987.

Diné of the Eastern Region of the Navajo Reservation. *Oral History Stories of the Long Walk, Hwéeldi Baa Hané.* Compiled and edited by title VII Bilingual Staff. Crownpoint, NM: Lake Valley Navajo School, 1991.

Dubofsky, Melvyn. "The Origins of Western Working Class Radicalism, 1890–1905." *Labor History* 7 (Spring 1966): 131–154.

Eichstaedt, Peter. *If You Poison Us: Uranium and Native Americans.* Santa Fe, NM: Red Crane Books, 1994.

Escobar, Arturo. *Encountering Development: The Making and Unmaking of the Third World.* Princeton, NJ: Princeton University Press, 1995.

Farella, John R. *The Main Stalk: A Synthesis of Navajo Philosophy.* Tucson: University of Arizona Press, 1984.

Fixico, Donald. *Termination and Relocation: Federal Indian Policy, 1945–1960.* Albuquerque: University of New Mexico Press, 1986.

Foley, Neil. *The White Scourge: Mexicans, Blacks, and Poor Whites in Texas Cotton Culture.* Berkeley: University of California Press, 1997.

Formes, Malia B. "Beyond Complicity versus Resistance: Recent Work on Gender and European Imperialism." *Journal of Social History* 28 (1995): 629–641.

Fox, Richard G., and Orin Starn. *Between Resistance and Revolution: Cultural Politics and Social Protest.* New Brunswick, NJ: Rutgers University Press, 1997.

Frisbie, Charlotte J. "Traditional Navajo Women: Ethnographic and Life History Portrayals." *American Indian Quarterly* 6 (Spring/Summer 1982): 11–33.

Gabaccia, Donna. *Militants and Migrants: Rural Sicilians Become American Workers.* New Brunswick, NJ: Rutgers University Press, 1988.

García, Mario T. "Americans All: The Mexican American Generation and the Politics of Wartime Los Angeles, 1941–45." In *The Mexican American Experience: An Interdisciplinary Anthology,* edited by Rodolfo O. de la Garza et al., 201–212. Austin: University of Texas Press, 1985.

———. *Mexican Americans: Leadership, Ideology, and Identity.* New Haven, CT: Yale University Press, 1989.

García, Matt. *A World of Its Own: Race, Labor, and Citrus in the Making of Greater Los Angeles, 1900–1970.* Chapel Hill: University of North Carolina Press, 2001.

Gilbreath, Kent. *Red Capitalism: An Analysis of the Navajo Economy.* Norman: University of Oklahoma Press, 1973.

Glen, Evelyn Nakano. *Unequal Freedom: How Race and Gender Shaped American Citizenship and Labor.* Cambridge, MA: Harvard University Press, 2002.

González, Deena. *Refusing the Favor: The Spanish-Mexican Women of Santa Fe, 1820–1880.* New York: Oxford University Press, 1999.

Goodman, David, and Michael Redclift. *From Peasant to Proletarian: Capitalist Development and Agrarian Transitions.* New York: St. Martin's Press, 1982.

Goodman, James M. *The Navajo Atlas: Environments, Resources, People and History of the Diné Bikéyah.* Norman: University of Oklahoma Press, 1982.

Gordon, Linda. *Heroes of Their Own Lives: The Politics and History of Family Violence: Boston, 1880–1960.* New York: Viking Press, 1988.

Grier, Beverly. "Pawns, Porters, and Petty Traders: Women in the Transition to Cash Crop Agriculture in Colonial Ghana." *Signs: Journal of Women in Culture and Society* 17 (Winter 1992): 304–328.

Grinde, Donald A., and Bruce Johnson. *Ecocide of Native America: Environmental Destruction of Indian Lands and Peoples.* Santa Fe, NM: Clear Light Publishers, 1995.

Gringeri, Christina E. *Getting By: Women Homeworkers and Rural Economic Development.* Lawrence: University Press of Kansas, 1994.

Gusfield, Joseph R. "Tradition and Modernity: Misplaced Polarities in the Study of Social Change." *American Journal of Sociology* 72 (January 1967): 361.

Gutierrez, David. *Walls and Mirrors: Mexican Americans, Mexican Immigrants, and the Politics of Ethnicity.* Berkeley: University of California Press, 1995.

Gutiérrez, Ramón A. *When Jesus Came, the Corn Mothers Went Away.* Stanford, CA: Stanford University Press, 1991.

Gutman, Herbert. *Work, Culture, and Society in Industrializing America.* New York: Vintage Books, 1976.

Hall, Thomas D. "Patterns of Native American Incorporation into State Societies." In *Public Policy Impacts on American Indian Economic Development,* edited by C. Matthew

Snipp, 23–38. Albuquerque: Native American Studies, Institute for Native American Development, University of New Mexico, 1988.

———. *Social Change in the Southwest, 1350–1880.* Lawrence: University Press of Kansas, 1989.

Harmon, Alexandra. *Indians in the Making: Ethnic Relations and Indian Identities around Puget Sound.* Berkeley: University of California Press, 1998.

Harris, Betty J. "Ethnicity and Gender in the Global Periphery: A Comparison of Basotho and Navajo Women." *American Indian Culture and Research Journal* 14 (1990): 15–38.

Harvey, David. *The Condition of Postmodernity: An Enquiry into the Origins of Cultural Change.* Oxford: Blackwell, 1989.

Hedlund, Ann Lane. "Give-And-Take: Navajo Grandmothers and the Role of Craftswomen." In *American Indian Grandmothers: Traditions and Transitions,* edited by Marjorie M. Schweitzer, 53–78. Albuquerque: University of New Mexico Press, 1999.

———. "'More of Survival than an Art,' Comparing Late-Nineteenth and Late-Twentieth-Century Lifeways and Weaving." In *Woven by the Grandmothers: Nineteenth-Century Navajo Textiles from the National Museum of the American Indian,* edited by Eulalie H. Bonar and National Museum of the American Indian, 47–68. Washington, DC: Smithsonian Institution Press in association with the National Museum of the American Indian, Smithsonian Institution, 1996.

Henderson, Eric B. "Navajo Livestock Wealth and the Effects of the Stock Reduction Program of the 1930s." *Journal of Anthropological Research* 45 (Winter 1989): 379–403.

———. "Skilled and Unskilled Blue Collar Navajo Workers: Occupational Diversity in a Native American Tribe." *Social Science Journal* 16 (1979): 63–80.

Henderson, Eric B., and Jerrold E. Levy. *Survey of Navajo Community Studies, 1936–1974.* Lake Powell Research Bulletin, no. 6. Los Angeles: University of California, Los Angeles, Institute of Geophysics and Planetary Physics, 1975.

Hill, Herbert. "The Problem of Race in American History." *Reviews in American History* 24 (June 1996): 189–208.

Hill, Sarah H. *Weaving New Worlds: Southeastern Cherokee Women and Their Basketry.* Chapel Hill: University of North Carolina Press, 1997.

Hill, Willard Williams. *The Agricultural and Hunting Methods of the Navajo Indians.* Yale University Publications in Anthropology, no. 18. New Haven, CT: Department of Anthropology, Yale University, 1938.

Hobsbawm, Eric, and Terence Ranger. *The Invention of Tradition.* New York: Cambridge University Press, 1983.

Hosmer, Brian C. *American Indians in the Marketplace: Persistence and Innovation among the Menominees and Metlakatlans, 1870–1920.* Lawrence: University Press of Kansas, 1999.

Hosmer, Brian, and Colleen O'Neill, eds. *Native Pathways: American Indian Culture and Economic Development in the Twentieth Century.* Boulder: University Press of Colorado, 2004.

Hoxie, Frederick. *The Final Promise: The Campaign to Assimilate the Indians, 1880–1920.* Lincoln: University of Nebraska Press, 1984.

————. *Parading through History: The Making of the Crow Nation, 1805–1935.* New York: Cambridge University Press, 1995.

Hurtado, Albert. "Hardly a Farmhouse or a Kitchen without Them: Indian and White Households on the California Borderland Frontier, 1860." *Western Historical Quarterly* 13 (1982): 245–270.

Iverson, Peter. *Diné: A History of the Navajos.* Albuquerque: University of New Mexico Press, 2002.

————. *The Navajo Nation.* Norman: University of Oklahoma Press, 1982.

Iverson, Peter, and Monty Roessel, eds. *"For Our Navajo People": Diné Letters, Speeches, and Petitions, 1900–1960.* Albuquerque: University of New Mexico Press, 2002.

Jacobson, Cardell K. "Internal Colonialism and Native Americans: Indian Labor in the United States from 1871 to World War II." *Social Science Quarterly* 65 (1984): 158–171.

Jaimes, M. Annette. "American Racism: The Impact on American-Indian Identity and Survival." In *Race,* edited by Steven Gregory and Roger Sanjek, 41–61. New Brunswick, NJ: Rutgers University Press, 1994.

James, George Wharton. *Indian Blankets and Their Makers.* 1914. Reprint, New York: Dover, 1974.

Jensen, Joan, and Darlis Miller. *New Mexico Women: Intercultural Perspectives.* Albuquerque: University of New Mexico Press, 1986.

Jensen, Joan M. *Loosening the Bonds: Mid-Atlantic Farm Women, 1750–1850.* New Haven, CT: Yale University Press, 1986.

Joe, Jennie R., and Dorothy Lonewolf Miller. "The Dilemma of Navajo Industrial Workers." *Nature, Society, and Thought: A Journal of Dialectical and Historical Materialism* 4 (1991): 303–330.

Johnson, Broderick, ed. *Navajos and World War II.* Tsaile, AZ: Navajo Community College Press, 1977.

————. *Stories of Traditional Navajo Life and Culture, Alk'idą́ą́' Yę́ę́k'ehgo Diné Kééda- hat'íńę́ Baa Nahane'.* Tsaile, AZ: Navajo Community College Press, 1977.

Johnson, James P. *The Politics of Soft Coal: The Bituminous Industry from World War I through the New Deal.* Urbana: University of Illinois Press, 1979.

Johnson, Susan Lee. *Roaring Camp: The Social World of the California Gold Rush.* New York: W. W. Norton, 2000.

Jorgensen, Joseph. "Indians and the Metropolis." In *The American Indian in Urban Society,* edited by Jack O. Waddell and O. Michael Wilson, 66–113. Boston: Little, Brown and Company, 1971.

————. *Oil Age Eskimos.* Berkeley: University of California Press, 1990.

Jorgensen, Joseph, Richard O. Clemmer, et al. *Native Americans and Energy Development.* Cambridge, MA: Anthropology Resource Center, 1978.

Kammer, Jerry. *The Second Long Walk: The Navajo-Hopi Land Dispute.* Albuquerque: University of New Mexico Press, 1980.

Kelley, Klara B. *Navajo Land Use: An Ethnoarchaeological Study.* Orlando, FL: Academic Press, 1983.

Kelley, Klara B., and Peter Whitely. *Navajoland: Family Settlement and Land Use.* Tsaile, AZ: Navajo Community College Press, 1989.

Kelley, Klara B., and Harris Francis. *Navajo Sacred Places.* Bloomington: Indiana University Press, 1994.

Kelly, Lawrence C. *The Assault on Assimilation: John Collier and the Origins of Indian Policy Reform.* Albuquerque: University of New Mexico Press, 1983.

———. *The Navajo Indians and Federal Indian Policy, 1900–1935.* Tucson: University of Arizona Press, 1968.

Kerber, Linda K. "Separate Spheres, Female Worlds, Woman's Place: The Rhetoric of Women's History." *Journal of American History* 75 (June 1988): 9–39.

Kern, Robert, ed. *Labor in New Mexico: Unions, Strikes, and Social History since 1881.* Albuquerque: University of New Mexico Press, 1983.

Kessler-Harris, Alice. *Out to Work: A History of Wage-Earning Women in the United States.* New York: Oxford University Press, 1982.

———. "Treating the Male as 'Other': Redefining the Parameters of Labor History." *Labor History* 34 (Spring/Summer 1993): 190–204.

Klein, Laura F., and Lillian A. Ackerman. *Women and Power in Native North America.* Norman: University of Oklahoma Press, 1995.

Kluckhohn, Clyde. *Navaho Witchcraft.* Cambridge, MA: Peabody Museum, 1944.

———. "The Philosophy of the Navajo Indians." In *Ideological Differences and World Order,* edited by F. S. C. Northrop, 356–384. New Haven, CT: Yale University Press, 1949.

Kluckhohn, Clyde, and Dorothea Leighton. *The Navaho.* Rev. ed. Cambridge, MA: Harvard University Press, 1974.

———. *The Navajo.* Cambridge, MA: Harvard University Press, 1946.

Knight, Rolf. *Indians at Work: An Informal History of Native American Labour in British Columbia, 1858–1930.* Vancouver, BC: New Star Books, 1978.

Kvasnicka, Robert M., and Herman J. Viola, eds. *The Commissioners of Indian Affairs, 1824–1977.* Lincoln: University of Nebraska Press, 1979.

LaDuke, Winona. *All Our Relations: Native Struggles for Land and Life.* Cambridge, MA: South End Press, 1999.

———. "Natural and Synthetic and Back Again." In *Marxism and Native Americans,* edited by Ward Churchill, i–iix. Boston: South End Press, 1983.

Lamphere, Louise. "Historical and Regional Variability in Navajo Women's Roles." *Journal of Anthropological Research* 45, no. 4 (1989): 431–456.

———. *To Run after Them: Cultural and Social Bases of Cooperation in a Navajo Community.* Tucson: University of Arizona Press, 1977.

Leacock, Eleanor, and Mona Etienne, eds. *Women and Colonization: Anthropological Perspectives.* New York: Praeger, 1980.

Levy, Jerrold E., Eric Henderson, and Tracy J. Andrews. "The Effects of Regional Variation and Temporal Change on Matrilineal Elements of Navajo Social Organization." *Journal of Anthropological Research* 45, no. 4 (1989): 351–377.

Lewis, David Rich. "Reservation Leadership and the Progressive-Traditional Dichotomy: William Wash and the Northern Utes, 1865–1928." *Ethnohistory* 38 (Spring 1991): 124–148.

Lewis, Earl. *In Their Own Interests: Race, Class, and Power in Twentieth-Century Norfolk, Virginia.* Berkeley: University of California Press, 1991.

Lichtenstein, Nelson. *Labor's War at Home: The CIO in World War II.* New York: Cambridge University Press, 1982.

Limerick, Patricia Nelson. *The Legacy of Conquest: The Unbroken Past of the American West.* New York: W. W. Norton, 1987.

———. "What on Earth Is the New Western History?" In *Trails: Toward A New Western History,* edited by Patricia Nelson Limerick, Clyde A. Milner II, and Charles E. Rankin, 81–88. Lawrence: University Press of Kansas, 1991.

Lindsey, Donald F. *Indians at the Hampton Institute, 1877–1923.* Urbana: University of Illinois Press, 1995.

Littlefield, Alice. "Indian Education and the World of Work, 1893–1933." In *Native Americans and Wage Labor: Ethnohistorical Perspectives,* edited by Alice Littlefield and Martha Knack, 100–121. Norman: University of Oklahoma Press, 1996.

Littlefield, Alice, and Martha Knack, eds. *Native Americans and Wage Labor: Ethnohistorical Perspectives.* Norman: University of Oklahoma Press, 1996.

M'Closkey, Kathy. "The Devil's in the Details: Tracing the Fingerprints of Free Trade and Its Effects on Navajo Weavers." In *Native Pathways: American Indian Culture and Economic Development in the Twentieth Century,* edited by Brian Hosmer and Colleen O'Neill, 112–132. Boulder: University Press of Colorado, 2004.

———. *Swept under the Rug: A Hidden History of Navajo Weaving.* Albuquerque: University of New Mexico Press, 2002.

Mallon, Florencia. *The Defense of Community in Peru's Central Highlands: Peasant Struggle and Capitalist Transformation, 1860–1940.* Princeton, NJ: Princeton University Press, 1983.

———. "Gender and Class in the Transition to Capitalism: Household and the Mode of Production in Central Peru." *Latin American Perspectives* 13 (Winter 1986): 147–174.

Marx, Karl. *The Eighteenth Brumaire of Louis Bonaparte.* New York: International Publishers, 1969.

McDonald, Peter, and Ted Schwarz. *The Last Warrior: Peter McDonald and the Navajo Nation.* New York: Orion Books, 1993.

McNitt, Frank. *The Indian Traders.* 1st ed. Norman: University of Oklahoma Press, 1962.

McPherson, Robert. *Sacred Lands, Sacred View.* Salt Lake City, UT: Signature Books and Charles Redd Center for Western Studies, Brigham Young University, 1992.

Meriam, Lewis. *The Problem of Indian Administration.* Baltimore: Johns Hopkins Press, 1928.

Meyer, Melissa L. *The White Earth Tragedy: Ethnicity and Dispossession at a Minnesota Anishinaabe Reservation, 1889–1920.* Lincoln: University of Nebraska Press, 1994.

Mitchell, Joseph. "Mohawks in High Steel." In *Apologies to the Iroquois,* edited by Edmund Wilson, 1–36. New York: Farrar, Straus and Cudahy, 1959.

Mitchell, Rose. *Tall Woman: The Life Story of Rose Mitchell, a Navajo Woman, c. 1874–1977,* edited by Charlotte Johnson Frisbie. Albuquerque: University of New Mexico Press, 2001.

Momaday, N. Scott. "Foreword." In *Between Sacred Mountains: Navajo Stories and Lessons from the Land*, compiled and edited by Rock Point Community School, vol. 11 of *Sun Tracks*, edited by Larry Evers, vii–viii. Tucson: University of Arizona Press, 1982.

Montejano, David. *Anglos and Mexicans in the Making of Texas, 1836–1986*. Austin: University of Texas Press, 1987.

———. "Is Texas Bigger than the World System?: A Critique from a Provincial Point of View." *Review* 4 (Winter 1981): 561–606.

Montgomery, David. *The Fall of the House of Labor*. New York: Cambridge University Press, 1987.

———. *Workers' Control in America: Studies in the History of Work, Technology, and Labor Struggles*. New York: Cambridge University Press, 1979.

Moore, Henrietta L. *Feminism and Anthropology*. Minneapolis: University of Minnesota Press, 1988.

Moore, John H. "Cheyenne Work in the History of U.S. Capitalism." In *Native Americans and Wage Labor: Ethnohistorical Perspectives*, edited by Alice Littlefield and Martha C. Knack, 122–143. Norman: University of Oklahoma Press, 1996.

Morris, Irvin. *From the Glittering World: A Navajo Story*. Norman: University of Oklahoma Press, 1997.

Moses, L. G. *Wild West Shows*. Albuquerque: University of New Mexico Press, 1996.

Mullin, Molly H. *Culture in the Marketplace: Gender, Art, and Value in the American Southwest*. Durham, NC: Duke University Press, 2001.

Nash, June. *We Eat the Mines, and the Mines Eat Us: Dependency and Exploitation in Bolivian Tin Mines*. New York: Columbia University Press, 1979.

Nickelson, Howard B. *One Hundred Years of Coal Mining in the San Juan Basin, New Mexico*. New Mexico Bureau of Mines and Mineral Resources, Bulletin 111. Socorro: New Mexico Institute of Mining and Technology, 1988.

Omni, Michael, and Howard Winant. *Racial Formation in the United States, from the 1960s to the 1980s*. New York: Routledge and Kegan Paul, 1986.

Ortiz, Roxanne Dunbar. *Economic Development in American Indian Reservations*. Santa Fe: Native American Studies, University of New Mexico, 1979.

Ortiz, Simon J. "Starting at the Bottom." In *Woven Stone*, vol. 21 of *Sun Tracks*, edited by Larry Evers and Ofelia Zapeda, 297–298. Tucson: University of Arizona Press, 1992. Albuquerque, NM: Institute for Native American Development, 1980.

———. "Grants to Gallup, New Mexico." In *Woven Stone*, vol. 21 of *Sun Tracks*, edited by Larry Evers and Ofelia Zapeda, 261–282. Tucson: University of Arizona Press, 1992.

Paci, C. D. James, and Lisa Krebs. "Local Knowledge as Traditional Ecological Knowledge: Definition and Ownership." In Brian Hosmer and Colleen O'Neill, eds., *Native Pathways: American Indian Culture and Economic Development in the Twentieth Century*, 261–282. Boulder: University Press of Colorado, 2004.

Page, Vicki. "Reservation Development in the U.S.: Peripherality in the Core." In *Native American Resurgence and Renewal: A Reader and Bibliography*, edited by Robert N. Wells Jr., 354–388. Metuchen, NJ: Scarecrow Press, 1994.

Painter, Nell Irvin. "The New Labor History and the Historical Moment." *International Journal of Politics, Culture and Society* 2 (Spring 1989): 367–370.

Parman, Donald L. *The Navajos and the New Deal.* New Haven, CT: Yale University Press, 1976.

Parsons, Talcott, and Neil J. Smelser. *Economy and Society: A Study in the Integration of Economic and Social Theory.* Glencoe, IL: Free Press, 1956.

Pascoe, Peggy. *Relations of Rescue: The Search for Moral Authority in the American West, 1874–1939.* New York: Oxford University Press, 1990.

Patterson, Thomas C. *A Social History of Anthropology in the United States.* New York: Berg, 2001.

Paul, Doris A. *The Navajo Code Talkers.* Philadelphia: Dorrance and Company, 1973.

Pérez, Emma. *The Decolonial Imaginary: Writing Chicanas into History.* Bloomington: Indiana University Press, 1999.

Peters, Kurt M. "Continuing Identity: Laguna Pueblo Railroaders in Richmond, California." *American Indian Culture and Research Journal* 22, no. 4 (1998): 187–198.

———. "Watering the Flower: Laguna Pueblo and the Santa Fe Railroad, 1880–1943." In *Native Americans and Wage Labor: Ethnohistorical Perspectives,* edited by Alice Littlefield and Martha Knack, 177–197. Norman: University of Oklahoma Press, 1996.

Pickering, Kathleen Ann. *Lakota Culture, World Economy.* Lincoln: University of Nebraska Press, 2000.

Pinxten, Rik, and Claire Farrer. "On Learning: A Comparative View." *Cultural Dynamics* 3, no. 3 (1990): 223–251.

Powers, Willow Roberts. *Navajo Trading: The End of an Era.* Albuquerque: University of New Mexico Press, 2001.

———. *Stokes Carson: Twentieth-Century Trading on the Navajo Reservation.* Albuquerque: University of New Mexico Press, 1987.

Pred, Allan Richard, and Michael Watts. *Reworking Modernity: Capitalisms and Symbolic Discontent.* New Brunswick, NJ: Rutgers University Press, 1992.

Prucha, Francis Paul. *The Great Father: The United States Government and the American Indians,* abr. ed. Lincoln: University of Nebraska Press, 1986.

Radford, Jeff. *The Chaco Coal Scandal: The People's Victory over James Watt.* Corrales, NM: Rhombus Publishing Company, 1986.

Reh, Emma. *Navajo Consumption Habits. For District 1. 1939.* University Museum of New Mexico State University Occasional Papers, Number 9, edited by Terry R. Reynolds. Las Cruces, NM: New Mexico State University, 1983.

Reichard, Gladys. "Human Nature as Conceived by the Navajo." *Review of Religion* 6 (1943): 353–360.

———. *Navajo Religion.* Princeton, NJ: Princeton University Press, 1950.

———. *Navajo Shepherd and Weaver.* New York: J. J. Augustin, 1936.

———. *Social Life of the Navajo Indians.* Vol. 7. New York: Columbia University Press, 1928.

Reno, Philip. *Mother Earth, Father Sky, and Economic Development: Navajo Resources and Their Use.* Albuquerque: University of New Mexico Press, 1981.

Richardson, Gladwell, and Philip Reed Rulon. *Navajo Trader.* Tucson: University of Arizona Press, 1986.

Robbins, Lynn. "Navajo Labor and the Establishment of a Voluntary Workers Association." *Journal of Ethnic Studies* 6 (Fall 1978): 97–112.

———. *Navajo Participation in Labor Unions.* Lake Powell Research Project Bulletin. Los Angeles: University of California, Los Angeles, Institute of Geophysics and Planetary Physics, 1975.

Robbins, William. *Colony and Empire: The Capitalist Transformation of the American West.* Lawrence: University Press of Kansas, 1994.

Rock Point Community School, comp. and ed. *Between Sacred Mountains: Navajo Stories and Lessons from the Land.* Vol. 11 of *Sun Tracks,* edited by Larry Evers. Tucson: University of Arizona Press, 1982.

Roediger, David R. *The Wages of Whiteness: Race and the Making of the American Working Class.* New York: Verso, 1991.

Roessel, Robert A., Jr. "Navajo History, 1850–1923." In *Handbook of North American Indians,* vol. 10, edited by Alfonso Ortiz, 519–520. Washington, DC: Smithsonian Institution, 1983.

Roessell, Ruth. *Women in Navajo Society.* Rough Rock, AZ: Navajo Resource Center, Rough Rock Demonstration School, 1981.

Roessel, Ruth, and Broderick Johnson. *Navajo Livestock Reduction: A National Disgrace.* Chinle, AZ: Navajo Community College Press, 1974.

Roseberry, William, and Jay O'Brien. *Golden Ages/Dark Ages: Reimagining the Past in Anthropology and History.* Berkeley: University of California Press, 1991.

Rosenbaum, Robert J. *Mexicano Resistance in the Southwest: "The Sacred Right of Self-Preservation."* Austin: University of Texas Press, 1981.

Rosenzweig, Roy. *Eight Hours for What We Will: Workers and Leisure in an Industrial City, 1870–1920.* New York: Cambridge University Press, 1983.

Rosier, Paul C. *Rebirth of the Blackfeet Nation, 1912–1954.* Lincoln: University of Nebraska Press, 2001.

———. "Searching for Salvation and Sovereignty: Blackfeet Oil Leasing and the Reconstruction of the Tribe." In *Native Pathways: American Indian Culture and Economic Development in the Twentieth Century,* ed. Brian Hosmer and Colleen O'Neill, 27–51. Boulder: University Press of Colorado, 2004.

Rostow, W. W. *The Stages of Economic Growth: A Non Communist Manifesto.* New York: Cambridge University Press, 1960.

Rubenstein, Harry R. "The Great Gallup Coal Strike of 1933." *New Mexico Historical Review* 52 (July 1977): 173–192.

———. "Political Repression in New Mexico: The Destruction of the National Miners' Union in Gallup." In *Labor in New Mexico: Unions, Strikes, and Social History since 1881,* edited by Robert Kern, 85–142. Albuquerque: University of New Mexico Press, 1983.

Ruffing, Lorraine Turner. "Dependency and Underdevelopment." In *Economic Development in American Indian Reservations,* edited by Roxanne Dunbar Ortiz, 91–113. Albuquerque: Native American Studies, University of New Mexico, 1979.

———. "Navajo Mineral Development." *Indian Historian* 11 (Spring 1978): 28–39.

Ruiz, Vicki. *From out of the Shadows, Mexican Women in Twentieth-Century America.* New York: Oxford University Press, 1999.

Ruiz, Vicki, and Susan Tiano. *Women on the United States–Mexico Border: Responses to Change.* Boston: Allen and Unwin, 1987.

Sacks, Karen. "State Bias and Women's Status." *American Anthropologist* 78 (September 1976): 565–569.

Sánchez, George. *Becoming Mexican American.* New York: Oxford University Press, 1993.

Saragoza, Alex M. "Recent Chicano Historiography: An Interpretive Essay." *Aztlán* 19 (Spring 1988–1990): 1–77.

Sasaki, Tom T. *Fruitland, New Mexico: A Navaho Community in Transition.* Ithaca, NY: Cornell University Press, 1960.

Schwarz, Maureen Trudelle. *Molded in the Image of Changing Woman: Navajo Views on the Human Body and Personhood.* Tucson: University of Arizona Press, 1997.

Scott, Catherine. *Gender and Development: Rethinking Modernization and Dependency Theory.* Boulder, CO: Lynne Rienner Publishers, 1995.

Scott, James. *Domination and the Arts of Resistance: Hidden Transcripts.* New Haven, CT: Yale University Press, 1990.

Scudder, Thayer. *No Place to Go: Effects of Compulsory Relocation on Navajos.* Philadelphia: Institute for the Study of Human Issues, 1982.

Sears, Paul. "Gallup Merchants Like It—When Indians Come to Town." *New Mexico Business,* November 1954, 2–8.

Shanin, Teodor. *Peasant and Peasant Societies.* New York: Basil Blackwell, 1987.

Shoemaker, Nancy. *Negotiators of Change: Historical Perspectives on Native American Women.* New York: Routledge, 1995.

Smith, Sherry L. *Reimagining Indians: Native Americans through Anglo Eyes, 1880–1940.* New York: Oxford University Press, 2000.

Soja, Edward W. *Postmodern Geographies: The Reassertion of Space in Critical Social Theory.* New York: Verso, 1989.

Spaulding, Karen. *Huarochirí: An Andean Society under Inca and Spanish Rule.* Stanford, CA: Stanford University Press, 1984.

Spence, Clark C. *Mining Engineers and the American West: The Lace-Boot Brigade, 1849–1933.* Moscow: University of Idaho Press, 1993.

Starr, Kevin, and Richard J. Orsi, eds. *Rooted in Barbarous Soil: People, Culture, and Community in Gold Rush California.* Berkeley: University of California Press, 2000.

Stern, Steve. "Feudalism, Capitalism, and the World System in the Perspective of Latin America and the Caribbean." *American Historical Review* 93 (October 1988): 829–872.

Stern, Steve, Frederick Cooper, Florencia Mallon, Allen F. Isaacman, and William Roseberry. *Confronting Historical Paradigms: Peasants, Labor, and the Capitalist World System in Africa and Latin America.* Madison: University of Wisconsin Press, 1993.

Stillwell, Paul. *The Golden Thirteen: Recollections of the First Black Naval Officers.* Annapolis, MD: Naval Institute Press, 1993.

Stocking, George W., Jr., ed. *Romantic Motives: Essays on Anthropological Sensibility.* Madison: University of Wisconsin Press, 1989.

Stoler, Ann L. "Making Empire Respectable: The Politics of Race and Sexual Morality in 20th Century Colonial Cultures." *American Ethnologist* 16 (November 1989): 634–660.

Streib, Gordon F. "An Attempt to Unionize a Semi-Literate Navajo Group." *Human Organization* 11 (Spring 1952): 23–31.

Takaki, Ronald T. *Strangers from a Different Shore: A History of Asian Americans.* Boston: Little, Brown and Company, 1989.

Thomas, David Hurst. *Skull Wars: Kennewick Man, Archaeology, and the Battle for Native American Identity.* New York: Basic Books, 2000.

Thomas, Wesley "Shił Yóół T'ool: Personification of Navajo Weaving." In *Woven by the Grandmothers: Nineteenth-Century Navajo Textiles from the National Museum of the American Indian,* edited by Eulalie H. Bonar, 33–42. Washington, DC.: Smithsonian Institution Press in association with the National Museum of the American Indian, Smithsonian Institution, 1996.

Treat, James. "Intertribal Traditionalism and the Religious Roots of Red Power." In *Native American Spirituality: A Critical Reader,* edited by Lee Irwin, 270–294. Lincoln: University of Nebraska Press, 2000.

Trennert, Robert A. *The Phoenix Indian School: Forced Assimilation in Arizona, 1891–1935.* Norman: University of Oklahoma Press, 1988.

Trotter, Joe W., Jr. *Black Milwaukee. The Making of an Industrial Proletariat, 1915–45.* Urbana: University of Illinois Press, 1985.

Ulrich, Laurel Thatcher. *A Midwife's Tale: The Life of Martha Ballard, Based on Her Diary, 1785–1812.* New York: Vintage Books, 1990.

Underhill, Ruth. *The Navajos.* Norman: University of Oklahoma Press, 1956.

Van Kirk, Sylvia. *Many Tender Ties: Women in Fur-Trade Society, 1670–1870.* Norman: University of Oklahoma Press, 1980.

Vizenor, Gerald. "Ishi Obscura." *Hastings West-Northwest Journal of Environmental Law and Policy* 7 (Spring 2001): 299–305.

Vlastos, Stephen. *Peasant Protests and Uprisings in Tokugawa, Japan.* Berkeley: University of California Press, 1986.

Vogler, Lawrence, Dennis Gilpin, Joseph K. Anderson, et al. *Gallegos Mesa Settlement and Subsistence: A Set of Explanatory Models for Cultural Resources on Blocks VIII, IX, X, and XI, Navajo Indian Irrigation Project, Vol. 3.* Navajo Nation Papers in Anthropology, no. 12. Window Rock, AZ: Navajo Nation Cultural Resource Management Program, 1982.

Vogt, Evon. *Navajo Veterans: A Study of Changing Values.* Papers of the Peabody Museum of American Archaeology and Ethnology, vol. 41, no. 1. Cambridge, MA: The Museum, 1951.

Waddell, Jack O. *Papago Indians at Work.* Tucson: University of Arizona Press, 1969.

Wagner, Sallie R., and Albuquerque Museum. *Wide Ruins: Memories from a Navajo Trading Post.* Albuquerque: University of New Mexico Press, 1997.

Walker, Cherryl, ed. *Women and Gender in Southern Africa to 1945.* London: J. Currey, 1990.

Walker, Kathy Le Mons. *Chinese Modernity and the Peasant Path: Semicolonialism in the Northern Yangzhi Delta*. Stanford, CA: Stanford University Press, 1999.

Wallerstein, Immanuel. *The Modern World System: Capitalist Agriculture and the Origins of the European World Economy in the Sixteenth Century*. New York: Academic Press, 1974.

Weaver, Jace. *Defending Mother Earth: Native American Perspectives on Environmental Justice*. Maryknoll, NY: Orbis Books, 1998.

Weigle, Marta. "Insisted on Authenticity." In *The Great Southwest of the Fred Harvey Company and the Santa Fe Railway*, edited by Marta Weigle and Barbara Babcock, 47–59. Phoenix: Heard Museum, 1996.

Weisiger, Marsha. *Sheep Dreams: Environment, Identity, and Gender in Navajo Country*. Seattle: University of Washington Press, forthcoming.

Weiss, Lawrence D. *The Development of Capitalism in the Navajo Nation: A Political-Economic History*. Minneapolis, MN: Marxist Educational Press, 1984.

West, Elliott. *Contested Plains: Indians, Goldseekers, and the Rush to Colorado*. Lawrence: University Press of Kansas, 1998.

White, Richard. *Middle Ground: Indians, Empires, and the Republic in the Great Lakes Region, 1650–1815*. New York: Cambridge University Press, 1991.

———. *The Roots of Dependency: Subsistence, Environment, and Social Change among the Choctaws, Pawnees, and Navajos*. Lincoln: University of Nebraska Press, 1983.

Whitt, Laurie Ann. "Cultural Imperialism and the Marketing of Native America." In *Contemporary Native American Cultural Issues*, edited by Duane Champagne, 169–192. Walnut Creek, CA: AltaMira Press, 1999.

Wilkins, David E. "Modernization, Colonialism, Dependency: How Appropriate Are These Models for Providing an Explanation of North American Indian 'Underdevelopment'? *Ethnic and Racial Studies* 16 (July 1993): 390–419.

Wilson, Alan, and Gene Dennison. *Navajo Place Names: An Observer's Guide*. Guilford, CT: Jeffrey Norton Publishers, 1995.

Witherspoon, Gary. *Language and Art in the Navajo Universe*. Ann Arbor: University of Michigan Press, 1977.

———. *Navajo Kinship and Marriage*. Chicago: University of Chicago Press, 1975.

———. "Navajo Social Organization." In *Handbook of North American Indians*, vol. 10, edited by Alfonzo Ortiz, 530–531. Washington, DC: Smithsonian Institution, 1983.

———. *Navajo Weaving: Art in Its Cultural Context*. Mna Research Paper 36. Flagstaff: Museum of Northern Arizona, 1987.

Wolf, Eric R. *Envisioning Power: Ideologies of Dominance and Crisis*. Berkeley: University of California Press, 1999.

———. *Europe and the People without History*. Berkeley: University of California Press, 1982.

———. *Peasants*. Englewood Cliffs, NJ: Prentice-Hall, 1966.

———. *Peasant Wars of the Twentieth Century*. New York: Harper and Row, 1969.

Woodman, Nancy. "The Story of an Orphan." In *Navajo Historical Selections*, edited by Robert Young and William Morgan, 65–68. Phoenix, AZ: Phoenix Indian School Print Shop, 1954.

Wyman, Leland C. *Blessingway*. Tucson: University of Arizona Press, 1970.

Yazzie, Ethelou, ed. *Navajo History*. Chinle, AZ: Navajo Curriculum Center, Rough Rock Demonstration School, 1971.

Young, Robert W. *The Navajo Yearbook of Planning in Action*. Window Rock, AZ: Navajo Agency, 1955.

Zolbrod, Paul G. *Diné Bahane': The Navajo Creation Story*. Albuquerque: University of New Mexico Press, 1984.

PH.D. DISSERTATIONS

Bsumek, Erika Marie. "Making 'Indian-made': The Production, Consumption, and Construction of Navajo Ethnic Identity, 1880–1935." Rutgers University, 2000.

Fanale, Rosalie. "Navajo Land and Land Management: A Century of Change." Catholic University, 1982.

Garcilazo, Jeffrey Marcos. "Traqueros: Mexican Railroad Workers in the United States, 1870–1930." University of California, Santa Barbara, 1995.

Hosmer, Brian Cooper. "Experiments in Capitalism: Market Economics, Wage Labor, and Social Change among the Menominees and Metlakahtlans, 1860–1920." University of Texas, Austin, 1993.

Luebben, Ralph A. "A Study of Some Off-Reservation Navaho Miners." Cornell University, 1955.

Moore, Laura Jane. "The Navajo Rug Trade: Gender, Art, Work, and Modernity in the American Southwest, 1870s–1930s." University of North Carolina, Chapel Hill, 1999.

Morton, Brian Jackson. "Coal Leasing in the Fourth World: Hopi and Navajo Coal Leasing, 1954–1977." University of California, Berkeley, 1985.

Muskett, Milford. "Identity, *Hózhǫ́*, Change, and Land: Navajo Environmental Perspectives." University of Wisconsin, Madison, 2003.

Uchendu, Victor. "Seasonal Agricultural Labor among the Navajo Indians: A Study in Socio-Economic Transition." Northwestern University, 1966.

Weisiger, Marsha. "Diné Bikéyah: Environment, Cultural Identity, and Gender in Navajo Country." University of Wisconsin, Madison, 2000.

Wilkins, Teresa Jo. "Producing Culture across the Colonial Divide: Navajo Reservation Trading Posts and Weaving." University of Colorado, 1999.

Young, Robert Allan. "Regional Development and Rural Poverty in the Navajo Indian Area." University of Wisconsin, 1976.

FILMS AND VIDEOS

Galan, Hector. *The American Experience: Los Mineros*. Boston: WGBH Educational Foundation and WNET, 1992. Video recording.

McLeod, Christopher. *In the Light of Reverence*. Oley, PA: Bullfrog Films, 2001.

Spitz, Jeff. *The Return of Navajo Boy*. Berkeley: University of California, Extension Center for Media and Independent Learning, 2000.

WEB SITES

Energy Information Administration: www.eia.doe.gov/cneaf/nuclear/page/umtra/ mexican_hat_title1.html. Accessed August 14, 2004.

Office of Miss Navajo Nation: http://www.missnavajo.navajo.org/history.html. Accessed August 4, 2004.

UNPUBLISHED PAPERS

Adams, William Y. "Early Navajo Experiences in Seasonal Wage Work." Paper delivered at the 14th Annual Navajo Studies Conference, Diné College, Tsaile, Arizona, April 2–5, 2003.

Boyden, Richard. "Breaking the Color Bar in Wartime Bay Area Shipyards, 1941–1942." Unpublished paper, February 1992.

Gilpin, Dennis. "The Navajo Coal Mines: Industrial Archaeology on the Navajo Indian Reservation." Paper presented at the 1987 Navajo Studies Conference, Northern Arizona University, Flagstaff, Arizona, February 19–21, 1987.

INDEX